A VISION SPLENDID

A VISION SPLENDID

The Influential Life of William Jellie
A British Unitarian in New Zealand

revised edition

Wayne Facer

Blackstone Editions

Blackstone Editions
Toronto, Ontario, Canada
www.BlackstoneEditions.com

© 2017, 2018 by Wayne Facer
All rights reserved
Published 2017. Revised edition 2018
Reprinted with corrections, 2019

978-0-9816402-6-6

Front cover image courtesy of the Rusty Snapper Café, Kawhia, New Zealand. Artist unknown.

For
Dorothy and Rex
In Memoriam

Contents

Illustrations	ix
Note on the Revised Edition	xiii
Foreword *by Peter Lineham*	xiv
Preface *by David Steers*	xvi
Acknowledgements	xvii
Introduction	xix

Part One: The Origins of William Jellie's Views on Society

1. From Carrickfergus to London and Oxford	3
2. A New World Vision	13
3. Religious Socialism and Social Change	26
4. Two English Ministries	42

Part Two: The Twentieth Century Ministries

5. In New Zealand: Auckland	51
6. In New Zealand: Wellington	74
7. Return to England	89

Part Three: Exchanging the Pulpit for the Lectern

8. In New Zealand: Timaru	103
9. The Poor Person's University	112
10. The Epilogue	127

Contents

Appendixes

   1. William Jellie's Synopsis of Philip Wicksteed's Lectures on Social Problems in the Light of Economic Theory   139

   2. Forward Movement Literary Society Lectures   156

   3. William Jellie's Public Education Courses   159

   4. Addresses by Rev. James Chapple at the Rationalist Association Sunday Evening Public Meetings   167

   5. Office Holders of the First and Second Unitarian Congregations and the Auckland Unitarian Church   170

Glossary   174

Notes   179

Bibliography   245

Index   271

Illustrations

Unless otherwise indicated, images are from collections of members of the Jellie family.

William Jellie, England, c.1896 — *frontispiece*

University Hall, Gordon Square, London — 2
  Courtesy of Harris Manchester College

Farm Hill House at Carrickfergus — 4
  Courtesy of the Deborah Yea Partnership Limited

James Martineau, portrait by George Frederic Watts — 7
  From James Drummond, *The Life and Letters of James Martineau* (London, 1902)

Philip Wicksteed — 14
  From C. H. Herford, *Philip Henry Wicksteed: His Life and Work* (London, 1931)

Mrs Humphry Ward (Mary Augusta Arnold) — 33
  Wellcome Library, London, under Creative Commons Attribution only licence CC BY 4.0. L0003411. Photograph by Barraud. Iconographic Collections Library reference no.: ICV No 27768

John Trevor — 36
  From John Trevor, *My Quest for God* (London, 1897)

Rose and Harry Atkinson — 38
  Courtesy of the Alexander Turnbull Library, reference MS-Papers-0071-18 William Ranstead papers

Illustrations

Stamford St Chapel From Emily Sharpe, *Unitarian Churches, with Explanatory Remarks* (London, 1901)	43
Ipswich Unitarian Chapel From Emily Sharpe, *Unitarian Churches, with Explanatory Remarks* (London, 1901)	47
William Jellie, portrait at his Ipswich ministry	48
William Jellie in 1905	50
Thomas Henry White, architect Author's collection	57
Auckland Unitarian Church plan by Thomas H. White Courtesy of the School of Architecture, University of Auckland. Thomas H. White Collection, WH2, Architecture Archive, University of Auckland Library	58
Auckland Unitarian Church in the 1930s Auckland Unitarian Church Collection	58
Laying the foundation stone of Auckland Unitarian Church Auckland Unitarian Church Collection	59
Newly engaged Ella Macky and William Jellie, 1905	62
Ella and William's wedding at Darlimurla, 1906 Courtesy of the Devonport Museum	63
Sir Robert Stout Auckland Unitarian Church collection	65
Sir George Fowlds With permission of the University of Auckland historical collection. Part 2. MSS & Archives 97/5, 6/1/1/4. Special Collections, U. of Auckland Libraries and Learning Services	65
Rev. Dr and Mrs Tudor Jones Auckland Unitarian Church collection	71
Rev. and Mrs William Kennedy Auckland Unitarian Church collection	84
Rev. Richard Hall Auckland Unitarian Church collection	85

Illustrations

Sir Robert Stout's farewell letter to William Jellie   88
  Courtesy of the Auckland War Memorial Museum Library,
  Auckland Unitarian Church collection, MS 91/72 Series C

Joseph and Mary Macky   93
  National Library of New Zealand, Ref: PAColl-1076

Sinking the Lusitania, 1915   95
  German painting: Bundesarchiv, DVM 10 Bild-23-61-17/
  CC-BY-SA 3.0

William, Hilary, Ella, and Margaret in England
during World War I   97

Bookplate for the Jellie book collection   102
  Reproduced with permission of Special Collections,
  University of Auckland Libraries and Learning Services

Rev. James Chapple   105
  Auckland Unitarian Church collection

Rev. Clyde Carr, MP   110
  From *Members of the New Zealand House of Representatives,
  25th Parliament, 1935-1938*

William Jellie's bust of Dante   116
  Author's collection

Revs. William and Wilna Constable   125
  Auckland Unitarian Church collection

Rev. Dr Cyprus Mitchell   128
  Auckland Unitarian Church collection

John Jellie on the *HMS Emperor*, 1944   132

Rev. Lincoln Gribble   134
  Author's collection

William Jellie in his study   136

William Jellie, James Chapple, and Richard Hall
at the Unitarian Hall, Timaru   *back cover*
  Auckland Unitarian Church collection

Note on the Revised Edition

Chapters 1-5 have been revised in this edition. Some text in these chapters has been rearranged in order to strengthen the thematic structure of the book. In the course of this rearrangement, the order of chapters 3 and 4 has been reversed.

Chapter 4, "Two English Ministries," is new in this edition. It replaces the previous chapter 3, "Entering the Unitarian Ministry". It incorporates additional material about William Jellie's ministries in London and Ipswich, and about his life as a young minister in London.

Foreword

It is a great pleasure to commend to readers this account of the life of William Jellie. In his life Jellie encompasses a number of the most interesting riddles in New Zealand history. For this reason this is a book that deserves attentive reading.

Firstly, this is an excellent introduction to the significance of Unitarians in New Zealand history. Unitarians have not really hitherto received the thorough historical investigation that one might have expected. This is largely a question of scale; for the Auckland congregation is the only one that lasted long. Jellie also served as pastor in Wellington and in Timaru and thus had a broader experience than any other pastor. In effect the Unitarians had their most significant impact through the work of Jellie, in the three locations where he served as pastor. Yet the story is more than this, because Jellie had connections with people of liberal and rationalist religious outlooks of various kinds, and thus his story unlocks a more general trend.

Secondly, the story in the process unlocks the personal side of what one might call intellectual aspect of New Zealand history. Jellie came to New Zealand attracted by its reformist reputation, and he immediately linked up with many leaders of these radical reforms. These links continued through his very long subsequent life as a pastor, lecturer, writer and thinker. It is sometimes contended that New Zealand reformism was instinctive and undoctrinaire. Perhaps this depends on the definition of undoctrinaire, but the story of William Jellie indicates that there is more to the story than that. William Jellie was highly interested in modern social analysis, as the fascinating discussion in this book of the influence on him of his tutors at Manchester College indicates.

Foreword

In New Zealand he took part in spirited discussions on reform issues. Wayne Facer shows that reformists debated a very broad range of issues, and that liberal theological and social theories were part of that discussion.

Thirdly this is a biography which has inhabited the life and the mind of the subject extremely well. Biographies are easier when there is great activity and action, but such was not the way of William Jellie. Moreover in Jellie's case private papers were not numerous. Consequently Wayne Facer has gone to great effort and expense to track down some puzzling threads of this story. His writing took him to England, and took him into archives as well as to reminiscences with people carrying the last memories of the grand old man.

Finally this is by no means a book just about New Zealand. Who knows what William Jellie might have done had he remained in England? The rich account of Jellie's Unitarian College, and in particular the influence on his life of the respected economist Philip Henry Wicksteed, indicates a real likelihood for him making a significant contribution in that setting. Wicksteed's social thinking illustrates the important ways in which advanced liberal religious thought interacted with early socialist ideas. Given the paucity of study of this aspect of advanced liberalism, this book has significance for the study of late Victorian and Edwardian thought.

The book now available is both serene and clear, and this is a great tribute to a very dedicated author. I very much hope that readers will enjoy this work as much as I have!

Peter Lineham
Professor of History
Massey University

Preface

Wayne Facer has written an absorbing biography of a hitherto little known but nevertheless fascinating and important person. Through meticulous research in both New Zealand and the UK the author illustrates the pioneering life of this minister and educator.

Born in county Down, Ireland, in 1865 and described by his family as "Irish through and through", William followed an uncle into the Unitarian ministry. A relatively small but theologically radical denomination, Unitarians placed great store on the value of an educated ministry and Jellie received an excellent education at Manchester College. The author draws out the influence of this education upon Jellie especially through the person of Philip Henry Wicksteed (1844-1927). Through Wicksteed, Jellie developed a love of Dante and literature in general as well as a belief in politically progressive causes and the need for direct intervention in society in favour of the poor. Serving in ministries in both England and New Zealand, where a contemporary journal described him as preaching "sermons and addresses so far superior to the ordinary", he became a key figure in the establishment of Unitarian churches and institutions in New Zealand. After retirement from the ministry he embarked upon a new career as a lecturer for the Workers' Education Association.

We owe a great debt to the author who has traced the varied course of Jellie's long career, bringing him vividly to life in the context of his times, his ideas and principles, his family and friendships and the institutions and organisations which he supported.

Rev. Dr David Steers
Editor of Faith and Freedom, *a journal of progressive religion published at Harris Manchester College, Oxford*

Acknowledgements

There are many people to thank for their interest, help and advice. Sue Killoran, Fellow Librarian at Harris Manchester College, Oxford, made me welcome during my visits over many years, fulfilled numerous requests for information and provided important archival material. David Verran and CJ Simmons at Auckland City Library were unfailing in finding reference and archival material. Mary Cobeldick, formerly Collections Registrar at the Alexander Turnbull Library, has been invaluable in locating information. Various librarians at the Massey University Library have been conscientious in finding material often difficult to obtain. The Librarians of the University of Auckland Special Collections and School of Architecture provided archival material.

The family of William and Ella Jellie have made an indispensable contribution. Their late children Margaret, Mary and John were very helpful, in conversations and by making documents available. When one of William's Manchester College notebooks was discovered, John's wife Nancy graciously donated it to the Library at Harris Manchester College. Margo Osborne, daughter of the late Hilary Jellie, kindly loaned me family documents and when visiting brought me material from Brisbane. William's grandson David and his wife Yvonne were an important link, loaning me a substantial collection of papers that their aunt Mary had amassed and a number of William's work books.

I have been fortunate in receiving help from a number of people with their own particular fields of expertise. The Rev. Andrew Hill, with his long-standing interest in Unitarian history, answered my many queries with knowledge and patience. The late Rev. Dr Len Smith, formerly Principal of Unitarian College, Manchester, kindly sent information and discussed questions about religion and socialism. My good friend Dr Bill Cooke has been unstinting in his advice and suggestions. Barbara Holt

Acknowledgements

arranged for the Auckland Unitarian Church historical records to be held at the Auckland War Memorial Museum Institute Library, ensuring their preservation, and since I began writing has kindly provided me with other references. Dr Peter Becroft kindly loaned me copies of his father's WEA programmes which largely coincided with William Jellie's involvement in the organisation. The Rev. Dr John Nelson provided information about William Jellie's uncle John Jellie. The Rev. Daphne Roberts and her husband the Rev. John Roberts went to considerable effort to find information about William Jellie's time at Southport, for which I am very grateful. Mr Howard Hague, former Archivist at the General Assembly of Unitarian and Free Christian Churches, Essex Hall, London, scheduled the archival holdings relating to New Zealand and made copies of those I wanted. John Maindonald kindly gave me files that he had used in writing a history of the Auckland Unitarian Church. Lincoln Gribble, who played such an important role in the church, generously donated his papers and a number of books to me. Dr Laurie Guy loaned me his early family journals, which provided important insights. My friend David Ross provided valuable technical assistance. Murray Darroch kindly reviewed an earlier version of the text and made many helpful suggestions.

Without the patience, care, knowledge and friendship of Professor Peter Lineham this book would not have been written. The skill and dedication of Lynn Hughes, editor of Blackstone Editions, made this book a reality.

Introduction

George Bernard Shaw's idea of a successful biography was a book entitled *Queen Victoria: by a personal acquaintance who dislikes her*.[1] According to this view, a biography is a story about the life of someone famous, preferably with some scandal and intrigue thrown in. But I much prefer to think that the cardinal purpose in writing biography is to discover and record a past that we might otherwise forget. As Dietrich Bonhoeffer wrote:

> But who bothers at all now about the work and achievements of our grandfathers, and how much of what they knew have we already forgotten? I believe that people will one day be quite amazed by what was achieved in that period, which is now so disregarded and so little known.[2]

A biographer is also a historian, trying to place the subject in the context of a certain time and place. A life must always be seen within its context. Historian Stephen E. Koss wrote:

> A self-respecting biographer must plunge deep into the history of his subject's period, if only to distinguish between the particular and the universal, and to evaluate testimony. In the process, he cannot help but contribute to an understanding of some aspect of the society to which his subject belonged.[3]

The biographer has the same armamentarium of methodology and technique as other historians. What is different, however, is the use of the prism of one individual's life to illuminate our view of history.

Introduction

Writing about William Jellie (1865-1963) means writing about a period of ninety-eight years, of which over forty were spent in the United Kingdom and over fifty in New Zealand. For more than thirty years William Jellie undertook ministries in both England and New Zealand. Then, at nearly sixty years of age, he devoted his next fourteen years to adult education, becoming a tutor for the Workers Educational Association in Auckland.

Part One of this book, "The Origins of William Jellie's Views on Society", traces his intellectual development. Jellie grew up in Ireland before the creation of the Irish Republic and attended the Royal Belfast Academical Institution. At Manchester New College, then co-located with University College in University Hall, London, he took a London University B.A. and studied to become a Unitarian minister. In Jellie's last year of study, Manchester College relocated to Oxford as a private hall. (Another century would pass before it became a full college of Oxford University).

One of the greatest influences on Jellie's view of life was Philip Wicksteed, his teacher, mentor and friend. Philip Wicksteed preached a gentle form of socialism in response to the need for change he saw in late nineteenth-century British society. This approach had great value in gaining support for the ideas of religious socialism through thoughtful intellectual persuasion rather than by delivering a strident message; a lesson not lost on William Jellie.

There is particular relevance in the course on sociology, economics and social problems that Wicksteed introduced into Manchester New College during William Jellie's final year of study. This course was probably the first of its kind to be introduced into a theological college.[4] While Wicksteed's course contained much information of the sort that could be found even today in introductory courses in economics and sociology, he also emphasised that inequality and human suffering in this world should be addressed in a principled manner by Unitarian clergy. I was fortunate in having access to William Jellie's own accounts of the course, contained in two large hardbound foolscap books now located in the Library at Harris Manchester College, Oxford. This material has allowed me to discuss Wicksteed's ideas in detail and to examine them within their historical context. An appendix contains Jellie's summary of each lecture.

Introduction

Upon completing their studies, most of Jellie's classmates went on to comfortable middle-class appointments. One exception was John Trevor (1855-1929), who left College early to become assistant to Philip Wicksteed and then went on to establish the Labour Church movement. The other exception was William Jellie. He took on one of the most demanding tasks any novice minister could face, surrounded by dire human need in an impoverished part of the City of London. He spent six years working at the Stamford Street Chapel while at the same time overseeing the Blackfriars Domestic Mission associated with the church. This was the area into which the university settlements would later come, starting with Toynbee Hall, followed by the Salvation Army. William Jellie and the Unitarian mission were already there.

It was when I was working on the penultimate chapter in this section, "Religious Socialism and Social Change," that an understanding of Wicksteed and the position of some of the other Unitarians of the period started to coalesce. This understanding was significantly helped by the work of Dr Len Smith, former Principal of Unitarian College Manchester. In addition to his very useful work on John Trevor, his book *Religion and the Rise of Labour* proved to be particularly insightful.

Part Two deals with William Jellie's twentieth century ministries, both in New Zealand and England. The question to be answered here is why he came to New Zealand. New Zealand at that time was known as the land of state socialism. As his old professor, J. Estlin Carpenter, wrote to Jellie on the eve of his departure: "Socially and politically, I imagine that you will find many interesting experiments going on in advanced democracy."

When William Jellie arrived in Auckland in 1900 one of the first sermons he gave was on the "Principles and Doctrines of Unitarians", in which he said: "The seat of our religious authority is the human mind and conscience, which were given to us by God for use ... Nothing is of force which does not commend itself to our mind and conscience. This is the ultimate tribunal which man can rely upon for the test of truth and right." He went on to advocate "freedom of thought, freedom of inquiry, freedom of speech, freedom of worship." When he discussed the relationship between conduct and opinion, he made it clear that deeds

Introduction

were far more important than systems of belief. The place of Christ within Unitarian theology did not depend on beliefs in doctrines about Jesus that grew up after his death; Christ had the position of master, teacher and leader in Unitarian thought.[5]

Upon his arrival in Auckland Jellie set about building the Unitarian movement, which led within two years to the construction of the church that still stands in Ponsonby Road. This in itself was no mean achievement. During his ten years in Auckland Jellie promoted the Unitarian cause in other centres, particularly Wellington, and he developed friendships with prominent New Zealanders, such as Sir Robert Stout (1844-1930) and Sir George Fowlds (1860-1934). Stout, then Chief Justice, was known for his freethought views, and had declared his Unitarianism during the 1896 election.[6] Fowlds, variously MP, single tax campaigner and President of Auckland University College, was twice chairman of the Congregational Union and a tolerant promoter of liberal religion and social reform: a good ally who assisted Unitarianism and William Jellie over many years.

Jellie's ministries in Auckland, Wellington, and Southport in Lancashire cover a period of twenty-one years. I hoped to be able to use Jellie's weekly sermons to trace his intellectual work and development during this period. Not every sermon would be based on a religious text: he was just as likely to draw inspiration from literature, art and science.[7] Often his sermons would form a series on a theme such as the plays of Shakespeare or the poetry of Robert Browning. Imagine my amazement at finding that only twelve sermons have survived! How could this be? I estimated that he should have produced 1200 during his time as a working minister in New Zealand.

In these circumstances it is usual for suspicion to fall on the family as the most likely culprits. The English biographer Michael Holroyd tells a tale that is all too familiar: a writer in his eightieth year asked Holroyd to be his literary executor, remarking that as soon as he was dead Holroyd "had better race down and gather up his unpublished papers." When the gentleman died some years later, Holroyd set off to meet the widow. When he was about two miles off he saw some white smoke rising up ahead. He arrived to find the widow flinging the last of the writer's correspondence with his first wife onto the bonfire.[8] Holroyd managed to save only a handful of letters.

Introduction

The William Jellie story is just about as startling. In the Mary Richmond collection of papers in the Alexander Turnbull Library I came across the following letter, which she received from Jellie in 1943:

> Turning towards sunset, one gets rid of a lot of old collected stuff, to save labour for those who have one's affairs to settle. Destroying some old papers today I came across a MS [manuscript] that may be of interest to you, if only to peruse and put in the waste basket. It is the MS of my address that I gave at the funeral of your sister, thirty years ago — so long as that — yet it seems but a little while ago, so vivid is my recollection. Perhaps you may not be able to read it; it was hastily scribbled, if so no matter. It may as well come to an end in Wellington as in Auckland.⁹

So there we have it. When he was in his seventy-eighth year William Jellie was tidying up, expecting he was helping his wife and children by destroying his papers. Of course he could not know he would live another twenty years, mainly in good health, or that other people would be intensely interested in what he wrote. He was in good company: Charles Dickens, Thomas Hardy and Henry James all burnt their papers before they died. Initially one thinks that someone who burns their papers or diaries has something to hide. Sometimes this is true. In Jellie's case it seems to have been no more than a belief that later readers would find his work out of date and "old hat", and that he was helping his family.

As a matter of fact, the Jellie family went to great lengths to preserve William's papers. His widow Ella sent all the papers she thought might be important to Manchester College, Oxford after his death. There was only one exception to the good work she did and we can forgive the vagaries of an elderly lady: Professor Winston Rhodes contacted her seeking correspondence between William Jellie and his protégé Frederick Sinclaire, about whom Rhodes was writing a biography, only to find that Ella had destroyed the correspondence.¹⁰ This is one item amongst the lacunae found as the William Jellie story unfolded.

Part Three, "Exchanging the Pulpit for the Lectern", begins with the two years Jellie spent at the Timaru Unitarian church. The Timaru church was founded by the Rev. James Chapple, a friend and fellow Unitarian minister of William Jellie's. The title for this book was inspired by one

Introduction

written by James Chapple. In 1924 Chapple visited England, where two of his books were published: *A Rebel's Vision Splendid* and *The Divine Need of the Rebel*.[11]

During his time in Timaru, Jellie became president of the South Canterbury branch of the Workers Educational Association. The WEA was an organisation set up to provide higher education to working-class people who were unable to attend university. It attracted criticism from time to time because of its left-leaning programmes and during the Depression the government slashed its funding; this was only reversed with the election of the first Labour government. Upon his return to Auckland — by now in his sixtieth year and at a time when many people start to think of retirement — Jellie began a new career as Tutor in the Auckland WEA.

William Jellie was by upbringing, education and inclination a scholar, and the chapter called "The Poor Person's University" explores this aspect of his life. (We are fortunate that John Jellie, the youngest son of William and Ella, preserved his father's WEA papers, which are now housed in the University of Auckland Library.) The greatest number of Jellie's courses were on aspects of English literature, followed by Dante, then social and political change in Europe. His workbooks show an enormous amount of preparation, reading and range of sources.

At the WEA, Jellie worked alongside a number of fellow Unitarians, such as Norman Richmond, the second WEA director; John Beaglehole; Hubert Becroft, a lecturer at Auckland Teachers College; and John Guy. Becroft and Guy were members of Jellie's Auckland congregation. Other Unitarian ministers, such as William Constable and Ellis Morris, followed him into the WEA. These ministers kept their ministries while contributing to the WEA. Jellie was unusual in leaving the ministry and going into teaching. The only other comparable case is that of Frederick Sinclaire, who did the same in Australia, giving up the church and teaching at the WEA and later at the University of Western Australia at Perth, finally accepting a chair in English at Canterbury University College. How fascinating it would have been to read the Sinclaire-Jellie correspondence and gain an insight into their thinking about this change in their careers.

Introduction

"The Epilogue" covers a surprisingly long period, from the outbreak of World War II until 1963. Jellie was physically able and mentally alert throughout most of this time, taking on the ministry again for the Auckland Church, giving adult education lectures to a variety of organisations and pursuing a strong defence of secular education. It was only towards the end of this period that his strength declined, interfering with his ability to work in his beloved garden. These later years were also a time for William Jellie to contemplate New Zealand's Unitarian history and reflect on a long life well spent.

Part One

The Origins of
William Jellie's Views on Society

University Hall, Gordon Square, London, where Manchester New College was located with University College, University of London

1

From Carrickfergus to London and Oxford

William Jellie was born on 25 July 1865 at Tullyhubbert in Comber, County Down.[1] His father, Robert Jellie, was a farmer and the son of a farmer from Ballyknockan, Saintfield, County Down. Robert was thirty-five years old when he married nineteen-year-old Letitia Turkington at the Moneyrea Non-subscribing Presbyterian Church on 4 July 1864.[2] Her father, John Turkington, was a gun maker from Carrickfergus.

William was the eldest child, followed by a brother, John, and two sisters, Elizabeth and Jane.[3] According to family lore, Robert Jellie went to America and did not return.[4] There is no record of when Robert left the family or why. However, when William entered the Royal Belfast Academical Institution in 1879 at the age of fourteen, his parent or guardian is recorded as "Mrs R. Jellie" and Carrickfergus was given as her address.[5]

William spent four years at the Royal Belfast Academical Institution. It is most likely he was a boarder rather than a day boy. He received an honourable mention in the Classical Department in his first year,[6] and two years later won a prize of £3 in the Intermediate examination for 1881.[7] When he left the Institution he went to live at Carrickfergus with his paternal uncle, the Rev. John Jellie (1824-1918).

John Jellie had been a student at the Institution between 1845 and 1849, when it had a collegiate department providing education to a university level. He completed the requirements of a General Certificate, which was accepted as the equivalent of a university degree.[8] However, no general certificates were awarded after 1839

Chapter 1

because of a theological controversy, and the collegiate department closed in 1849.[9] John Jellie then decided to train for the ministry of the Non-subscribing Presbyterian Church of Ireland. After completing his theological training in 1852 he had ministries at Glenarm, Ravara, Moneyreagh, York Street and Templepatrick. John Jellie was described as "an eager exponent of advanced Unitarianism". He and his friend Franklin Bradley (1831-1909) refused to follow a new code requiring answers to prescribed questions at the time of his own installation in 1859 and Bradley's ordination by the Bangor Presbytery.[10]

John Jellie's first wife, Elizabeth Dunn of Glenarm, died in 1860, during the time of his Moneyreagh ministry. Later, during his York Street ministry (1862-1873), he married Eliza Sweeny of Belfast, with whom he had five children. His last ministry was at Cairncastle from 1875 to 1880. He spent his subsequent years at Farm Hill House, Carrickfergus. Three years after retiring he was appointed a Justice of the Peace. When he received this appointment it was observed that he enjoyed "the distinction of being the first Irish Non-subscribing minister who, in his retirement from the duties of his profession, has attained the honours of the magistracy".[11]

Farm Hill House at Carrickfergus,
where William often stayed with his uncle Rev. John Jellie

From Carrickfergus to London and Oxford

John Jellie would have provided a male role model for the young William. He may have helped with his education, encouraging Letitia to send him to the Institution and possibly helping financially. Raising children on her own must have been particularly trying for Letitia, and she was bound to welcome the interest shown in her eldest son's welfare by his uncle. William probably spent his holidays with his uncle, and he was certainly living at Farm House when he finished his schooling.

On 5 April 1884 William wrote to the Rev. James Martineau (1805-1900), Principal of Manchester New College in London, seeking admission as a divinity student.[12] He said he had "passed the Matriculation examination of the University of London in January 1884, having been returned in the first division." He included three character references; one at least had known him from childhood.[13] The College then sent a telegram to John Jellie, who replied that William "has been living in my house for a considerable length of time" and that he was "extremely studious, and most anxious to become a useful minister in connection with the Unitarian body." He went on to explain that he had not previously provided a testimonial because as a relative he might be considered an interested party.[14] The next month William travelled to London, where he had three days of entrance examinations in Greek, Latin, English and Mathematics. The College Principal, James Martineau, declared that the professors "were unanimous in their favourable judgment of [Jellie's] papers and his *viva voce* work".[15]

Manchester New College was housed in University Hall, Gordon Square, London. The Hall, which opened in 1849, was built with funds subscribed by the Unitarian Congregations of Great Britain as a permanent Memorial to the passing of the Dissenters' Chapels Act 1844, to "perpetuate in the most useful form the great principle of unlimited religious liberty". Manchester New College had an affiliation with the University of London going back to 1840, when a Royal Warrant was "granted to Manchester New College, to issue Certificates to Candidates for Degrees in the University of London".[16] The University of London had been established in 1836. Its Royal Charter gave it the right to grant degrees without doctrinal subscription or any religious test, and also permitted the affiliation of outside Colleges with the University. In 1853 Manchester New College moved from Manchester to occupy University Hall jointly with University College.[17]

Dr James Martineau was in his last year as Principal of the College when Jellie joined the Session of students at University Hall on 1 June 1884. After forty-five years of service to Manchester New College, Martineau resigned on Michaelmas, 29 September 1885. Dr James Drummond (1835-1919) succeeded Martineau, who then became President of the College, a position he held until 1888. The teaching staff of James Drummond, J. Estlin Carpenter and Charles Barnes Upton (1831-1920) did not increase until Philip Wicksteed (1844-1927) was appointed five years later. Wicksteed would become a lifelong mentor and friend and his ideas were to have a profound effect on Jellie's world view.

Manchester New College students were in residence with University College students, whatever their religious persuasions. Accommodation at the Hall proved popular and there were always more applicants than places available. Manchester New College reported:

> There are 54 in the Hall, and 4 waiting outside and joining in the Hall life by day, bringing the community to 58 ... The 54 students in the Hall itself are classified as follows: 10 Manchester New College students (4 of whom are in receipt of the special grant), 15 General University College students, 17 Medical and Scientific students, and 12 Indian Civilians.[18]

The year before Jellie arrived, Professor Henry Morley had been appointed Principal of University Hall and he set about reorganising the rooms into bed sitters with basic furniture. University Hall could accommodate up to forty students, and Morley planned to increase that number to fifty. A contemporary report said that Morley "has thrown himself into the development of Collegiate life in University Hall with a zeal and energy that could not be surpassed. Not only has his influence filled the Hall to overflowing but it has given him a strong personal hold upon all the students in his charge."[19]

The cost of residence at University Hall for the three-term year ranged from £60 7s. 6d. to £78 7s. 6d. The difference was in the room rent, depending on whether a room was large or small and whether it was shared. The balance of the costs went on the board fee of £34 13s. which

From Carrickfergus to London and Oxford

*James Martineau, Principal of Manchester New College from 1869 to 1885
This portrait by George Frederic Watts hung in the College library
when Jellie was a student.*

covered breakfast, lunch, dinner and tea, and the term fee of £3 3s. for coal, gas and laundry. There was also a library fee of £1 11s. 6d.

William Jellie was undertaking a six-year period of study. His first three years were spent as an undergraduate student studying for a University of London B.A. The B.A. subjects approved by Manchester New College were Greek and Latin, German or French, and one science subject. In addition students were required to study a Mental Philosophy course under Professor Charles Barnes Upton, comprising Psychology and Logic, which was approved by London University for the degree. Further study was required in Hebrew, but this did not count towards the London B.A.

There was provision for Manchester New College to pay the University College course fees and University Hall costs for four undergraduates each year. (For those not residing at University Hall, a grant was available.) There was a similar provision for four theological students each year. To obtain one of these awards undergraduates had to sit an examination in May each year and theological students in September.[20] It is not recorded whether Jellie received an award, called an Exhibition, but it is likely, given his scholastic ability and the number of awards available. In his first year he was one of two new students.[21]

At the end of his first year Jellie was on the list of those who achieved Academical Distinctions: in his case a sixth certificate in English.[22] In his second year he was again placed on the list of Academical Distinctions, receiving First Class in Intermediate Arts for London University and a third certificate of first class in English in University College.[23] It is noteworthy that Jellie studied and did well at English and Arts, as these subjects were not part of those prescribed by Manchester New College. Unless he was able to include them as approved options he would have had to pay the university fees for them himself. In his last year he completed his B.A. in the second division with third class honours in French.[24]

Jellie's next three years were devoted to theological study. The Session for 1887-88 opened with an address by the Rev. J. E. Carpenter, Professor of Ecclesiastical History and Comparative Theology. Jellie was one of four students commencing their theological studies. By this time University Hall had become the social centre of University College life and the Annual Report expressed its satisfaction with "the increasing degree in which Manchester New College Students have intermingled with the young laymen in the Hall ... these satisfactory results have been largely due to the admirable influence of Professor Morley." But the Report noted that Professor Morley would "retire from his Principalship of the Hall at the end of next Session — that is, in June, 1889" and concern was raised about how the Hall would fare under a new Principal.[25]

One of the University College students Jellie was friendly with was William Rothenstein (1872-1945). After studying at University College he went to Oxford University and later, when Principal of the Royal College of Art, was knighted. His warm reminiscence provides an insight into student life at University Hall:

> It was from my companions at University Hall, then a students' hostel, that I got my keenest mental stimulus. The Hall, of which Henry Morley was Warden, was shared by students of University College and

Unitarian students belonging to Manchester New College. I confess I found the atmosphere there warmer and kindlier than at the Slade. Perhaps because I was a very small boy among much older men, I found everyone welcoming and helpful. I enjoyed the communal life, the keen talk and the varied interests. Henry Morley himself was a wide-viewed scholar and the kindest of men. In his family circle at Haverstock Hill I was warmly received. A familiar figure at the Hall was Dr Martineau, whose portrait by Watts hung in the library. Older students of University College were Frank Heath, Gregory Foster, Digby Besant, William Jellie and G. F. Hill. I was a raw provincial lad, ignorant, ill-disciplined but eager for knowledge, and these patient friends opened my eyes to many aspects of *dichtung* and *wahrheit* [poetry and truth] ... I enjoyed meeting men who were following other pursuits, medicine, science, history, philosophy and theology. There was much good talk after dinner in men's rooms, and good talk is a thing I have always enjoyed.[26]

Divinity students were usually required to reside in University Hall and we know Jellie continued to reside there, for he recorded that he had lived at the Hall for five years.[27] It is also likely he received another Exhibition, which would have paid his fees and costs. The Exhibition was renewed each year so long as the holder was diligent in his studies and remained in good health. The course Jellie studied included Theology, Historical and Comparative Religion, Hebrew Language, and Literature and Philosophy. In addition, all staff and students attended daily religious services in the Library, except for weekends and Mondays. Students led these services in rotation. There were regular exercises in elocution and composition of prayers and sermons.

In Jellie's second year two events occurred that would have a significant effect on him. The first was straightforward enough: Manchester New College, already concerned about the imminent departure of Professor Morley from University Hall, decided to move to Oxford. This decision was facilitated by the passing of the Universities Tests Act 1871. This Act abolished religious tests at Oxford, Cambridge, and Durham Universities, and their halls and colleges. (It had been led through Parliament by the Liberal MP John Duke Coleridge (1820-1894), who in 1883 as Lord Chief Justice presided over the Foote blasphemy case, which will be discussed later.) For Unitarians and other dissenting Christians who had been shut out of College Fellowships of the most prestigious universities, the time was ripe to reposition their academic status. The implications of the move to Oxford were seen as benefitting staff through academic recognition, and providing the opportunity for students to take Oxford degrees.

The second event was the provision of a course of sociology lectures delivered weekly by Rev. Philip Henry Wicksteed on society and the human condition. These lectures formed the environment in which Jellie lived and studied for his final year. Jellie's extensive course notes exist for *A Course of Lectures on Social Problems in the Light of Economic Theory*.[28] He attended an introductory lecture in December 1888; the first lecture of the course proper was given in January 1889, the last in December. A donation of £100 paid for the course so students were able to attend free. In Jellie's final year at College, Wicksteed's course was underwritten for a further five years and Wicksteed was appointed to the teaching staff as a Lecturer on Social Economy. These lectures aroused a "considerable interest" amongst the theology students and other people, not enrolled at Manchester New College, who had been admitted to the course.[29]

Wicksteed was an outstanding scholar. After taking an M.A. at University College, London, with a gold medal in classics, he had a number of ministries in Unitarian chapels, his last at Little Portland Street, London (1874-1897), where he was joined by Jellie's classmate John Trevor as his assistant minister. For many years he was a University Extension Lecturer. He was particularly known for his work as a Dante scholar over a period of forty years.[30] He also made major contributions to economic theory. He was interested in the ethics of commercial society. His first work dealt with distribution and marginal productivity. These ideas were developed further in his 1913 Presidential address to the British Association. Today his contribution to modern economic thought is seen as part of the "Austrian" school of economics.[31] He was a close friend of George Bernard Shaw and had sympathy with the Fabians. When his friend John Trevor formed the Labour Church movement in 1891, Wicksteed became a member and provided financial support.

Wicksteed began his University Extension teaching while Jellie was a student in London; the first course he gave was on Dante, at Wimbledon in 1887. From that time until 1915 he lectured extensively for the Oxford, Cambridge, London, Liverpool and Manchester university extension centres, most frequently on Dante. Jellie would have had ample opportunity to attend any number of Wicksteed's Dante lectures,[32] and it is reasonable to assume that he did so. It is also plausible that the example of his mentor may have fired Jellie's own interest in later studying Dante as well as the deep involvement he would develop in adult education.[33]

The Session for 1889-90 began on 15 October 1889 in temporary premises at 90, High Street, Oxford. (University Hall was sold to the Trustees of Dr Williams' Library, which is housed there to this day.)[34] Mansfield College had just vacated what were described as "convenient and commodious" rooms, and Manchester New College remained there until its permanent buildings were ready in 1893.[35] Benjamin Jowett (1817-1893), the Greek scholar and former Vice-Chancellor of Oxford University, was among those who welcomed the College to Oxford. Other notable academics who welcomed it included Max Muller (1823-1900), the German scholar of comparative religion and mythology; the Scots-born philosopher Edward Caird (1835-1908); and the classical scholar Gilbert Murray (1866-1957). The last three subsequently served as Visitors to the College.

Although the integration of the College into Oxford University would be a gradual process extending over many years,[36] from the time of its arrival it found varying degrees of acceptance:

> Oxford University co-operated with the new College in several ways. College students were invited to attend lectures at New College and meet the Professors and the examinations in Responsion subjects [the first examination Oxford students must pass before taking any degree] were undertaken by an Oxford Tutor. The College Professors held an "At Home" in each term in which their students could meet other Oxford men. The Discussion Society was open to the public as were the Evening Lectures on Theology given by Dr Carpenter. The fact that an average of seventy people joined the Chapel Services each week is further evidence that the College was by no means a small isolated community.[37]

Chapter 1

One aspect of student life that did suffer was the missionary tradition of service. The location at Oxford made it difficult to continue the practical experience that had been obtained by College students during their vacation, since the days of Martineau as Principal, and even before. Dr Drummond, the Principal, said, "The removal to Oxford has inevitably crippled one portion of our work. Neither the time at our disposal, nor the circumstances amid which we are placed, allow the students to obtain the practical experience which they found among the Congregations, Sunday Schools and Missionary agencies of London." In an attempt to overcome the problem, Dr Drummond asked the Missionary Associations to help to provide work for students during the long vacation and "to pay them two guineas a week."[38]

The College's move to Oxford provided a number of opportunities: it supported academic development and recognition of its staff; it helped the College to attract staff of high standing and scholastic achievement; and it enhanced the standing of the College.[39] The significance of this academic association may not have been foremost in the mind of the 24-year-old William Jellie, but it would remain with him for the rest of his life.[40]

2

A New World Vision

The idea of addressing the problems of poverty and social inequality had been slowly taking hold in advanced religious thinking in nineteenth-century Britain. This was a time when conventional religious opinion, in the form of the Church of England, insisted that inequality was the natural order of society and poverty was a necessary part of God's plan. It even went so far as to express these sentiments in verse three of the popular hymn *All Things Bright and Beautiful*, written by the wife of the Archbishop of Armagh:

> The rich man in his castle,
> The poor man at his gate,
> God made them, high or lowly,
> And ordered their estate.

Hymnals did not begin removing this verse until 1900.

The theological basis for this inertia was buttressed by socio-economic factors. The period between the demise of Chartism in the middle of the nineteenth century and the long depression of the 1880s had been largely, though not entirely, free of social ferment.

Philip Wicksteed, the Unitarian minister, economist, Dante scholar and ardent social reformer, saw major deficiencies with existing economic theory because of its failure to explain the causes of economic depression and to account for the extremes of wealth and poverty. His views were reinforced by his wife Emily (née Solly, 1845-1924) and his father-in-law Henry Solly (1813-1903), a Unitarian minister active in many radical causes including Chartism, universal suffrage, the co-operative movement, antislavery and workingmen's clubs.

Chapter 2

Philip Wicksteed

The turning point for Wicksteed came with the publication of Henry George's book *Progress and Poverty* in 1879. Wicksteed imbibed the ethical underpinnings of George's theory, namely that the problem of poverty can be traced to private property in land, and that the mechanism of a single land tax could be used to redistribute wealth. This focussed Wicksteed's thinking on the welfare of the individual citizen and led directly to the ideas for his course, *Social Problems in the Light of Economic Theory*.

The decision to allow Philip Wicksteed to introduce such a course at Manchester New College involved the coincidence of three factors. First, Wicksteed was well known to and on friendly terms with the staff at Manchester New College. In particular, his old friend, J. Estlin Carpenter, professor of ecclesiastical history and an authority on biblical criticism and comparative religion, had been appointed vice-principal when James Martineau retired as Principal in 1885.[1] Wicksteed's biographer, Professor Charles Herford, observed, "The large social intelligence of Wicksteed's friend, Estlin Carpenter, insensibly widened these horizons [of social philosophy] wherever he worked and taught ... In Wicksteed, the organised social thinking of Positivism played an analogous part."[2] And so Wicksteed proposed a course of lectures to his old College.

Secondly, there was the structure of the Unitarian denomination, which came together in annual meeting but did not exercise control over the College.[3] This meant that matters concerning theological education were largely in the hands of the Principal and academic staff.[4]

Thirdly, the particular attitude toward religious inquiry that prevailed in Unitarian belief facilitated Wicksteed's proposal. Here was a College that professed a belief in free inquiry into religious matters, and was, from 1805, the only Dissenting institution of higher learning that attracted students from throughout the entire country, without requiring subscription to any creed. (The absence of any religious test or subscription to doctrine or creed in the dissenting academies was in sharp contrast to the requirements that existed at the time for matriculation at Oxford and degree conferment at Cambridge, which effectively barred those with dissenting views from the universities.[5]) The free inquiry that was so much part of the Unitarian tradition also laid stress on the importance of human reason, knowledge and individual conscience. According to Jean Raymond and John V. Pickstone, writing in *Truth, Liberty, Religion: Essays Celebrating Two Hundred Years of Manchester College*, this ensured that the Unitarian position

> could withstand opposition, it being the end-result of reason in theology ... [and] that natural sciences, in as much as they served as a paradigm of free enquiry, were of peculiar concern to Unitarians. The Priestleyan model of man, as a knowing and worshipping being, had been central for their science and for their rational theology. It was on this central question that a "shift in intellectual temper" came to interact with the growing specialization and professionalization of knowledge.[6]

Wicksteed was invited to inaugurate his course of lectures by giving the opening address to the 1888-89 session of the College.[7] His address on "The Place of Sociology in the Circle of Theological Studies", attended by all the students, was later published. In addition, members of the public could enrol for a fee of 10s. 6d. This suited Wicksteed's interest in adult education. For Wicksteed there was no question "of the propriety, indeed the necessity" for students studying for the Christian ministry to examine the problems of sociology. Here Wicksteed used the word "sociology" in a sense that incorporates both the study of social problems and the science that investigates the nature, structure and development of society.

A feature of Wicksteed's address, which recurs later in his lectures, is the involvement of ethics: "For human conduct — the subject of the science of ethics — everywhere rests upon and is everywhere conditioned by social relations and institutions." And he goes on to say that in large cities, people may not be aware of personal wrongdoing, but "we may be complacently bearing our part in acts which, with a collective weight of gathered oppression, fall upon the helpless and the wretched." This was another theme he would return to: the unintentional collective effect that could harm others. In stating this he also asked a fundamental question: "how far the structure and institutions of this 'society' are inflexibly determined by the laws of nature, how far they may be moulded and re-moulded by man?"[8] By asking this he was able to open up the issues of reform and social change.

Wicksteed argued for an important connection between religion and sociology. He told his listeners that Jesus entered into personal relationships when he gave "his great world-renewing principles. It was his special and immediate task to preach to the poor and powerless the truth that there and then, without waiting for any outward change or revolution, they might live the life of communion with God." The belief that soon after his death Jesus would return, and the existing order of domestic and social relations would pass away, was a complete mistake. It is, in fact, "the very negation of the central teaching and principle of Jesus, and…has done more than anything else to cramp and thwart the beneficent influence of Christianity." It has caused Christians to renounce the world rather than redeeming it, while all the time treating as permanent the institutions of public and social life. For Wicksteed any distinction between the church and the world was "pernicious".[9]

In his *Three Essays on Religion*, John Stuart Mill had described nature as a huge slaughterhouse, which negated the idea of a benevolent deity.

Wicksteed said that the issues of scepticism and declining interest in religion had to be faced fairly and their sources examined. He thought that the root cause of much scepticism was disbelief in the possibility of regenerating society. The answer was to believe that the world was capable of being moulded "into full accordance of God's law, and that Sociology can only be truly studied when baptized in the spirit of religion".[10]

> But this is not all. We profess in our College to examine any belief that is submitted to us, not for the sake of showing that it is false, but for the sake of inquiring whether it is true. We must not shrink from the application of our principles here. "The Bible, and the Bible only..." has long ceased to be our motto. The Bible word, "God is love," will not help us if it is contradicted by reason and experience. We have rejected the authority of the Church, and the ecclesiastical doctrine that God revealed his character and purpose when the Word was made flesh in Jesus... Where then, are we to seek the authentic revelation of God? In the utterances and the constitution of the human mind, and in the conditions of human life.[11]

Wicksteed believed that a complete course of theological studies must include the study of the moral and mental condition of humanity. Auguste Comte, he pointed out, had said that religion was necessary for a fruitful study of society; similarly, the study of social life was an essential part of theological studies. "Comte saw far and deep when he denounced, as materialistic and immoral, the study of industry apart from the general structure and purpose of society... Sociology, then, bereft of religion, is without a goal, and the blight of perpetual sterility is upon it. Theology, bereft of Sociology, is remote from the actual life of men, and is smitten with unreality. On the union of these two depends the future of humanity."[12]

Following this opening address, students attended Wicksteed's lectures each Friday afternoon at 3 PM. William Jellie, then in his second year of theology study, was one of only nine students in the class, so there was ample opportunity for Wicksteed and the students to get to know each other well. The College Committee thought the students would "derive great benefit" from the lectures, as Wicksteed was "so deeply versed in his subject," and that "no less advantage will be gained by them from personal contact with his quickening and inspiring indi-

Chapter 2

viduality".[13] Wicksteed set a high expectation for his students' readings in the course. When the class was told to read Auguste Comte and Herbert Spencer,[14] Jellie made a note "but make personal observations"; so Wicksteed was expecting the students to relate these ideas to other knowledge they had.

The first ten lectures were given under the heading "Elements of Sociology". In the first lecture Wicksteed introduced ideas on land tax from Henry George's *Progress and Poverty*. As the class continued to explore human social development Wicksteed relayed the significance of language, its origins and cultural characteristics. The basis for this section was the *Introduction to the Science of Language*, published in two volumes in 1880 by Archibald Henry Sayce (1845-1933), Professor of Comparative Philology at Oxford University and an expert in Middle Eastern languages.[15]

Next Wicksteed dealt with the social aspects of property. While he did not examine how the notion of natural rights arose, Wicksteed pointed out that Jeremy Bentham had said that "some kind of universal principle of moral criticism was needed that could cut through the partiality of the status quo and the abstract talk of 'natural rights' that supplied its moral rationale."[16]

Because Darwin had shown that family life occurred generally among higher animals, Wicksteed maintained that the maternal instinct was the basis for altruism. The term "altruism" was coined by Comte and derived from the Italian *altrui*, meaning to or of others.[17] Wicksteed does not appear to have extended the idea of altruism beyond the family to the general level in society.

Somewhat surprisingly for the times in which he lived, Wicksteed included a segment on what in modern parlance would be called human sexuality. "Efficiency of civilization is gauged by its power in transforming the sexual life ... literature, romance, poetry, which stirs feelings is built upon the relationship of the sexes." He referred to the work of Dr Elizabeth Blackwell (1821-1910), who he said "attempts to direct this passion in positive ways." Blackwell, upon her return to England from America in 1869, spent much of her time promoting the health and hygiene of women, health education in schools, and education about sex and moral issues, especially in her publication *The Human Element in Sex*.[18] Wicksteed also took a modern view of gender issues. The subjugation of women by men was, he thought, the "most awful form of human tyranny". He pointed out that women's inferior status was based on the notion of property: "Woman is the property of the father, next given [literally during the wedding service by her father] to the husband. No claim of chastity is laid on the man, only the woman as [sex outside marriage] is a breach of property rights." He observed, "These ideas of property do not satisfy modern people."[19]

Wicksteed recognized that Government must have sufficient ability to regulate its members and enforce its laws, and that this ability ultimately rests on physical force. Government must protect the person and property; but how much government is needed beyond that? Here Wicksteed referred to the work of Thomas Hill Green (1836-1882).[20] Green was an Oxford University professor of philosophy of the idealist school and a critic of empiricism and naturalism. His political philosophy, aimed at providing a cogent theory to underpin Liberalism, is sometimes seen as an early theory of the welfare state.[21] By breaking with the ideas behind classical Liberalism and replacing them with ideas about equality and freedom, Green contributed to the development of ethical socialism.[22] His friends included leading dissenting clergymen such as Hugh Price Hughes (1847-1902), the founder of the *Methodist Times*, and the Unitarian James Martineau. To the consternation of some orthodox religious believers, Green argued that England's national religion cut across denominational boundaries and was pluralistic in character — an important position to hold in an increasingly democratic age.[23]

Writing about the legislative programme of the Liberal Party, in a famous lecture Green recounted the liberals' struggles to establish political freedom from aristocratic privilege and economic freedom versus protectionism. The current phase was concerned with social freedoms. Green defined social freedom as a positive power: freedom with rational and moral purpose. This type of freedom involved genuine citizenship, and the progress of society was to be measured by its growth. Such freedom would allow members of society to make the best of themselves. Nevertheless he thought State regulation in matters such as the sale of alcohol, housing, land ownership, employment conditions and education was justified to protect citizens' interests.

Chapter 2

Wicksteed asked whether it is a function of government to protect the moral sense from outrage. He acknowledged that in doing so there is a great danger that the state, becoming involved in censorship, will act in a tyrannical way. The illustration he gave is that of George William Foote (1850-1915),[24] the well-known freethinker, who had recently experienced "the suppression of anti-religious polemics". Foote was the editor of the *Freethinker*, which he had established in 1881. Incensed at the refusal to allow fellow rationalist Charles Bradlaugh (1833-1891)[25] to take his seat in the House of Commons when he wished to affirm and not take an oath, Foote launched an attack on Christianity in the form of a series of cartoons depicting Biblical scenes, published in various editions in 1882. Charged with "wickedly and profanely devising and intending to asperse and vilify Almighty God, and to bring the Holy Scriptures and Christian Religion into disbelief and contempt",[26] he was found guilty on a retrial (the first jury failing to agree) and sentenced to one year's imprisonment for the crime of blasphemous libel. A call to reduce his sentence was signed by many illustrious scientific, literary and public figures, including eleven clergymen, one of whom, the Rev. Stopford Brooke, was a prominent Unitarian.[27] A third trial occurred, while Foote was still in prison, with Bradlaugh also a defendant but tried separately. Bradlaugh was acquitted and Foote's jury could not reach a verdict.[28] These trials were to have far-reaching consequences for the law of blasphemy; in 1883 Lord Chief Justice Coleridge changed the definition of the crime, namely: "I now lay down as law, that, if the decencies of controversy are observed, even the fundamentals of religion may be attacked without a person being guilty of blasphemous libel."[29] So the manner of expression, rather than the subject matter, now became the test.

The trials had a galvanizing effect on other Unitarians; for example, the Rev. William Sharman (1841-1889) became secretary of the Society for the Repeal of the Blasphemy Laws.[30] In 1887 the noted Unitarian MP and jurist, Courtney Stanhope Kenny (1847-1930), introduced his Religious Prosecutions Abolition Bill, which sought the repeal of laws restricting the expression of religious opinion.[31] Whatever these Unitarians may have thought about Foote's subject matter, they saw a greater principle involved, that of freedom of thought and the publication of ideas concerning religion. The ongoing publicity surrounding this *cause célèbre* could not have been lost on the students of Wicksteed's class.

In his next lecture Wicksteed examined the relationship between education and spiritual power. Human beings, he said, were "only human in society and learning is required to associate with other human beings". Language is needed for the transmission of culture; technical education allows workers to produce what others want; artistic and literary people contribute to the higher life. Further, he recognised that education can lead to change, and that "every change in education should leave the way to further change".[32] Following up on the comments in his previous lecture about the danger of the state enforcing laws against "moral outrage" and the iniquity of censorship, he concluded this lecture by raising the question of the separation of the church and state.

The final lecture in this series looks at the place of economics in sociology. Here students were introduced to the work of Nassau W. Senior (1790-1864), a classical economist who argued that governments were responsible for human welfare, while economics studied the creation of wealth, and that the two spheres were separate. The ideas of the American economist Francis Amasa Walker (1840-1897) were presented. An opponent of Henry George, Walker rejected the wage fund doctrine, which said that the amount set aside for labour costs was predetermined. His theory of profits showed that labour benefited from innovation and that gains of the employer are not at the workers' expense. The economist William Stanley Jevons was quoted as saying that political economy "deals with wealth of nations and aims at teaching what should be done that the poor may be as few as possible". Students were then referred to Wicksteed's own text, *Alphabet of Economic Theory*. Wicksteed argued that a redistribution of wealth would ensure better conformity between price and marginal want, which would produce "economic harmony" of inestimable importance.[33]

Between December 1888 and May 1889 Wicksteed delivered the remainder of his course. He began by giving the students the tools to understand the political economy around them: his section on "Social Problems in the Light of Economic Theory" provided an introduction to the mathematics needed to understand the economics involved. Students were directed to an article in *The Quarterly Journal of Economics*

Chapter 2

which provided a Jevonian critique of David Ricardo's doctrine of value and a general description of the marginal economics of the Austrian school.[34] The laws of diminishing and increasing returns were covered in the following lectures.[35] The latter lecture also presents the case for labour specialization and argues for free trade. The theme of free trade is continued, with the view that free trade helps maintain peace between countries.[36]

Wicksteed next turned to the contentious topic of population.[37] Thomas Malthus had argued in the early nineteenth century that doubling the population does not result in doubling food production. Thus, measures to control population were required in order to avoid the misery associated with overpopulation. Excess population growth, Malthus argued, implied a readiness to emigrate.[38] Wicksteed appears to have accepted the Malthusian analysis without dissent because he saw the opportunities for underpopulated areas of the British Empire to absorb more people as a possible solution to the problem.

Wicksteed then considered the issue of low wages.[39] He taught that oversupply of poor workers caused them to compete against each other, resulting in depressed wages. For example, he saw refugees granted asylum in London as a source of cheap labour competing with English workers, but he said that "Jewish clothing firms are [not] the worst." And since women and children were the worst-paid workers, "their employment often deprives men of work." So poor women and children make life difficult for poor men! This form of economic theory points to the worker as the cause of his or her own suffering. Wicksteed's solution to low wages was for workers to leave low wage industries, but just how this was to be done he did not say. His answer would come in his last lectures, on utopian socialism.

Three more lectures followed on land, explaining the cases for and against nationalisation.[40] Agriculture, Wicksteed postulated, was "the natural equilibrating industry" in society, so it was important to keep it open to all workers who wished to take part in it. But why, he asked, were men leaving the land and swarming into London? The answer he gave was private ownership of land, which can drive tenant farmers off the land when uneconomic rents are charged. (He could have looked back to another contributor, the various Enclosure Acts beginning in the eighteenth century.) And so he asked, who is the primitive proprietor of the soil? This fundamental question leads to a series of arguments for public ownership: the land premium belongs to the community; public ownership of land would allow other taxes to be abolished; it would remove the need for public debt. All of these points would have been discussed when Wicksteed introduced Henry George to the class in his first lecture. To introduce the case against nationalisation Wicksteed turned to Arnold Toynbee (1852-1883),[41] who had made his name as an economic historian of the "industrial revolution", a term he was credited with coining. Toynbee said, "I agree with George that it has been a mistake to sell land to private individuals instead of keeping it for the use of the people", but he objected to land nationalization policies unless there was full compensation. Here Wicksteed referred his students to the work of his brother Charles Wicksteed (1848-1931), who advocated full compensation funded against the security of the land, paying current interest until the principal had been repaid.[42]

The last two lectures in this section concerned socialism. Wicksteed turned to a contemporary author whom he regarded as the most intelligent writer about the society of the future: Edward Bellamy (1850-1897), an American socialist who had published the first nine chapters of Marx's *Capital* in 1893 under the title *Marx's Theory of Value Complete*.[43] Marx's *Capital* did not capture the popular imagination as Henry George's *Progress and Poverty* had done or as Bellamy's novel *Looking Backward 2000-1887* was destined to do. The book's principal character, Julian West, wakes in the year 2000 after sleeping for 113 years. He finds a new society that guarantees the needs of all its citizens; the unequal economic and class structure of the nineteenth century has been eliminated. Citizens work toward the benefit of society as a whole and the nation's wealth and industrial organisations are held in a single national trust.[44] What did Wicksteed's students make of their lecturer's endorsement of such a utopian future? If it was a view they shared, we do not know.

The final section of Wicksteed's course, "Ethical and Theological Aspects of Sociology," comprised three lectures.[45] Wicksteed recognised that no one political economic model could represent the entire world, although his lectures had proceeded as though the English model was the only one of importance. Wicksteed claimed that people desire wealth for moral and emotional reasons, which moves the study of economics to the ethical area. Ministers of religion, he believed, have a responsibility to be a transforming influence on others. The idea that happy and pure homes come at the price of degrading other homes or pushing competitors over the edge is unacceptable. It is in investigating these issues that sociology and economics bear on theology. Wicksteed's lectures raised a prescient question: Is there enough room on the planet for all of humanity? Can selfish motives be socialized? For a ministry to be helpful, he said, it must have a real and vital connection with everyone.[46]

The new world view that Wicksteed offered his students promoted social justice; recognised inequality based on social and economic class as unethical; advocated a living wage for workers, gender equality, and freedom of thought; and prefigured the welfare state that would appear in some countries in the twentieth century. In doing so Wicksteed motivated his students to see beyond the Zeitgeist of their time and place and to believe in ideals yet to be realised.

Of the students who attended Wicksteed's first year's lectures about whom information is available, only William Jellie was motivated to undertake a pastorate with a mission. In the year Wicksteed's course began there were four final-year students who would have completed his course:[47] Arthur William Fox (1863-1945), whose first ministry was at the Longsight Unitarian Chapel, Manchester, 1889-1894; E. D. Priestley Evans, who went to the Loughborough Unitarian Chapel in Leicestershire, 1889-1890 (although he had had earlier ministries in Wales before coming to Manchester New College); Thomas Nicholson, who went to Birmingham as an assistant minister at the Church of the Messiah, 1889-1892;[48] and Frank Parnell. Parnell was also in his final year; no trace can be found of him after he left College.[49] Another classmate, Daniel Rees (1865-1938), went from Oxford on a Hibbert Scholarship[50] to the universities of Berlin, where he completed an M.A., and Leipzig, where he completed a Ph.D. Upon his return he took up a ministry at Strangeways Unitarian Chapel, Manchester.[51] The remaining student in Jellie's class, Salomon Csifo, came from Transylvania and no follow-up is possible.

A New World Vision

The exception to this pattern is Jellie's classmate John Trevor (1855-1930).[52] John Trevor was already thirty-two years old when he entered College for a year's study. He had left College by the time Wicksteed commenced his course and was working as Wicksteed's assistant at Little Portland Street Chapel in November 1888. There he was able to study the social problems that so obviously interested Wicksteed; and their discussions no doubt increased Trevor's drive to undertake changes in society. This first found expression when, while at his next charge (Upper Brook Street Chapel, Manchester, June 1890 to November 1891), he set about founding the Labour Church.[53] In him, Wicksteed had, according to his biographer, "recognized a man who, otherwise frail and ineffectual, possessed something of poetic and prophetic power".[54] John Trevor did not need Wicksteed's lectures to inspire him.

3

Religious Socialism and Social Change

For the ideas of socialism and social change to flourish, new ideas had to take hold. The most important of these was the idea that pauperism, with its attendant dirt, disease and destitution, was the consequence of poverty and not its cause. The cause had to be sought in the social structure of society and ways had to be found to introduce profound changes to society. For this shift in thinking to occur in a religious context, a new view or reinterpretation of theology was required. In examining these issues this chapter will concentrate on Unitarian developments, though not to the exclusion of other influences,[1] as it seeks answers to the question: what was the Unitarian contribution to religious socialism and social change?

Unitarian responses to the poverty, deprivation, destitution, ill health and social neglect of a large proportion of the British population began much earlier. Outbreaks of typhus fever in Manchester in the 1790s, associated with the large cotton-spinning factories and the workers' dilapidated, unsanitary and overcrowded dwellings, were a cause for action. John Ferriar and his colleague Thomas Percival[2] led a campaign for an extension to the infirmary, which culminated in the founding of England's first fever hospital, the Manchester House of Recovery — although the campaign was also motivated by considerations other than the wellbeing of the poor, including the fear that the disease would spread from the poor to the better-off classes.[3] Not quite so obvious was the radical notion that the poor as well as the rich should have access to medical care when sick.

Some forty years later, in 1831, Manchester had its first cholera epidemic. James Phillips Kay, Secretary of the Manchester Board of Health, worked in a dispensary where he treated the poor in their homes, gaining experience similar to Ferriar's. He used his position to advocate better conditions for working classes. Like Ferriar and Percival, Kay was a Dissenter with strong Unitarian connections.[4]

The Manchester Ministry to the Poor, renamed the Manchester Domestic Mission in 1836, was founded by Unitarians in 1833.[5] The Rev. William Gaskell (1805-1884) was on its committee from 1833 until he died in 1884; from 1841 he also acted as Secretary. His wife, the novelist Elizabeth Gaskell (1810-1865), used material from the annual reports of the Society in her fiction; whole sections are reproduced in her novel *Mary Barton*, which gave a radical account of the hardship faced by workers.[6]

Further Unitarian domestic missionary societies followed. A second London society was founded in 1835, followed by societies in Liverpool in 1836, Bristol in 1839, Leeds and Birmingham in 1844, and Leicester in 1845.[7] Belfast started a society in 1853. The North End Domestic Mission, the second in Liverpool, began in 1859. New societies were still being formed well into the 1880s: a society was founded in Nottingham in 1883 and in Croydon in 1886.

The domestic mission movement had some notable features. Despite the Unitarian desire to cooperate with other denominations, they were usually shunned and so operated alone.[8] The missions were non-sectarian and many societies stated explicitly that they would not proselytise. Education was usually seen as one of the most important functions, whether it was the establishment of a Sunday school which also provided secular education on weekday evenings or a "Ragged School" aiming to give basic education to neglected children, often delinquents with criminal parents. Other forms of education and training, such as the Mechanics Institutes, were frequently initiated and supported.[9] Moreover there was a move from moralism to reform. The issue of poverty was discussed in terms of wages, political economy and the social consequences of an unreformed factory system.[10] Savings schemes were set up to help the poor to budget. Individual families were befriended and help was given to find employment. Paid male missionaries were introduced, increasing numbers of whom were trained ministers, often replacing volunteer visitors.

The Unitarians had decided in 1854 to establish a college dedicated to training ministers to work among the poor — itself a unique move among the Nonconformists. The Unitarian Home Missionary Board was established in Manchester in 1854 for the training of home missionaries,

Chapter 3

an area not being addressed by Manchester New College. "Our Institution aims at training those who shall be fitted to labour among the poor, to speak to 'the common people' and to bring Unitarian Christianity to the hearts and homes of the great mass of society", the Board proclaimed.[11]

The Unitarian Home Missionary Board was established the same year that the results of the religious census of 1851 were published. The report by Horace Mann, *Census of Religious Worship England and Wales*, was published in January 1854, and documented what many who worked in the domestic missions had found from experience: namely, that the working classes were largely indifferent to religion. It has been suggested that this report may have been a catalyst that led to the Board's foundation.[12] Two inaugural sermons were preached on 4 December 1854, one by Rev. John Relly Beard (1800-1876), the new Board Principal, the other by the Rev. William Gaskell, who supported the venture and became Literary Tutor.[13] Beard had a history of bringing education to the masses and had founded a Unitarian Village Missionary Society in Manchester.[14]

Six years later, at the second annual conference of ministers educated at the Unitarian Home Missionary Board, held in Manchester on 24 January 1861, Rev. William Binns, one of the first graduates, presented his paper "Unitarianism, its Mission and its Missionaries". In it he argued:

> The working class history of the last fifty years will be more helpful to us in missionary enterprises than will the classical histories from the first landing of the Roman legions, or the earliest traces of the Cymri [the Welsh race]. Chartism, Socialism, and the different phases of religious unbelief, strikes, Luddite riots, trade unions, and the co-operation movement, are all fraught with deep significance, and represent popular dissatisfaction with what is conceived to be injustice, and attempts to make what is harmonise better with ideas of what ought to be.[15]

He then went on to describe how the social problems of the day must be dealt with. The missionaries, he said, must understand that in the unwritten history of the working class they will find warfare, patriots who have toiled in vain for the workers, and periods during which utopian experiments had been tried and failed and many had lost all their savings. Furthermore, he said:

> We must apply Christianity to the solution of great questions. If its intensely human spirit be fairly exhibited, it will win allegiance from

multitudes who now regard it as a mere priestly creed, offering a doubtful heaven, but powerless to lessen the sorrows of earth. Messrs. Maurice and Kingsley, the Christian Socialists, and the managers of Working Men's Colleges, have done a world of good by their enterprises. They have shown that religion is not divorced from life; and have secured a respectful hearing for their faith by the practical Christianity of their works.

This endorsement for the socialism of F. D. Maurice should come as no surprise; it would sit well with the ethos of his listeners. Although Frederick Denison Maurice (1805-1872) was an Anglican clergyman, his was Broad Church Anglicanism. The Broad Churchmen took a rational approach to religion and were interested in science and modern discoveries in the higher criticism of the Bible. They were known for their attempts to relate Christian teaching to the social and economic conditions prevailing in nineteenth-century Britain. The spread of influence and ideas between the Unitarians and Broad Churchmen went both ways.[16] Maurice can be regarded as the spiritual leader of the first wave of nineteenth-century Christian socialism. He attracted a group of followers, including another Anglican clergyman, Charles Kingsley (1819-1875), who went to the Chartist demonstration at Kennington Common in 1848 with John Ludlow and later referred to himself as a Chartist; Edward Vansittart Neale (1810-1892), who spent a lifetime working for the co-operative movement, especially in the North of England; Thomas Hughes (1822-1896), who worked for co-operatives and supported trade unions; and John Malcolm Forbes Ludlow (1821-1911), who had been in Paris during the 1848 revolution, had knowledge of French co-operatives and for many years was chief registrar of friendly societies. These last three had read for the bar at Lincoln's Inn, where F. D. Maurice, as chaplain, had encouraged the discussion of social questions and work amongst the poor. They gave concrete content to Maurice's theology of social change: providing working-class education, establishing co-operative workshops for tailors and other oppressed trades, and agitating for social reform.

Henry Solly, the father-in-law of Philip Wicksteed and founder of Working Men's Clubs, regarded himself as a disciple of F. D. Maurice, whom he thought was one of his century's greatest Englishmen.[17] Solly had attended the initial meeting which was to establish the Working

Chapter 3

Men's College in London. Maurice and Solly exchanged sermons, gaining ideas from each other. This congeniality between the two men would have been strengthened by F. D. Maurice's Unitarian background. Maurice was the son of a Unitarian minister and raised a Unitarian, but his family harmony was disrupted when two of his seven sisters changed their religious views, followed by their mother. F. D. Maurice entered Cambridge University, which had no religious test for matriculation, and studied law. Because he would not subscribe to the Thirty-Nine Articles, he left without a degree. When his own religious views changed to Anglicanism, he decided to become a Church of England clergyman and entered Exeter College at Oxford University. However, the Unitarian influence never left him. His biographer David Young described it in *F. D. Maurice and Unitarianism*: "Maurice built his own understanding of the Christian faith on Unitarian foundations. Throughout his life, he consistently affirmed the unity of God and the universality of love. His theological tree received fresh grafts and new branches, but none the less its Unitarian origins remained substantially recognizable."[18]

The second wave of Christian socialism (sometimes called the "revival" of Christian socialism) was more gradual than the first. It had multiple initiatives and emerged even while much of the first wave continued, particularly in the form of educational initiatives.[19] Concern about the dangerously widening gulf between the poor and the well-off classes led to discussion at Oxford University on ways to address the issue. Suggestions included the need for educated middle-class men to spend time among the poor if they were to have credibility and advance practical solutions. There was a mood of dissatisfaction with existing social and religious institutions. Samuel Barnett (1844-1913), an Anglican clergyman, proposed a peaceful solution (he was well aware of the revolutionary alternatives) in his speech at St John's College, Oxford, in November 1883, just after publication of "The Bitter Cry of Outcast London", which had focused much attention on the problem.[20]

In London, the settlement movement, as it became known, began when Barnett established Toynbee Hall in 1884.[21] Named after Arnold Toynbee, the economic historian who had died the year before, the Hall was organised on a non-sectarian basis, "creedless" to its critics. The intention was for university graduates and undergraduates to reside at

Whitechapel, where they could undertake charitable work, agitate for local government services and teach university extension courses. The next settlement, established by Keble College in 1885, was Oxford House in Bethnal Green. This, in contrast to Toynbee Hall, was a settlement with a distinctively Christian flavour.

The Women's University Settlement was founded in 1887. Women came to work at the non-sectarian settlement from Girton and Newnham Colleges at Cambridge University, from Lady Margaret and Somerville Colleges at Oxford University, and from Bedford and Royal Holloway Colleges at the University of London.[22] The Unitarians had a connection to this settlement with the honorary membership of the Rev W. Copeland Bowie (1855-1936),[23] who for many years was secretary of the B&FUA. In 1889 the settlement was joined by Octavia Hill (1838-1912), a housing and social reformer who had already undertaken work in Deptford and Southwark at the behest of Anglican ecclesiastical commissioners "embarrassed to find the church had become a slum landlord".[24]

In 1889 the magnitude of the problem to be faced was documented by the publication of the first volume of *Life and Labour of the People of London* by Charles Booth (1840-1916).[25] Booth's massive study of poverty in London drew on the services of young men and women at the Toynbee settlement and continued over fifteen years. Booth's cousin Beatrice Potter (1858-1943), who later married Sidney Webb (1859-1947), worked on the project for him; her reports on dock labour and the tailoring trade appeared in the report under her own name. One of Booth's researchers, Clara Collett (1860-1948), knew Philip Wicksteed in the 1880s and 1890s,[26] which could have given him access to information about the research in progress and may well have fuelled his responses about the conditions of the poor. The report found that poverty affected one third of the people of London and was attributable to industrial depression, competition, unemployment and low wages.

The Wesleyan settlement of Bermondsey, which had religious work as its focus, followed in 1890. The Congregationalists opened two settlements: Mansfield House in Canning Town in 1890 and Browning Hall in Walworth in 1895.[27] In contrast to these later settlements, Toynbee Hall had developed a radical left-wing flavour. The residents were almost exclusively from Oxford and Cambridge Universities and many had

Chapter 3

adopted the idealist philosophy of T. H. Green. They participated in the 1889 dock strike, helping with relief funds and providing a public platform for strike leaders.[28] Two years later Toynbee men supported the busmen's strike. Conferences were held at Toynbee Hall on old-age pensions, friendly societies, co-operatives, trade unions, unemployment, strikes and socialism. According to Leonard Smith in *Religion and the Rise of Labour*, "the Settlement was associated with the emergence of the New Unionism, which was attempting to organise the hitherto unorganised unskilled labourers and to extend Unionism amongst the skilled and semi-skilled."[29]

Students at Manchester New College had assisted with missionary work in London for many years. After the College moved to Oxford, the Principal, Dr Drummond, asked the Unitarian London Domestic Missionary organisations to provide work for his students during the long vacation. This project was aided when Mrs Humphry Ward, the successful novelist and Unitarian sympathiser, decided to found a university settlement.

Mrs Humphry Ward, née Mary Augusta Arnold (1851-1920), was the granddaughter of Dr Thomas Arnold, the influential headmaster of Rugby School. Her husband, Humphry Ward, was then a Fellow of Brasenose College, Oxford. Her most popular novel, *Robert Elsmere* (1888), tells the story of an Anglican clergyman whose faith journey takes him from traditional Christianity towards acceptance of Unitarian beliefs. She attended the services of the Unitarian minister Dr Stopford Brooke until his chapel closed in 1895 and she gave a number of lectures at Unitarian events. She raised funds for philanthropic causes and from 1881 to 1898 served on the Council of Somerville Hall, one of Oxford's earliest women's colleges.[30]

In the autumn of 1889 Mrs Ward visited Toynbee Hall. This visit crystallized her ideas about founding a hall based on the new theology. She decided to rent rooms at University Hall "for two students for their use during the Oxford vacations — to work among the poor of London."[31] She turned to the premises of University Hall, Gordon Square, recently occupied by Manchester New College, which by 1890 was home to Dr Williams' Library, and arranged to rent the "gloomy dormitory and cavernous common rooms".[32] The Hall was close to Bedford Square, both squares having been built on the Duke of Bedford's

Mrs Humphry Ward (Mary Augusta Arnold)

estate in Bloomsbury, while the slums of St Pancras and King's Cross reached its edges. The nearby Cartwright Gardens appeared on Charles Booth's map as the penultimate grade of poverty.

Mrs Ward persuaded Philip Wicksteed to become warden of the Hall, despite his doubts about the enterprise. By October 1890 ten residents had been selected. During 1891 and 1892 a course of Sunday lectures was offered to the public, mainly by Wicksteed, supported by other notable Unitarian scholars including James Martineau. Wicksteed, however, continued to have doubts. He did not believe the Hall was doing the work that it set out to do, and later confided to Mrs Ward's daughter, Janet Trevelyan (1879-1956), that he felt uneasy all the time.[33]

Wicksteed's misgivings were well founded, as the Hall faced a rebellion by its residents, who rejected the role Mrs Ward gave them as students of "modernism", the Christian theism she hoped to propagate.[34] Some of the residents were more interested in a Marxist interpretation of class and poverty. They sought answers as to why poverty existed and how it could be removed. So the residents raised their own funds to rent a small building in Marchmont Street in the slum neighbourhood behind Tavistock Square. In Marchmont Hall, children were entertained, boys' and girls' clubs organised, music provided and socialist ideas discussed. Marchmont Hall was secular, had sixteen residents, and welcomed working-class people. This unofficial hall was highly successful. For Mrs Ward the writing was on the wall and she decided to abandon University Hall in favour of creating a new settlement closely modelled on Marchmont Hall. Having raised the building funds from the well-known philanthropist Passmore Edwards (1823-1911),[35] she persuaded the Duke of Bedford to provide a large plot of land on the corner of Tavistock Square.

The Passmore Edwards settlement was opened in 1897, much to the relief of Philip Wicksteed, who resigned as warden at University Hall. The settlement provided adult education, concerts, debates and sporting events. Its greatest success was in early childhood education for the poor parents of the district. By the end of 1897 there were 650 children coming to each Saturday session and by the end of 1898 there were 800. This success lived on into the twentieth century.

One reason why Wicksteed would have been happy to see his role in the settlement end was the demands he had felt for some time as the chief supporter of the Labour Church. "The Labour Church rested on Wicksteed's broad shoulders as long as I was connected with it", John Trevor wrote.[36] Wicksteed had, in one sense, provided a catalyst for the formation of the Labour Church. In 1891 Trevor attended the triennial National Conference of Unitarian, Free Christian, Presbyterian and other Non-Subscribing Churches at Essex Hall in London. There he heard addresses on the subject "The Church and Social Questions" by the trade union leader Ben Tillett (1860-1943)[37] and Philip Wicksteed. Tillett "burst on the audience like a Titan"[38] with his speech about the needs of the working class and the failure of the churches, but it was Wicksteed who described the basis for radical social reconstruction:

> All questions of industrial organisation are to be regarded simply and without qualification from the point of view of the worker ... [A]ll who do not in the strictest sense "make" their living must stand or fall by the

simple test of whether they make life more truly worth living to the hewers of wood and the drawers of water.[39]

Upon Trevor's return to Manchester he met a working man, a regular attendee at his church, who told him he could no longer attend: "He liked me, he liked my sermons, but he could not stand the atmosphere of the Church. He could not breathe freely."[40] Trevor told the man that if he could not find a home in the Church, it was no home for him either. His next step was to form the Manchester and Salford Labour Church, which he did while still minister of Upper Brook Street Free Church. The church allowed Trevor access to a room one night a week for choir rehearsal and use of the harmonium for his Labour Church services. Support within his existing congregation came mainly from younger and poorer members. Trevor may have thought this amounted to a majority, but there was unexpected opposition from Edward Vansittart Neale. Neale, as we have already seen, was outstanding in the first wave of Christian socialism as a leader in the co-operative movement. He was a warden at the church, having been attracted by the open and informed approach of the minister before Trevor. While he disagreed with Trevor's Labour Church services, he did so in a kind and tolerant manner.

By the end of 1891, after founding the Labour Church, Trevor realized that he was unable to continue his Labour Church work and carry on his ministry at Upper Brook Street. He decided to resign while still enjoying good relations with his former congregation.[41] The theology that John Trevor advanced was that God was in the Labour movement here and now. It was a form of ethical socialism with its roots in an immanentist world view. It claimed that the divine was present in this world, thus removing the distinction between the sacred and secular; it emphasized the universal brotherhood of all persons; and it saw Jesus as a man whose mission was to uplift the downtrodden in society.[42]

John Trevor, it has been noted, remained committed to his Unitarian ideals. He did not abandon them when he formed the Labour Church movement; he gave them an outlet that he believed served the working class.[43] This is an important observation, as some have seen his resignation from Upper Brook Street as a renunciation of Unitarianism. However, he never severed his links with Unitarianism and continued to act as a supply minister into the early 1920s.

Chapter 3

John Trevor

Wicksteed was second only to Trevor in importance to the Labour Church. He provided funds;[44] he held a discussion group at University Hall to expound its ideals and arranged for Trevor to come and speak; on 3 February 1892 he gave a sermon at the Labour Church in Manchester, which he subsequently wrote about in the *Labour Prophet*:

> I had the rare privilege of conducting a service for the Labour Church. I was struck at once with the purposeful air with which the six or seven hundred members of my congregation gathered. They were of all classes, but the great bulk I took to be workmen. We had, I think, the most genuine and spontaneous religious service in which I ever engaged.[45]

This was the first of many addresses Wicksteed would give. He also wrote for the Labour Church organ *Labour Prophet*, which Trevor established in 1892, and contributed articles in *The Inquirer*. One of his most significant publications was *What Does the Labour Church Stand For?* in which he asserted that whenever the labour movement looks to its principles it is inspired by the abolition of privilege. He then proceeded to criticise the churches for accepting the existing social order.

He pointed out the shallowness and hypocrisy of accepting my "working class brother" as religiously equal when he is alienated in all other spheres of life. "The true militant labour-democrat" he said, "cannot feed his religious life in fellowship with those whose conception of the kingdom of God is not only different from, but radically incompatible with his own", and he concluded, "If, then, the labour Movement is to find religious utterance, there must be a Labour Church."[46]

In 1893 John Trevor became chairman of the Labour Church Union, with the able support of the New Zealander Harry Atkinson (1867-1956)[47] as general secretary. Organisation was necessary as the movement had spread rapidly across the country from Bradford to York, with the greatest concentration in the northern counties of Lancashire, Yorkshire and the midlands.[48] Church leadership was not limited to Unitarians: Quakers, Congregationalists and Wesleyan Methodists could all be found, although Unitarians with socialist sympathies comprised most of the ministers. The number of Labour Churches continued to expand, especially after the involvement of Robert Blatchford (1851-1943), owner of the socialist newspaper *Clarion*, who founded the Manchester and Salford Independent Labour Party in 1892. Independent Labour Party branches and Labour Churches were often virtually inseparable, with common membership and meetings that were hard to tell apart. John Trevor soon realized that if he was to preserve the religious ideology of the Labour Church there must be a clearer separation between the two. To this end a conference was held in London in January 1893, at which the Independent Labour Party became a national movement. It adopted the Manchester and Salford Independent Labour Party constitution prepared the previous year, which, according to Harry Atkinson in a letter to Wicksteed's biographer, came about in the following way:

> Although Blatchford [did] the writing, much of the inspiration came from John Trevor. He it was who had the idea that the different elements in the movement towards socialism in Manchester at that time should be got together. So we had two leading spirits from the Social Democratic Federation, Evans and Purvis, two from the Fabian Society, Settle and Dugdale, he [John Trevor] and I [Harry Atkinson], his assistant, from the Labour Church, and the great man of the day, Blatchford, of the *Clarion*. I have not seen any evidence yet which weakens my

Chapter 3

Rose and Harry Atkinson

belief that the starting of the Manchester and Salford I.L.P. under such auspices and in such a manner was the true inauguration of the Third Party movement and the beginning of the British I.L.P.[49]

John Trevor suffered a period of ill health following the deaths of his second son in June and his wife Eliza in December 1894. He married Annie Higham on 20 March 1895 and soon afterwards moved to London, looking to establish Labour Churches there.

A meeting of some forty friends was held in Dr Williams' Library on 12 July 1895. It is reasonable to assume that William Jellie would have been invited and would have attended this meeting, as his mentor Philip Wicksteed had played an important part in the organisation. Jellie, as we will shortly see, was active in meetings of London Unitarians.

John Trevor thought Dr Williams' Library could form an intellectual centre for the Labour Church movement. To this end he made a proposal to the Trustees of the Library that he hold regular Sunday meetings there, on the express understanding that the Library would have no responsibility for the ideas or doctrines of the Labour Church. The arrangement was made, but at the last minute it was cancelled by the trustees of the Library, and the Labour Church was not allowed to meet there, much to the embarrassment of John Trevor and his supporters.[50]

Although it would not have been apparent then, the Labour Church movement had already reached its peak, with 54 congregations in 1895. From that point on there was a continual decline, so by 1902 there were only 22 churches.

London was never to be the success John Trevor hoped for, although other Unitarian ministers gave considerable support to the Labour Church at their meetings. The Rev. Stopford Brooke at a London ministers' meeting on 20 November 1893 asked his colleagues to take the side of the working classes as opposed to the privileged classes.[51] At the triennial National Conference of Unitarians, Free Christian and other Non-Subscribing Congregations held in Manchester in April 1894, the Rev. Charles Hargrove read a paper on "The Churches and the Poor", in which he asserted that the church had a duty to act on unemployment, bad housing and the conditions that bred vice. He rejected economic competition and argued that charity was not effective. What was needed, he said, was "a revolution of peaceful ideas if the Churches do their part and take a lead, and Christ heads the movement; but revolution violent and subversive if they uphold the existing confusion and preach peace where there is no peace".[52] The speech was received with applause. John Trevor and Philip Wicksteed were among those who took part in the following discussion, nearly all of whom were Unitarians who supported the Labour movement.[53] Only one clergyman spoke against Hargrove's ideas.

The 1894 annual meeting of the B&FUA at Essex Hall, London, saw a discussion following a paper by the Rev. James R. Beard on "Pioneer Work at Home". In the course of the discussion the Rev. W. H. Lambelle from Newcastle said, "Attention should be given in a marked manner to Labour. [Hear.] The Labour Church was all on one side and if its upholders said they had no creed the Unitarians said that they had no creed, but were bound together by the fatherhood of God and the brotherhood of man." He was followed by the Rev. H. W. Perris from Hull who said that in Hull they had a Labour Church with a congregation of 200 working men. "He felt a great disappointment that Unitarians were not elastic enough to take into their circle these men. [Hear, hear.] Personally, he had a profound belief that the work of the Labour Church would go on." William Jellie was in attendance, having conducted the devotional service that preceded the meeting.[54]

The annual meeting in the following year saw a discussion on "The Social Implications of our Faith", with the Rev. G. St Clair of Cardiff maintaining that Christ was a social reformer and teacher of brotherhood rather than a socialist — a view discussed subsequently by Philip Wicksteed from a different perspective.[55] H. Bond Holding, a Unitarian lay preacher and member of the executive committee of the Fabian Society who was prominent in the Labour Church, urged the Unitarian Lay Preachers Association to support the London Labour Church.[56]

William Jellie, as we know from his correspondence with the Rev. Brooke Herford, was active in 1896 in organising a Unitarian meeting in London.[57] He appears to have been present at more than one meeting in 1896: he corresponded with Brooke Herford about one meeting in March, and with James Martineau about another meeting in May.[58]

The meeting in question was that of the London Unitarian Ministers on 27 May 1896, at which Wicksteed, in a clever move that linked the twin evils of class and racial prejudice — "The human race is *not* born for the few" — persuaded his colleagues to vote unanimously in expressing opposition to Britain's treatment of native people in British colonies. He argued that "The history of race oppression has been still more horrible than the history of class oppression ... the struggle that puts the British workman in command of his own destinies also puts him in command of the destinies of hundreds of millions of the 'subject-races'..."[59]

There can be no doubt that William Jellie heard this argument and voted for it. And he went further, having read Fabian publications including those written by Beatrice and Sidney Webb. It was in the writing of Beatrice Webb that he identified with a sentiment for the common good, so much so that he recorded it in his collection of quotations:[60]

> In the life of the wage earning class, absence of regulation does not mean personal freedom. Fifty years' experience shows that factory legislation, far from diminishing individual liberty, greatly increases the personal freedom of the workers who are subject to it. Everyone knows that the Lancashire woman weaver, whose hours of labour and conditions of work are rigidly fixed by law, enjoys, for this very reason, more personal liberty than the unregulated [in Notting Hill][61] laundry woman. She is not only a more efficient producer, and more capable of associating with her fellows in Trades Unions, Friendly Societies, and Co-operative

Stores, but an enormously more independent and self-reliant citizen. It is the law, in fact, which is the mother of freedom.[62]

As the nineteenth century was drawing to a close, the nature of social change was determined by the reality of poverty and the responses to that reality. The work of the Unitarian domestic missions, which had been developed over 70 years earlier amongst the poorest of the poor, was not restricted to soup kitchens. In addition to helping to address immediate wants, the missions aimed to introduce skills that could help people to find employment and, through the provision of basic education, to increase the chance of another generation being lifted from poverty. The establishment of the Unitarian Home Missionary Board was a significant commitment in this area.

The settlement movement in which the Unitarians were involved, like other philanthropic movements, has been seen as trying to deal with a problem that really required large-scale intervention by the state. Although this criticism could be fairly levelled at philanthropy generally, the movement did have some success at the local authority level, lobbying for improved public water supply and sanitation. Perhaps a greater indirect achievement was the awareness of the reality of poverty that it gave the young university-trained people who passed through the settlements. This was an experience they carried for life and were able to use to influence others.

However, it was in the Labour Church movement that the Unitarians played their greatest part in promoting social change. While not all Unitarians embraced it, and certainly many opposed it (while others saw involvement as a loss rather than a gain for Unitarianism), for a brief period of time this movement enjoyed a symbiotic relationship with the political Labour parties. Arguably it stimulated important ideas about social change and, by doing so from a religious perspective, contributed to the development of the Labour movement. The Labour movement would continue into the twentieth century and would introduce the greatest social changes seen in modern Britain, the welfare state. For this to be achieved required a revolutionary change in thinking. As Beatrice Webb put it, there had to be a "transference of the emotion of self-sacrificing service from God to man".[63]

4

Two English Ministries

William Jellie graduated from Manchester College, Oxford, in June 1890. His next step was to obtain a ministerial appointment, but where? In the event it was Stamford Street Chapel, with its associated Blackfriars Mission, that Jellie accepted as his first charge.[1] He succeeded the Rev. W. Copeland Bowie, who became secretary to the B&FUA.

The Stamford Street Chapel was well established by the time Jellie arrived in 1890. Built in 1823, the Chapel had united two congregations; Princes Street Chapel, Westminster, and St Thomas's Street Chapel, Southwark. The Chapel, located near the approach to Blackfriars Bridge, was an impressive structure; its portico was built in neoclassical design comprising six large Doric columns and pediment.[2]

When Jellie arrived at Stamford Street Chapel, he found a proud recent history. A former minister, Robert Spears (1825-1899), had hosted what was probably the first public meeting to support British women's suffrage on 6 April 1868.[3] Under Spears the Chapel had grown in the 1860s and 1870s; the Sunday school had 140 children enrolled, the headquarters of the London Unitarian Lay Preachers Union was located there and regular public meetings were hosted.[4] In 1882 there was need for more accommodation so the roof was removed and a hall capable of holding 500 children was built, which could be used for Sunday School.[5] The lecture hall was also used for public concerts. Membership of this thriving congregation required the payment of five shillings per annum and name entry in the register.[6] Newspaper advertisements began appearing in the "Preachers for Tomorrow" Unitarian section of the local paper in November 1890. The message was always the same:

Stamford St Chapel, where William Jellie was minister for six years

at Stamford-street, Blackfriars-road, S.E. the Rev. William Jellie, B.A. was conducting Sunday services at 11am and 7pm.[7]

Besides his usual ministerial duties there was an additional pastoral workload for Jellie: "Blackfriars Mission as part of the work of Stamford Street congregation — and in recent years the responsibility for it has been placed entirely on their minister's shoulders."[8] This responsibility arose in 1880 when the former Carter-Lane Mission became the Blackfriars Mission and the inhabitants from Collingwood Street and New Cut were amalgamated with Stamford Street Chapel. "The ministers of Stamford-street Chapel have had since the amalgamation entire charge."[9] Jellie had sole charge as both minister and missioner. It was not common to find a domestic mission associated with a chapel in this way.[10] But it was a role he embraced.

Blackfriars Mission was located near Blackfriars Bridge in the London Borough of Southwark. Charles Dickens had set his novel *Little Dorrit* — which George Bernard Shaw described as a more seditious book than *Das Kapital* — in the old Borough. Beneath the criticism of Victorian society it is an account of suffering that afflicted Dickens when his father was incarcerated in Marshalsea debtors' prison in Southwark.[11]

Chapter 4

The mission was aimed at the "neglected poor" of this somewhat crowded part of the city. Home visits were undertaken in an attempt to form friendships so that the problems of hunger, drunkenness and unemployment could be addressed.[12]

The Women's University Settlement, at 44 Nelson Square on the east side of Blackfriars Road, was in the heart of Jellie's domestic mission area and was his close neighbour, his residence being 20 Nelson Square, Blackfriars.[13] The settlement's focus was on activities to improve the welfare of women and children, initiatives that would have been underway by the time Jellie arrived at the Blackfriars mission.

Jellie had only been in his job a few years when another organisation, the Salvation Army, decided to undertake work in Blackfriars. They opened lodging houses and shelters for homeless men in 1892 in Blackfriars Road.[14] Their accommodation provided a place to sleep and wash and a slice of bread each night for upward of 800 men, but it was not without controversy. Some accused the shelters of unhealthy overcrowding,[15] which the Army denied. The medical officer of health for Southwark objected to the numbers of paupers admitted to the shelters, who then became a charge on the rates. In 1893 the cost had reached over £837 "so this so-called philanthropic enterprise," said *The Times*, "entails a heavy and indirect tax upon the ratepayers."[16] The introduction of yet another mission in Blackfriars after thirty years of Unitarian work must have been welcomed by Jellie. The immensity of the task in that area is reflected in the numbers so readily catered for by the Salvation Army as well as the cost to the ratepayers.

No doubt influenced by the conditions he encountered in his missionary work, Jellie showed a strong interest in wider social issues. In 1892 the local Member of Parliament is found addressing a meeting in the Chapel; and in 1893 Jellie took part in a public meeting at Lambeth addressed by David Lloyd George, MP speaking in favour of local control over the liquor trade. He claimed that the drink traffic was the root cause of "pauperism, crime and immorality."[17]

Jellie was also active in the B&FUA. In 1894 he conducted the devotional service at the opening of the sixty-ninth conference held at Essex Hall. He may well have been attracted by the conference topic on the first day: "Pioneer Work at Home". The conference discussed the new Labour Church at some length, with one speaker expressing the view that "the work of the Labour Church would go on."[18]

It may have been at this conference that Jellie first met the Earl of Carlisle, George Howard (1843-1911), who chaired the last session on day three.[19] Jellie became friendly with the Carlisles, particularly the Countess of Carlisle, Rosalind Howard (1845-1921), known as the "Radical Countess."[20] She was a supporter of women's rights and temperance. She was on the executive of the Women's Liberal Federation in 1890. Identifying with the radical wing of the Liberal party, at the 1892 party conference she confronted Gladstone over women's suffrage.

It is almost certain that Jellie was a visitor to the Carlisles' London home, where the guests would have been likely to entertain and stimulate him. In this circle he could have come across intellectuals and literati, some of whom he already knew. The English actor and dramatist William Poel (1852-1934) was an instructor to the Shakespeare Reading Society, founded by students of University College, London in 1887[21] when Jellie was a student at University Hall. It is reported that Jellie "was a friend of William Poel, tutor to actors of the quality of the Du Mauriers and the Terrys and often accompanied them to house parties where reading and acting were the done thing."[22] Exposure to such dramatic talent was not wasted on Jellie. He put it to good use soon after his arrival in New Zealand with members of the Auckland Unitarian Church and subsequently was to reach even greater heights in public performance.

We do not know how much contact Jellie had with his family in Ireland after he became minister at Stamford Street. Presumably he had the chance to return each year during his long vacation. On one such holiday during his fifth year working in London he went home to see his family in Carrickfergus. His reputation had preceded him and he was pressed into service at the Church of the Second Congregation, Rosemary Street Presbyterian Church, Belfast. An advertisement announced that "the Rev. William Jellie, B.A. (Lond.) of London will officiate tomorrow", Sunday 12 August 1894 at 11:30 a.m.[23] It may well have been considered something of a coup to have the young minister from London in the pulpit.

Chapter 4

The young man from the north of Ireland matured in many respects in his first ministerial position. He had developed within a circle of cultured friends who supported his social and personal interests; he had worked hard at his ministerial responsibilities and tackled the myriad problems presented by the Blackfriars Domestic Mission; he had pursued political reform that he thought would alleviate the hardship of the poor around him. As the B&FUA saw it, "he remained for six years and did very good work in a crowded and poor part of the Metropolis."[24]

The announcement that the Rev. W. Jellie had accepted the pastorate of the Ipswich Unitarian Chapel appeared in *The Times* on 25 May 1896. The Rev. Brooke Herford gave him encouragement and advice concerning his appointment: "the Eastern Co[unties] want more heart and spirit putting into them ... We dreadfully need strengthening there; ... That's why I want a man like yourself who knows something of the South to go there."[25]

Jellie probably took up his appointment in July 1896,[26] when he was just 31 years old. He began his ministry with a Sunday morning sermon, "Our Witness to God", and in the evening, "Are Unitarians Christians?"

The call to Ipswich may have seemed like a welcome relief from the demands of Stamford Street. The contrast between the two could not have been greater. Architecturally, the neoclassical style of the Stamford Street Chapel was exchanged for the Puritan-derived lines of a Meeting House built in 1700. The bustle and squalor found in the great metropolis was exchanged for a small county town in the east of England; the religious, educational, social and political societies available in London were replaced with the confines of rural town life.

From his arrival Jellie once again became involved in Unitarian organisation. A fortnight after his arrival the Eastern Union of Unitarian and Free Christian Churches held its two-day annual meeting in Ipswich. At the Sunday Chapel service Jellie preached on "The Household of God" in the morning and "Christian Unity" in the evening. On Monday there was a business meeting followed by an evening Recognition Service at which the Rev. Dr Brooke Herford preached. This was followed by a

Two English Ministries

Ipswich Unitarian Chapel

public meeting to welcome Jellie to his ministry in this town. At this conference he initiated a successful motion at the conference to support the appeal of the B&FUA for a mission to India.[27] Two years later, at the Eastern Union conference held in Norwich in 1898, he became joint conference secretary.[28]

It was at Ipswich that Jellie first began his involvement in adult education, something that would become a lifelong passion in New Zealand. He attended the first meeting of the Ipswich University Extension Society on 21 June 1898 and was elected to the committee. The Society began with 50 members and decided to introduce Cambridge Extension Lectures in Ipswich.[29] The first course of lectures attracted 138 students; nine entered the examination, all passing, three with merit. The second course attracted 105 attendances, 15 students entered the examination and nine passed.[30] There was much Jellie could learn from this successful start in adult education.

The B&FUA plans for Home Mission work revolved around a speaking tour by the Rev. Stopford Brooke. Between October 1897 and May 1898 he preached in thirty-four churches in England, Scotland and Ireland, giving a great stimulus to liberal religion.[31] Dr Brooke spoke at the Ipswich Unitarian Chapel early in 1898, assisted by Jellie. There were large congregations at both services, and Dr Brooke was

Chapter 4

listened to with great attention.[32] This no doubt gave a great boost to Jellie's ministry.

In 1899 attention was already being given to the forthcoming bicentennial celebration of the Ipswich Chapel. The Rev. Dr Stopford Brooke returned in November 1899 to preach a special service to raise funds for the bicentenary.[33] These were celebrations Jellie was destined to miss. He found the quiet provincial life too limiting and had resigned the previous month to accept a position in Auckland, New Zealand.

William Jellie, portrait at his Ipswich ministry of three years, before he left for New Zealand

Part Two

The Twentieth Century Ministries

William Jellie in 1905

5

In New Zealand: Auckland

In October 1899 the B&FUA invited William Jellie to go to Auckland, New Zealand. It was made clear in this offer that, should he so desire, he could return home to England after three years.

What was it that attracted Jellie to the Colony of New Zealand and caused him to travel half way round the world, leaving behind all the people and places familiar to him, to start a new venture in a new land? He would have known that in New Zealand the absence of an established church allowed all dissenting opinions to be freely held without legal disabilities, which had until recent times not been the case in the United Kingdom. This was certainly a factor in the minds of some who migrated. In 1883, a settler to the colony, John Bradshaw, wrote:

> Whatever other prejudices or civil disabilities the colonists have left behind, religious differences have not been lessened by any larger-minded uniformity induced by change of life and scene. Possibly, starting as they did on an altogether fresh basis, the several sects exercise more toleration towards each other than they used to do at home. The principle is fully recognized that every individual possesses a right to enjoy the perfect freedom of his religious convictions.[1]

The absence of inherited power and privilege with its attendant class structure could have been another consideration for Jellie. Despite the attempts by the New Zealand Company to import the British class structure into New Zealand, the colonising elite were unable to create the class structure they desired. This was not to say that elite groups did not emerge from time to time in pastoralist areas, commercial centres or politics. But importantly from the viewpoint of social opportunity, class distinctions were not strictly observed in New Zealand.[2] Although inherited titles and honours were recognized and transmitted in New Zealand, they did not provide the special status that they enjoyed in Britain.[3]

But what was perhaps most attractive to Jellie was the reputation New Zealand had in the minds of many regarding its progressive social reforms. "He knew the early days of the Fabian movement", wrote one who knew Jellie well.[4] The influence of his mentor and friend Philip Wicksteed reached George Bernard Shaw, the Fabian Society and the Labour Church.[5] The moral dimension that Wicksteed brought to bear in his discussions about socialism would have chimed with William Jellie's worldview, training and experience. Although we do not know how deeply Jellie's sympathies ran, it is reasonable to assume he looked favourably on the New Zealand developments.[6]

Most of the labour and industrial reforms so proudly promoted in New Zealand at the end of the nineteenth century had the hallmark of William Pember Reeves (1857-1932).[7] Reeves was Minister of Labour in the Liberal government of John Ballance (1839-1893),[8] which came into power on 24 January 1891. It was a Liberal government that enjoyed Labour support inside and outside Parliament for its reforms. When it came into power the country was still in the grips of the long depression which had begun in 1880 and would not be ameliorated until 1895. There had been increasing unemployment, especially among casual and seasonal workers, and real per capita income had declined between 1886 and 1893.[9] Mindful of the agitation that surrounded the Royal Commission into "sweating", which reported in 1890 recommending extensive workplace regulation,[10] Reeves ensured that a comprehensive review was made of labour legislation. The Factories Act of 1891 was one of the first pieces of legislation passed by the new government. It was extended in 1894, forbidding the employment of children less than 14 years of age, setting maximum hours of work and requiring registration of factories and an inspection regime. The Employers Liability Act 1891 enabled workers to obtain compensation for injuries received from operating dangerous machinery or because of employers' carelessness. The Shops and Shop Assistants Act 1894 controlled hours of work. Trade unions were given legal status with the ability to incorporate. Much attention was directed in the area of industrial reform. Writing in 1898, Reeves declared that the Industrial Conciliation and Arbitration Act 1894 had been passed in an endeavour "to settle Labour disputes between employers and Trade Unions by means of public arbitration" instead of the strike and the lock-out.[11] Most of these Acts were administered by the new Department of Labour organised by Reeves' ally and right hand man Edward Tregear (1846-1931).[12]

A number of the labour reform measures had been frustrated in the Upper Chamber, the Legislative Council. As a consequence the life term of appointment was changed to seven years, and the Council was allowed to elect its own Speaker, but continued to be a nominee chamber.[13] However when Ballance sought to appoint a dozen more Councillors, the Governor, William Hillier, fourth Earl of Onslow (1853-1911), accepted only eight appointments, saying the Liberals had no right to "swamp" the Council. Ballance refused to accept Onslow's decision or that of his successor Lord Glasgow and had the matter referred to the Colonial Office in London, who ruled in Ballance's favour.[14] Thus a further blow was struck that would aid the progressive reforms sought by the Liberal government. Following the death of Ballance, Reeves found Richard Seddon, the new Premier, less enthusiastic about his labour law reforms; so when he was offered the post of Agent General for New Zealand, Reeves accepted and left for London in January 1896.

William Jellie's colleagues also expected that Jellie would find in New Zealand a progressive society that looked after its members in a much fairer way than the one he would leave behind, which was infused by class and poverty. Professor J. Estlin Carpenter from Manchester College, who as we have seen was an early supporter of the Labour Church, wrote to him just before he left for New Zealand, saying, "I imagine that you will find many interesting experiments going on in advanced democracy."[15] For an observer in England during the last decade of the nineteenth century, reports about New Zealand's "experiments" would have been plentiful. An address to the Royal Colonial Institute on "State Socialism and Labour Governments in Australasia" in 1893 by the former Governor, the Earl of Onslow, claimed that developments in the colony were "in the direction in which the spirit of the age is everywhere tending" and should be followed when shown not to be harmful to Britain's commercial interests.[16]

Chapter 5

When William Reeves and his wife Maud (1865-1953)[17] arrived in London they publicly promoted New Zealand's reforms. Forming close friendships with Fabian luminaries such as Beatrice and Sidney Webb, George Bernard Shaw and H. G. and Jane Wells, Maud promoted women's suffrage, which had been achieved in New Zealand in 1893. (In contrast, women in Great Britain over the age of 30 and with property received the vote in 1918; however at the same time all men over 21 were allowed to vote. It was not until 1928 that all women were able to vote.) William Reeves meanwhile was active in writing and speaking about the New Zealand reforms. He was inundated with invitations to give lectures, free or paid, to all sorts of organisations. Most of them, naturally enough, were about New Zealand and his own reforms. Altogether he contributed a great deal towards reducing the general ignorance about New Zealand. His lectures were not his only addresses. His wit, clarity, brevity and apparently inexhaustible fund of amusing stories made him an admirable after-dinner speaker. In 1898 an English periodical described him as one of the best in London.[18] One lecture he gave about industrial arbitration on a Fabian platform in 1897 drew an audience of five hundred. The Fabian Society published his tract *The State and its Functions in New Zealand*,[19] in which he described land reforms in the form of perpetual lease schemes, national life insurance, a public trust office, compulsory secular education, compulsory acquisition of estates for subdivision and resettlement, as well as the labour reforms previously mentioned. This "Socialistic policy" had succeeded, he said, because the Liberals had the support of the Trade Unions. His later lectures and publications made reference to the old-age pension legislation, the first state pension in the English-speaking world.[20]

It was into this New Zealand society, emerging from the long depression, that William Jellie arrived in February 1900 to build the Unitarian cause. By the time he arrived he had a repertoire of skills that was surprisingly wide for a man of thirty-four: a variety of organisational and administrative experience, political savvy with an ability to engage politicians over social causes, experience working amongst both the slums of London and the soirees of the upper classes, Shakespearean acting, adult education, as well as the usual expertise found in a minister of religion: delivering sermons and addresses, officiating at services and providing pastoral care.

In his first public address, at two Unitarian services held in the Oddfellows Hall in Pitt Street, Auckland on 4 March 1900, William Jellie stated "at the very beginning what it is we set ourselves to do." First and foremost, he said,

> We want to build a church. Not an organisation that shall arrogate to itself supernatural privileges, or exclusive powers from God, but a place of worship, a place for prayer and praise, a place for the study and practice of religion, a place for the promotion of good conduct, a place for the study of truth, a place for the education of men and women in the ways of righteousness, as individuals, as members of a state, and as members of the human brotherhood of all races and nations. That is our idea of a church.[21]

He made it quite clear that the views of heaven and hell held by the orthodox churches were to be rejected. "We have a different meaning of the phrase," he said. "This Heaven and Hell are not postponed to some other life. They begin in this life." The purpose of Unitarianism lay in "helping men and women escape evil and misery in this life, and to attain good and happiness here and now".[22] His idea of escaping misery in this life and obtaining happiness here and now was congruent with the goal espoused by the Labour Church and the sentiments expressed by Philip Wicksteed. It was certainly a view Beatrice Webb wanted to see the churches embrace. However, Jellie did not describe just how he thought this aim should be achieved. He went on to expound another aim: "Though only one little church, standing alone, we shall endeavour to hold up an ideal of a true Catholic Church, that shall be tolerant to all, and able to rejoice in the good of all true workers for humanity." This ideal of tolerance was to sit alongside the concept of a rational theology, so that the facts and discoveries of modern research would be accepted, and science and religion "may no longer be opposing forces".[23] But it was in the following sermon that he dealt with the "Principles and Doctrines of Unitarianism" most clearly and forcibly:

> The seat of our religious authority is the human mind and conscience, which were given us by God for use, and wherein we recognise the voice of God. Nothing is of force which does not commend itself to our mind

and conscience. That is the ultimate tribunal which man can rely upon for the test of truth and right.[24]

Jellie saw a strong link between freedom, upon which he believed human progress depended, and the Unitarian position: "We advocate freedom of thought, freedom of inquiry, freedom of speech, freedom of worship." Freedom was practiced in Unitarianism by not requiring members of the congregation or ministers to subscribe to any particular set of beliefs or form of worship.[25] Another principle he discussed was the relationship between conduct and beliefs. Jellie stated that human conduct was far more important than human opinion. It was, he elaborated, the Unitarian belief that God's attitude towards humanity does not depend on whether our views are correct so much as the life we lead. "A man cannot help his opinions," Jellie said, "but he can help his conduct."[26] The position of Christ within Unitarian theology was covered: Unitarians see Christ as our master, teacher and leader and hold "in essence and spirit, Christ's conception of religion". Jellie said there was no need to believe doctrines about Jesus which he never taught and which grew up after his death: "it is the religion of the Lord's Prayer, the Sermon on the Mount, the Prodigal Son, the Good Samaritan, which Unitarians accept as most fully and clearly expressing that which they hold."[27]

Both services were well attended. Jellie recorded in his diary that there were forty people in the morning and seventy-five in the evening. Publication of the sermons in booklet form became the springboard to launch the church building fund in the following month.[28] Sold for one penny, with the sales going towards the fund, they proved so popular that a reprint of a further thousand copies was issued with a request for donations from friends and sympathisers throughout the Colony.

Jellie did not undertake this task alone. There were talented and generous people in the congregation who helped raise donations for the building fund, design the building and acquire the land. An accountant, Charles Newland (1863-1946), was Treasurer on the committee, providing financial advice and support throughout Jellie's Auckland ministry.[29] He and Jellie formed a legal committee, working with the church solicitor to draft a new set of Church Rules and a Trust Deed. Upon completion of their work a decision was made to incorporate the church under the Religious, Charitable and Educational Trust Boards Incorporation Act 1884.[30]

In New Zealand: Auckland

Thomas Henry White, architect

In regard to the main goal of getting a church building erected, perhaps no one was more important than Thomas Henry White (1843-1923), a musician and architect. An accomplished violinist, White originally came to the fore as leader of the church orchestra. He was born and educated in Birmingham and had studied in Paris before coming to New Zealand via Melbourne in 1863. He took up farming at Taupiri while practising architecture in Hamilton and Auckland, where he designed impressive buildings for both cities.[31] He was also a fine water colour painter. He had already designed a number of churches in New Zealand by the time he was asked to undertake the Auckland Unitarian Church project. There is no evidence that he designed churches outside New Zealand.[32] It was Thomas White and William Jellie who searched for suitable building sites around Auckland and settled on the city council leasehold site in Ponsonby Road. When White was elected chairman of the committee on 27 March 1901, it certainly made for easier planning and organisation so far as the building project was concerned, as the committee often met in his office in Victoria Arcade.

Chapter 5

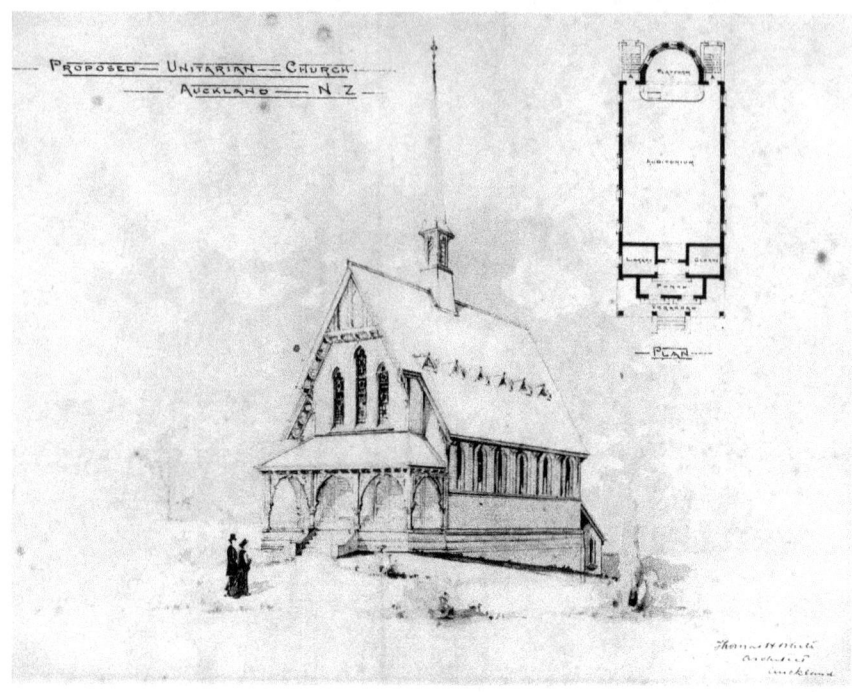

Auckland Unitarian Church plan by architect Thomas H. White, 1900

Auckland Unitarian Church
Original building before the front was altered in the 1930s

In New Zealand: Auckland

*Laying the foundation stone of Auckland Unitarian Church, 17 August 1901
William Jellie on left*

Following the resignation from the committee of Hugh McCready (1853-1933)[33] in October 1901, the vacancy was filled by Joseph Cochrane Macky (1855-1915), then in the last year of his term as mayor of Devonport (1896-1901).[34] It was a choice that was to have far-reaching consequences both for the church and for William Jellie. Five years later, Joseph Macky would become Jellie's father-in-law.

Joseph Macky came from a family which adhered to the Presbyterian tradition and had migrated from the north of Ireland around the middle of the nineteenth century. By the time he joined the Unitarians in his late forties, his life had had its share of success and sadness. Joseph had enjoyed political and commercial success. He was chairman of directors of a large trading enterprise, Macky, Logan, Caldwell Limited, which included the oldest men's clothing manufacturer in the Colony.[35] He married Isabella Campbell Kennedy (1849-1887) on 25 September 1878. They had four

Chapter 5

children, of whom three survived childhood. Their eldest child, Thomas Hugh Macky (1881-1965), was followed by Archibald Cameron Macky (1883-1884), Isabella (Ella) Wilson Macky (1885-1981) and John (Jack) Macky (1887-1977). Three years after the death of their baby son Archie, Joseph's wife Isabella died on 7 August 1887, aged 38 years.[36] A little over a year later, on 11 October 1888, Joseph married again, to Mary Birrell (1858-1915). In the interim it is likely Joseph received help from his family in caring for the children; his brother Thomas Lindsay Macky (1858-1936) and his wife Elizabeth were living in Hepburn Street, Ponsonby, at the same time as he was. By 1892 both families had settled in Devonport. Joseph and Mary had four children of their own: Stewart (1890-1946), Frank (1891-1975), Dorothy Mary (1894-1990) and Joseph Cecil Douglas (1899-1970). Mary was a caring and affectionate mother to the children of Joseph's first marriage. A family historian, Neil Macky, records that Mary "became a real mother to his children and a wonderful helpmate in the difficult years immediately following."[37]

What was it that drew Joseph Macky to the liberal religion of the Auckland Unitarian Church? Was it, as has been suggested,[38] simply intellectual doubts about the orthodox creeds? Or did it also involve personal factors, such as the tragic loss of his young wife and child?

Joseph Macky fell out with his Presbyterian church over the celebrated heresy trial of the Rev. Samuel James Neill (1851-1918). In 1874 Neill had been ordained by the Presbyterian Church in Ireland as a missionary to New Zealand, never having been ordained by a congregation in Ireland.[39] Shortly after his arrival in New Zealand, on 2 May 1875, he was inducted into the Presbyterian Church in Cambridge, Waikato. Two years later he became minister to the St James Presbyterian Church at Thames, where he enjoyed a ministry for the next seventeen years. However, problems emerged when he became involved with the Theosophy Society in 1893. He was initially charged with bringing a woman into the Thames district to promote Theosophy. When this could not be proved he was found guilty of improperly removing four members of his church committee, and in case this was insufficient to remove him he was also declared by the Auckland Presbytery to have departed from the teaching of the Church. The Rev. Neill then organised his own non-sectarian church, holding services in the Choral Hall at Auckland city on alternate Sundays. He continued to hold services in the Thames church for the next three years, until he abandoned it for greener pastures following the Australasian tour of American Theosophists in 1897.[40]

Throughout Rev. Neill's ordeal, Joseph Macky was his stalwart defender, appearing at all the hearings, and declaring at one hearing that "Mr Neill's life was beyond question."[41] When the decision was made to remove Neill from his ministry on 14 February 1894, Joseph Macky, described by *The Observer* as "a gentleman who is and always has been a moral example to every young Presbyterian in New Zealand", stated that "he for the first time in his life was ashamed of his Church".[42] What is not clear is whether Joseph Macky came to the defence of Rev. Neill because he was attracted to the idea of a liberating universalism *vis-à-vis* the constraints of Calvinist Presbyterianism, or simply because he thought the procedure used to try him was unfair. Whatever his motivation, Macky became a key figure in the fledgling Auckland Unitarian Church and a person of great significance in the life of William Jellie.

From Joseph Macky's wife, Mary, we have a picture of Jellie as he was when he arrived in the colony. He was a gentleman aged 34 years, of handsome appearance, dark haired with a dark moustache, bespectacled, and with an agreeable if slightly serious mien. Mary Macky described him as "such an unaffected straight forward man, that he never beats about the bush". Elsewhere she said: "He reads so beautifully, I never heard anyone give an author's meaning as he does." And after observing his pastoral work she wrote, "He is, I should think from what I saw that day, a skilful visitor of the sick."[43]

When the new church building was officially opened on 4 December 1901, Joseph Macky presided over the evening event, a public meeting interspersed with musical selections. The Rev. George Walters from the Sydney Unitarian Church and George Fowlds, Member of the House of Representatives, were the speakers. Macky continued to serve on the committee throughout the period of William Jellie's ministry. He was elected chairman 1902-03 and again in 1909-10, as well as being a Trustee of the Church.

By the time the two men were working closely over Church affairs, Joseph Macky knew that William Jellie had formed a romantic attachment with his daughter Ella. The Mackys had often invited Jellie to visit

Chapter 5

and stay with them at their Devonport house *Darlimurla,* and William and Ella had many opportunities to meet on these occasions. Shortly before Ella left for a trip to Europe and study at the Royal Holloway College on 9 March 1903, William made his feelings known to her parents.[44]

Royal Holloway College was an interesting choice for Ella's higher education. It had been opened in 1886 by Queen Victoria as an independent women's college. In 1900 it became a college of London University along with Bedford College, which had been established in 1849 by Unitarians. The association with a modern secular university was no doubt connected with the struggle for women to be admitted to degrees at Oxford and Cambridge. According to a history of Holloway College:

> Both Universities, after bitter debate, had refused to admit them [women], and in July 1896 a conference of Oxford and Cambridge committees, with all male membership, had advocated the foundation of a women's university, to be called "The Queen's University". The main objection to these committees was not to the higher education of women, but to their admission to full membership of the Universities through the granting of degrees, which would bring with it the right to participate in University policy-making and government.[45]

William and Ella kept in touch, writing to each other on a weekly basis. Much of their correspondence has survived. The Mackys meanwhile maintained constant social contact with William Jellie; he was a regular visitor to their house and attended numerous social engagements as their guest, in addition to the work he undertook with Joseph Macky on Church business. Within a week of Ella's

Newly engaged Ella Macky and William Jellie, 1905

In New Zealand: Auckland

Ella and William's wedding at Darlimurla, 1906

return, on 18 January 1905, the couple became engaged. A year later, on 30 January 1906, they married at *Darlimurla*.

How well did William Jellie's political opinions sit with his new family? An insight into their views is gained from Mary Macky's letter to her eldest son Tom in England:

> I am exceedingly glad to find you taking up the Capital Labour problem. I think you would find one thoroughly in sympathy with Dr [Charles] Strong. More so even than Mr. Jellie. Because the latter is content to stand aside, it seems to me, and patiently wait the results of the forces he so firmly and brightly believes to be working towards the settlement of all problems. Dr Strong suits my temperament more in that he *does*. [Emphasis in original.] He has taken part in every movement in Victoria towards breaking down the barriers you feel so keenly about. But he is an older man than Mr. Jellie. I remember well how great a turmoil Henry George's books threw us. I don't remember much of them now only that his views were lofty and sadly above the practices of the world.[46]

Chapter 5

Both Mary and Joseph Macky had followed Dr Charles Strong, reading his pamphlets and visiting his Australian Church when in Melbourne. Strong had rejected Calvinist Presbyterianism and formed a free religious fellowship ministering to a liberal religious congregation. He was an active reformer involved in the anti-sweating movement; he founded the Working Men's Club and was active in many other social reforms.[47] Jellie, it seems, was not so active a participant in social reform, though he was seen as having the sympathies of a reformer. Mary Macky seems to be attributing to Jellie the popular view of progress as a moral force for good in society. There could have been other considerations in his mind. He may have thought that the reforms achieved to date, and others spoken about by the Liberals, placed New Zealand in a class that did not warrant vigorous agitation. And perhaps he was aware that provocative views in this area could be divisive and inhibit the growth and development of his Church, which was his primary mission.

In the first decade under William Jellie's leadership the Church became known not only as a place of cultured liberal theology. It also achieved a high musical standard with its organ, employing organists of quality, and its choir, for many years under the leadership of William Gribble (1858-1939).

In August 1903 Joseph Macky suggested to the committee that an organ be purchased. Prior to this he and Jellie had for some time been making inquiries to determine what would be a suitable organ and visiting other churches to listen to organs and judge their performance. One that impressed them was built by George Croft (1871-1955) and installed in the Mt Eden Congregational Church.[48] Joseph Macky went to Croft's workshop in Eden Terrace and "was very much impressed with him and his work".[49] When the time came Joseph Macky recommended a Croft organ to the committee that August,[50] its style to be an "unusual double pipe facades divided on either side of the building facing across and down the church".[51] This was the first example in the Colony of the application of a tubular pneumatic action to a divided instrument. The detached console was of solid figured oak.[52] At some £400 the organ was more expensive than the one Croft built for St. Barnabas Anglican Church in

In New Zealand: Auckland

Mt Eden for £300, but Joseph Macky considered the money well spent and entered into a bond with the Trustees of the Church to cover the sum involved.[53] By May 1904 the organ was installed, much to the delight of the congregation, and was declared "one of the best in the colony".[54] Its inauguration was marked with three recitals which filled the Church to capacity, followed by a programme of regular recitals. "Its tone enhanced by the fine acoustic properties of the church, drew music lovers from all over the city: the monthly organ recitals were packed to the doors, gallery included, and on one occasion many were turned away."[55]

The Library that William Jellie oversaw included books on religion and many general topics as well. By the end of his time in Auckland there were over a thousand books and subscribers paid a penny a week to enjoy them. Jessie Heywood (1852-1947) was librarian for 25 years between 1906 and 1930 and her contribution to the intellectual life of the Church was immense.[56]

William Jellie showed political acumen as well as seeking ideological compatibility in the friendships he formed with two outstanding political figures of the day. It appears that he met George Fowlds (1860-1934)[57] and Sir Robert Stout (1844-1930)[58] in the first week in March 1901.[59] These two men had somewhat similar backgrounds: both were born in

Sir Robert Stout   *Sir George Fowlds*

Chapter 5

Scotland, George Fowlds in Ayrshire and Robert Stout in the Shetland Islands; and both of their families followed Scottish Presbyterianism. At home both men enjoyed the open and liberal discussions about current topics that prevailed, but with a difference. In the Stout household theology was more likely to be debated, whereas in the Fowlds house it was radical political ideas. Both men left the religion they were raised in. Robert Stout became a notable freethinker and helped form the Dunedin Freethought Association in 1880,[60] becoming its President, while George Fowlds became Chairman of the Congregational Union in 1899. One significant difference was in the relative wealth and position of their families; whereas Fowlds' father was a handloom weaver[61] and George was apprenticed to a clothier, Robert Stout's father was a merchant and landlord, which gave him an educational advantage early in life. However, when Stout went into politics in New Zealand he denounced the landlord system as a result of witnessing the eviction of tenant farmers in Scotland, and his political views were of the Liberal left in sympathy with the labour bloc.[62] He had publicly called for a Royal Commission following the exposure of the "evils of sweating", and had joined in support of the workers when he became a Trustee of the Tailoresses' Union.[63] Stout had been Premier twice before resigning from politics in 1898. The following year he was appointed Chief Justice of the Supreme Court. The same year George Fowlds entered Parliament as a representative for Auckland City.

Who could have effected the introductions or suggested that Jellie make contact with these men? One answer in the case of Sir Robert Stout could be his old friend John Gammell (1836-1913), a former Unitarian minister and retired educationalist, who had visited Jellie in March 1900.[64] In the case of George Fowlds it is possible that the mercurial Hugh McCready, the original church secretary, may have helped with an introduction, as he had his tailoring business in Queen Street while George Fowlds had his more extensive premises manufacturing and selling clothes on the corner of Fort and Queen Streets. In any event the meetings were propitious and Jellie was to find these friendships rewarding over many years. As we will see, both new friends would help in the development of the Unitarian movement, Sir Robert Stout in particular with Wellington.[65] When Jellie entered into a new career in education some twenty years later, the friendship he had forged with

George Fowlds was to prove valuable. In the meantime George Fowlds had moved to more radical positions. Fowlds, Stout and Jellie had some fundamental positions in common: belief in secular education and its defence from sectarian inroads;[66] belief in the importance of education as the vehicle to provide opportunity in society; and a desire for a just and fair society that rejected the inequities of the Old World.

In 1908 Jellie delivered an important series of sermons on the theme of science and religion. For a man of letters he showed an excellent grasp of current scientific knowledge as he sought to address "one of the great problems of the present day for thoughtful minds ... to reconcile the results of scientific discovery with the conceptions and practices of religion".[67] He approached the subject by referring to a newly published book, *The Bible of Nature* by Professor J. Arthur Thomson,[68] which Jellie asserted was a far larger Book of Revelation than the Bible ever was. He told his listeners that they were living at a time when radical changes were occurring in our thinking about the history of the universe — so much so that it is an "impossibility for the old theology to continue to exist". He first dealt with what was known about the origin of the universe; trying "in a few minutes to outline the story of one thousand millions of years" as he described how planets arose and how other solar systems continue to be created. He discussed how matter changes and evolves and what is known about its chemistry. He pointed out that science says nothing about God, nor does it ask why the universe has come into existence. Here Jellie argued that, because God cannot be outside creation, he must be "the Spirit, the Life, the Soul, as it were of the universe". At the same time he rejected the notion of miracles: "Miracles seem absurd to [the man of science] on the face of them."[69]

When he turned to the origins of life he made two points. First, he said that while it has not yet been demonstrated that life can arise from non-living matter, scientific experiments do not exclude the possibility that it has happened, or that it might be demonstrated in the future. "Personally, I am much inclined to believe that such a discovery will one day be made."[70] Secondly, he turned to the biology of life, describing the evolutionary theory of Charles Darwin and the influence of *The Origin of Species* on human knowledge. Darwin, he told his listeners, had collected a vast amount of evidence, which Jellie had found entirely borne out when he visited the Natural History Museum in London. He illustrated

Darwin's theory with references to species that evolved over time into a myriad of varieties from a common ancestor. Here he used the text *Extinct Animals* by Professor E. Ray Lankester (1847-1929), Director of the Natural History Museum 1898-1907, which was published in 1905. In looking at the evidence for the descent of species, including the fossil records, Jellie invited his listeners to contemplate the difficulties of the alternate explanation, "the special creation theory". That would require us to believe that millions and millions of living forms, looking similar to earlier forms, had been created in separate acts of creation, and that fossils ended up in rocks as a result of multiple cataclysms which annihilated earlier species, after which God began afresh.[71] He placed these ideas in the context of the new knowledge about the geological periods of the earth and the types of life forms that arose at different times.

Finally he turned to the place of humans in the scheme of nature. Here he wanted his listeners "not to take my word for gospel, or the word of any man". His purpose was to look for a few hints "as to how scientific investigation is trending, and what are the generally accepted conclusions, drawn from the facts discovered". Science, he told his listeners, says that man is an animal belonging to the primate family, and he discussed the common characteristics between man and ape: "not merely our physical structure and blood constitution, but our consciousness, the power of feeling, memory, thought, the power of looking forward and expecting something to come." But human morality, by which he meant "a clear conception of what is just and right in our relations with our fellow-men", was something that animals did not have.[72] Jellie then made what appears to be an important declaration of his own beliefs. This may not seem to be closely related to the parallel he was seeking to draw between science and liberal religion, until we learn that the audience to which it was delivered was mainly composed of working class men:

> ...man's dignity is totally independent of his origin. It is pure snobbery to judge of a man by his ancestry. Personally, I think more of a worthy man if he be the son of a poor, or even if he be the son of an unworthy parent. The greater is the credit due to him. And, similarly, there is no loss of dignity, really, if we have to regard man as the self-made son of poorer and less worthy parents.[73]

The significance of the "Modern Genesis" sermon series is threefold: first, it is one of only twelve of Jellie's sermons for which copies are still extant;[74] secondly it is the only one of these where he discusses modern science and its relationship to religious ideas; and thirdly it was noteworthy to church members at the time. For Jellie, preaching may have been "a matter of mind to mind, heart to heart, soul to soul",[75] but as Joseph Macky commented about an earlier sermon by Jellie on the same theme:

> Meanwhile our little church is progressing fairly well. The attendance at the evening service is especially encouraging, the building being quite crowded and the congregation is largely composed of people who, I fancy, have not been attending any church, a most thoughtful looking crowd mostly men and apparently belonging to the working classes. Mother likes Mr. Jellie's morning sermons best as more quiet and helpful and not so argumentative as the evening addresses but the latter are the most popular being a series of subjects taken from the first chapter of Genesis and having to do with the more modern or scientific story ... he does not hesitate and holds himself perfectly free to tell the wonderful story, really far more wonderful, as told by the deep patient searchings of science.[76]

In addition to these intellectual and cultural pursuits, there were many other activities for church members to engage in. Picnics at beaches and rambles with young people and camps, especially at Waiheke Island, were very popular. The record of Charlotte Mary Guy (1875-1957) provides accounts of some of these rambles.[77] William Jellie went on a ramble with Thomas White and five young ladies, including his then-fiancée Ella Macky, from Birkenhead to Kauri Point on 25 November 1905. On 9 December 1905 the ramblers went from Lake Takapuna to Devonport; this time William Jellie was accompanied by three other men and eight young ladies. They stopped for strawberries and cream en route, and at North Head Mr. Jellie left them to visit the Mackys. ("What time do the Mackys have tea on Saturday's?" Charlotte wonders in her journal.) On 13 January 1906 there was a ramble from Auckland to Penrose, a party of seven young ladies plus William Jellie and two other men, where they explored caves before returning to Newmarket.

There is a further record, also likely to be from Charlotte Guy,[78] of a camp at Waiheke Island, 5-14 February 1910. Fifteen girls went by ferry to Pegler's Bay at the eastern end of Waiheke Island, next to Cowes Bay. There they were met and brought ashore by Mary and George Pegler and William Jellie in "pulling boats." They found the tents already erected and

Chapter 5

the camp prepared: clotheslines, washbasins, hooks, fireplace and firewood, "everything that comfort or convenience could desire was already prepared for us." Ella Jellie was also there with the new baby Hilary, less than three months old, having been born on 17 December 1909.[79] The author recorded a scene that occurred early in the evenings when a solitary figure would emerge and take his swim: "'tis a sad sight to see a strongman, the father of a family and the Minister of a Congregation like ours, amiably splashing about in 3 feet of water, when he might have been breasting the wave like one of us!" The girls played tennis, hockey and cricket and did some tree climbing. One day they rowed to Cowes Bay where the Post Office was. Every evening they had music, having bought an orchestra of violins and mandolins with them. There was great excitement when they saw the white sails of the yachts in the bay bringing the boys to join them. Later they went fishing with the boys in their boats, a decided improvement over fishing off the rocks. On Saturday night there was group singing and "some of the boy's songs haunt my memory still." They composed their own song, *Won't you come back to Pegler's Bay*, which they sang as they steamed out of the bay on their way home.

While the Auckland church was thriving, all was not well in the Wellington Unitarian Church. Murmurs of discontent with the new minister, the Rev. Dr William Tudor Jones (1865-1946), had reached Jellie during 1907. Ever resourceful, Jellie sought to obtain an independent sounding of affairs from his trusted friend Mrs Annie Shawcross (née Smith, 1848-1927). She had been educated at Newnham College, Cambridge University and taught at Manchester High School for Girls before coming to New Zealand and marrying Edward Russell Shawcross (1838-1899). They were members of the congregation before Jellie arrived; both were on the management committee, and Edward Shawcross was chairman.

Mrs Shawcross stayed in Wellington for nearly a fortnight with friends, Mr and Mrs Andrews, who were former members of the church in Auckland. Upon her return she wrote William Jellie a report of her impressions.[80] She found William Tudor Jones and his wife Helen dedicated to their calling, but realised they had not been able to adapt well

In New Zealand: Auckland

Rev. Dr and Mrs Tudor Jones

to New Zealand: "Dr Jones cannot be self-controlled and silent at times, when it is seriously necessary he should be, and so brings trouble upon himself." She gave an example: "But Mrs Shawcross what would you do with the ones on your committee — the one not even believing that Jesus ever lived and the other not believing in God! They must go!" He had expected to remain for ten or fifteen years, but had already written to the secretary of the B&FUA asking to be released at the end of three. In fact, he confided to Mrs Shawcross, he would leave at the end of next week if he could! However, Dr Jones was an excellent preacher and appreciated by many. The problem lay in the relationship between the minister and the management committee. It required a great deal of tact on the part of the minister and his wife if they were to work together in harmony. Not helping matters was the behaviour of some of the congregation in forming cliques; the half dozen leading families in the church did not reach out a welcoming hand to others. Nor, it appeared, were those with money especially generous in their support.

This report was forwarded to the Rev. W. Copeland Bowie, secretary of the B&FUA, who said in his reply to Jellie that he was not surprised: "An impetuous Welshman cannot easily be calm and collected just at

Chapter 5

the times he ought to exercise restraint." He thought that Dr Jones, by returning early, was throwing away an opportunity that might not come his way again. He returned the report by Mrs Shawcross and said it should be kept in William Jellie's archives.[81] That same month Dr Tudor Jones wrote to Jellie to tell him that he had decided to leave after two years and three months, and had already given notice to the B&FUA. His main reason for leaving was the difficulties with some members of the committee, especially those who had no previous church connection.[82] Wellington had long been thought of as the second city ripe for a Unitarian church, and William Jellie had made a number of journeys there: in 1903, in 1904 and again in 1907 with Ella. His efforts, including lobbying the B&FUA, had led to the visit of the Rev. Charles Hargrove (1840-1918), which was instrumental in the appointment of Dr Tudor Jones; he must have been disappointed to learn that the enterprise, if not at risk, was at the very least facing difficulties.

So what are we to make of Jellie's proposal to the B&FUA a year later for a two-year exchange with an English minister, or even for a permanent successor to be found for his pulpit in Auckland? He had been married for two years now and having time away from Auckland could have appealed to both him and his wife, especially if it involved travelling to Britain. While they agreed that he should have a change, the B&FUA said, "whether temporary or permanent it is not easy to decide."[83]

By now William Jellie had completed over a decade of work at Auckland. He took stock of the achievements and state of the church for the B&FUA.[84] Auckland, he said, had just finished the most successful year's work in its history: Sunday morning attendances ranged from 40 to 50 and evening attendances were between 100 and 275, while the Sunday School roll stood at 112. The church building was debt free and consideration was being given to the provision of a social hall. The library, with over a thousand books as well as periodicals, had 50 subscribers. There were a number of societies and clubs organised by the Church, many meeting there during the week, including a young people's club, a Free Discussion Society, hockey teams, tennis club, rambler's club, Women's Society, Shakespeare Society,[85] Dickens, Burns and Browning societies and a choir. In addition there were regular socials and picnics.

Jellie explained that there was missionary work to be done, which he could not carry out because his time was completely taken with local work. To undertake this work he proposed a visit by either Rev. William George Tarrant (1853-1928), former editor of *The Inquirer* and then chairman of the Colonial Committee of the B&FUA, or Rev. Dr Lawrence Pearsall Jacks (1860-1955), then editor of the *Hibbert Journal*. He also proposed that a Colonial Scholarship be offered annually to local candidates for the Unitarian ministry so they could study at a colonial university before attending Manchester College, Oxford. This he thought would provide "a constant inducement to our young men and women to consider the ministry as a practicable profession." Continuing with his major concern with the supply of ministers, he suggested that "Home" students be prevailed upon "to devote themselves to colonial work, as in other churches they devote themselves to foreign missions."[86]

Being such a prominent spokesman for the cause of liberal religion in a colony of more than a million people brought rewards. Publication of *The Modern Genesis* attracted a review in the avant-garde journal *The Triad*:

> The Rev. W. Jellie, of the Auckland Unitarian Church, is certainly one of the best-read parsons Auckland can claim. He adds to a lucid style a depth of appreciation of modern problems, and his widely-trained mind presents us with results in sermons and addresses so far superior to the ordinary ... But it is matter of regret that Mr. Jellie's following is not larger and that all the work in inculcating the religion of the present day, of conducting worship clarified by scientific thought, should fall only upon his shoulders.[87]

Perhaps this work was no longer going to fall on his shoulders alone as a result of *The Triad* review. Within weeks of the review's appearance, Jellie received a letter from the Manse at St Andrews Presbyterian Church, South Canterbury. The Rev. James H. G. Chapple (1865-1947) wrote: "In reading a sermon of yours in 'Triad' it struck me how closely you approximated to my views ... I am a Presbyterian minister but have no right in the church. The Presbytery know of my heterodoxy & tried to shift me two years ago..."[88] Chapple had joined the New Zealand Socialist party in 1905. The events he referred to arose because of the support for working class interests he gave from his pulpit. The Timaru Presbytery tried to remove him in 1907, but failed in the face of overwhelming support he received from his parishioners: they voted 200 to 8 that he should stay.[89] Just how much William Jellie knew of this background is not known, but he would shortly find out a lot more about this radical clergyman.

6

In New Zealand: Wellington

In the absence of organised Unitarianism in nineteenth-century Wellington, many individual Unitarians were drawn into a movement that espoused a compatible social spirit of Christianity and put these views into action: the Forward Movement. By the time William Jellie visited Wellington he knew there was a cohesive group of Unitarians there who had come together through the Forward Movement and demonstrated their ability to work towards a common goal.

Born out of the long depression, unemployment and "sweated" labour resulted in abject poverty which was condemned in a number of sermons, such as that given by the Rev. William James Williams (1847-1936) at the Durham Street Wesleyan Church in Christchurch in 1888. Williams' sermon, "The Bitter Cry of Christchurch", described household goods sold bit by bit to buy bread, and homes where the bitter cry of cold and hungry children could be heard, while scores of able-bodied men were on the streets, wanting work but finding none.[1] A year later the Rev. Rutherford Waddell railed against sweated labour in Dunedin.

The cry was heard by two Congregational ministers, William Albert Evans (1857-1921) and Charles Henry Bradbury (1851-1914). Born in South Wales, Rev. Evans trained at Springhill College, Birmingham, attended classes in biology and philosophy at Cardiff University, and was ordained at Bridgend Church, Glamorgan in 1887. He arrived in Dunedin in 1888, then moved to Nelson and took charge of the Emanuel Congregational Church in 1890.[2] There he met Kate Milligan Edger (1857-1935), daughter of the Rev. Samuel Edger (1823-1882), who had been minister to the nonconformist Albertland settlement around the Kaipara area.[3] Kate Edger studied at Auckland and graduated B.A. from the University of New Zealand in 1877, the first woman in the British Empire to do so. She later graduated M.A. after studying at Canterbury University College and went on to become the first principal of Nelson College for Girls in 1883. When she married Rev. Evans in 1890 she resigned from this position. Her husband resigned his pastorate in 1893 and they moved to Wellington, where they were joined by the Rev. Charles Henry Bradbury.[4] Born in Lancashire and educated at Airedale College, Bradford, Yorkshire, Bradbury had one ministry before coming to New Zealand in 1887, following the early deaths of two wives, which "utterly unnerved him".[5]

Initially Charles Bradbury was the more politically active and radical of the pair. From the time of his appointment to the Linwood Congregational Church in Christchurch until he resigned to join the Evanses, he was embroiled in political activity. In 1891 he was on the executive of the Christian Ethical Society, of which the Rev. James O'Bryen Hoare (1835-1914) was secretary and treasurer.[6] The society's study programme for members and visitors of readings and lectures was divided into ethical, health and Fabian sections.[7] In 1891 Bradbury chaired meetings for the Heathcote Radical Association at which labour supporters spoke, and addressed a union meeting organised by the Canterbury Trades and Labour Council on socialism.[8] The next year he spoke out in favour of an unfettered women's franchise and appeared on the Liberal Association platform which included William Pember Reeves.[9] When he resigned his Linwood ministry he told his church quite directly the reason why:

> The church had grown fat and rich and had coddled itself to the verge of destruction; it had bowed itself to the mammon of this world, and "shunted" the poor till we now had little better than a democracy of howlers and scowlers. He had been asked to join a brother who proposed opening a mission in Wellington, and had accepted the call. He could not say exactly what form the mission might assume, but it would be Christian not "churchy." His desire had long been to get among the masses of the people, if by any means he might help to raise them to a true sense of manhood and womanhood, and a true citizenship. It was, he said, proposed to open the mission the first week in May.[10]

It had been expected that he would soon leave for Wellington, which he almost certainly did, so when we find him standing later that year

Chapter 6

in the General Election in Christchurch it seems that he returned from Wellington to go round the hustings. At Sydenham he addressed electors about the need for the State to save the country, supporting secular education against the "Irish Bible" (the Catholic Bible promoted in schools), supporting old age pensions and a State bank.[11] In the event William Pember Reeves headed the poll, William Whitehouse Collins came third and Rev. O'Bryen Hoare and Rev. Bradbury were unelected at fifth and sixth respectively.

In Wellington both Evans and Bradbury were working to attract support for the Forward Movement from some prominent Unitarians. The movement was non-sectarian; there was no creedal test, simply a willingness to work with like-minded people on a great humanitarian project. Enlisting members of the Atkinson and Richmond families to their cause meant getting people well connected in the Wellington establishment who could act to support and promote their aims. Judge Christopher William Richmond (1821-1895),[12] the patriarch of the family, wrote to his married daughter Alice Blake (1863-1944):

> We see a good deal of Mr. Evans ... He is on social questions a member of the Party of Progress, but not a socialist and a very moderate democrat — if indeed you can call him one at all. Bradbury is less cultured and philosophical — a very good fellow people say having strong sympathies with the wage earning class. The purpose of the mission seems to be to introduce something very like [John Hamilton] Thom's and [James] M[artineau]'s view of Christianity to our agnostic young men and to the working classes. They lecture every Sunday ... and are drawing fair audiences ... A homely looking little man [Mr. Evans] in a black coat in a lecture hall fitted for theatrical entertainments, with a strange pronunciation, must have very good matter in him and great spiritual power to compete, in the judgement of the crowd, with "the snowy handed" and his great organ and his surpliced choristers and other adjuncts ...[13]

Just what were the aims that this cause espoused? Two years after the movement's formation, in the first edition of its publication *The Citizen*, the Rev. Evans elaborated on their aims: "It affirms the fatherhood of God, and the sonship of man; it accentuates the law of service as the law of life; it asserts that rights and duties are correlative terms..." He believed that the Forward Movement could adopt the programme of the Mansfield Settlement, the Congregational university settlement opened in 1890 at Canning Town, London, which was set up to fight against selfishness, injustice, vice, disease, starvation, ignorance, and squalor and to build society based on mutual helpfulness and concern for all human life. (While he may have drawn inspiration from the settlement idea, the Forward Movement was not exactly the same thing. Each day, Bradbury and Evans came down from Mt Victoria to work in the slums; they did not live there, nor were there university students in Wellington to help them in their work.)

Evans described how the movement's aims would be achieved through educational policies: public lectures and study classes, cottage meetings, open air meetings, and children's groups. He also sought to organise men "for the purpose of supervising the administration of existing laws affecting the health and weal of the community".[14] This latter aim appears to provide ample scope for more direct political action.

The Literary Society lectures that took place between 1895 and 1896 in the Forward Movement Hall, previously Ballance Hall, in Manners Street, were well supported by Unitarian lecturers, who gave at least a third of them.[15] About two hundred people subscribed to these lectures, which in the main provided an introduction to nineteenth-century English literature. The public lecture programme was more varied. In one week in 1895 it included arithmetic, algebra, geometry, mechanics, English, shorthand, citizenship and socialism; there was no subscription but a donation was taken. The advertisement declared "Presidents — C. H. Bradbury, W. A. Evans".[16] The contents of all eight issues of *The Citizen*, the complete series published between 1895 and 1896, shows that of forty-five authored articles, seventeen (38 percent) can be identified as written by Unitarians. The Mutual Help Society, of which the future Mayoress of Wellington, Maria Annie Hislop (née Simpson, 1848-1909),[17] was a President, attended to the needs of poor families, providing clothing, bedding, boots and other necessities. The temperance message was strongly averred by the two clergymen and some of their supporters.

The wider family of Judge Richmond active in the Forward Movement included his daughters Mary (1853-1949) and Margaret Fell (née Richmond,1857-1933); his nephew and secretary Arthur Richmond Atkinson (1863-1935), a member of Parliament for Wellington South between 1899-1902; Arthur's wife Lily May Atkinson (née Kirk, 1866-1921); Judge Richmond's niece Dolla (Dorothy Kate) Richmond (1861-1935),[18] a professional artist and member of the Council of the New Zealand Academy of Fine Arts; and Maurice Wilson Richmond (1860-1919), another nephew of Judge Richmond's and a lawyer who was to become Professor of Law at Victoria University College.[19]

There were other well-known supporters, chief among them Sir Robert Stout and his law partner Dr (later Sir) John Findlay (1862-1929); Judge Herbert Frank Edger (1854-1909), the only son of the Rev. Samuel Edger and brother of Kate Evans; the Hon. Thomas Hislop (1850-1925), former Minister of Education and Justice who became Mayor of Wellington, and his wife Annie Hislop; Fred de la Mare, who was then a young civil service clerk and went on to become a lawyer and educationalist at Victoria University College; George Hogben (1853-1920) a close friend of Rev. Evans who joined the movement when he arrived in Wellington to take charge of the Department of Education; and (David) Ernest Beaglehole (1866-1946), an accountant. Over half the members of the management committee appear to have been Unitarians.[20]

The Forward Movement did pursue a broader political agenda along with its humanitarian and philanthropic work. Kate Evans organised a union for domestic servants in Wellington in 1898. She "sought to improve the working conditions of domestic servants through moral suasion of employers, and by the establishment of a clubroom and a benefit fund."[21] Her husband was the guiding force in establishing the New Zealand Workers Union in Wellington, although he was at pains to point out that it was not in his role as a leader in the Forward Movement; these activities were undertaken in his capacity as a member of the Workers Union.[22] A conference attended by unemployed delegates was held in the Forward Hall to discuss the issue of unemployment. Meanwhile the Rev. Bradbury was taking the message to the Congregational Union. In an address a year before he was elected chairman of the Union he said: "As they truly knew their faith they could only hail the advent of socialism and regret its tardiness. Socialism was the direct outcome of the Christian faith."[23] Evans appears to have become increasingly politicised through the situations he encountered in his work and his association with Charles Bradbury. Sharing a house and working together provided many hours for discussion between the two men. We next find Rev. Evans chairing a series of lectures in the Forward Hall on behalf of the Clarion Club, which he said was modelled on the Fabian Society to educate people about socialism.[24] Moreover the Clarionettes, as the club members called themselves, were instrumental in the formation of a Socialist Party in Wellington in 1901, of which the Rev. W. A. Evans was a foundation member.[25]

Life had not been easy for Charles Bradbury, or for Kate and William Evans (who had three sons to support), while they worked in the Forward Movement. There was no regular income for the men from their work in the slums or with the unemployed, despite their having undertaken some work at the request of the Wellington Charitable Aid Board.[26] For some years Kate Evans was the main earner in the household, running a private secondary school for girls during the day at the family home and coaching adult pupils in the evening. Eventually Charles Bradbury decided to return to regular parish work. In August 1897 he took up a pastoral appointment at the Prahran Independent Church in Melbourne, just over four years after he joined William Evans in Wellington to start the Forward Movement.[27] Rev. Evans soldiered on, but by 1904 the Forward Movement had run its course and he became pastor of the Newtown Congregational church, a position he held until 1921.[28]

During its existence the Forward Movement had served to benefit Unitarianism in a number of ways. Contact had been made with Harry Atkinson, who founded the Socialist Church in Christchurch; he addressed the Forward Movement on "Religion in its Relation to Labour", where he spoke about his experiences with John Trevor and the rise of the Labour Church in Britain.[29] The movement certainly forged a link with members of the Auckland Unitarian Church who looked favourably upon the activities in Wellington. On his visits to Auckland, William Evans stayed at Herne Bay with his sister-in-law Gertrude Evangeline Hemus (née Edger, 1852-1936) and her husband Charles Hemus (1849-1925). The Hemuses were active in the Auckland Unitarian Church and through them Evans met other church members. The Macky family were friends of the Hemuses and spent music and literary evenings at their home.[30] On one occasion Joseph Macky reported that:

Chapter 6

As usual we have all been over to morning church and the children to Sunday school as well ... We then went along to the Hemus's to see a Rev. Mr. Evans who is up from Wellington. He is minister to the Forward Movement church [sic] down there, a sort of branch of the Congregational Church but rather more progressive. He is all but Unitarian in his ideas and a very interesting man whom I hope to see more of in my future trips to Wellington.[31]

A few years later, just as the Forward Movement was beginning to peter out, a new cause was being organised. The Wellington Unitarian Society was formed in 1904 following the visit of Charles Hargrove, and in 1906 the Rev. Dr Tudor Jones took up his charge at the Wellington Unitarian Free Church. For those Wellington Unitarians involved it must have been a straightforward and welcome transition from the Forward Movement to the church. The Rev. Evans continued to spread the social gospel,[32] although he now believed it could only be realised through political action — a view that found sympathy with many Unitarians.

When William Jellie agreed to go to Wellington[33] to take over as minister following the departure of Dr Tudor Jones in February 1910, he faced two major tasks: first to reconcile the differing viewpoints on the management committee, some of whom had been so antagonistic to Dr Tudor Jones; and secondly to deal with the outstanding debt the church faced on its building. None of this would have appeared particularly daunting. He had dealt successfully with problems like this in the past. The Wellington church site was in the central city area and at a cost of £1,287 was considered a good price for the location.[34] A little more than a year after the land was bought, on 18 April 1909, the church was opened by Mrs Margaret Richmond Fell, the third daughter of Judge Richmond.[35] The church was designed by the well-known Wellington architect James Bennie (1873-1945)[36] and built by Adams and Smart for a reported cost of some £1,500.[37] It was designed in a Gothic style, with a massive doorway surmounting a flight of steps. The front was built in compressed red brick and faced with bluff bricks. The interior had a domed ceiling and graded floor, so the congregation could see and hear easily, and there was light from the roof which was asbestos tiled. The church could accommodate 400 people.[38]

Jellie's plan was to have the whole congregation work together on solutions to the church's problems. His first action was to have the committee call the congregation to a "Council of War." The state of affairs of the church was laid out and discussed and suggestions invited. The "Council of War" produced an interesting result, split along gender lines. A Unitarian Men's Club was formed, which held meetings of a "social and deliberative character." The Women's Alliance, on the other hand, formed separate working groups: a Work Committee to raise funds, a House-Keeping Committee for cleaning and decorating the church, a Visiting Committee to make calls on members, a Corresponding Committee to supply information to inquirers and keep in touch with distant Unitarians, and finally a Study Committee. Jellie followed up these plans by urging members to get into a team and work in a steady, united way "and in a year or two we shall look back in wonder upon the distance we have travelled and the loads we have carried."[39]

When Ella and William arrived with baby Hilary they settled into a house at 83 Roxburgh Street, Mount Victoria. During the year Ella Jellie had her "at home" times for casual visitors, usually on the third Tuesday of each month. This she continued with until October 1911, the month before their second child, Margaret Campbell Jellie (1911-2006),[40] was born. Ella resumed her "at home" times in March 1912. Being in Wellington meant more opportunity for William Jellie to see old friends, such as Sir George Fowlds. Fowlds had become a vice-president of the Society for the Protection of Women and Children, originally established in Auckland in 1893. In Wellington the Society had set up in 1897 with help from Kate Evans and Edward Tregear and enthusiastically supported by Unitarian women, including Annie Hislop, Lily Atkinson, Margaret Fell and Lady Stout. Aimed at providing help to deserted mothers and children, including unmarried mothers and their babies, it was a cause that William Jellie, having had his own difficult family experience, could readily identify with. He willingly agreed to give it his public support and became a vice-president.

By Jellie's second year in Wellington there was an experienced committee behind him, led by the articulate and intelligent Mary Richmond in the chair.⁴¹ The eldest of the nine children of Judge Richmond and his wife Emily, she had taught at Wellington Girls' High School, and then travelled to London where she trained in kindergarten teaching at the Froebel Institute. On her return to Wellington she started a scheme to provide poor children with pre-school education, after which she founded the Richmond Kindergarten Schools. At the time of William Jellie's ministry she was also a member of the Wellington Hospital and Charitable Aid Board.⁴² Additionally, the standing the church enjoyed in the wider community was enhanced by the support it received from members who were public figures, such as Sir Robert Stout and Professor Hugh Mackenzie, who could be called upon to provide a sermon, welcome a visitor or speak out on an issue; and on occasion they played a formal role as President of the church.⁴³

What did worry William Jellie at this time was the lack of growth in new members. The attendance at the services was satisfactory, with morning services attracting around 200; however Jellie was concerned that there was little growth in membership. In 1912 the roll stood at 99 members.⁴⁴ It was a theme he would return to in the *Calendars*, pointing out the benefits and ease of joining: "You have only to express your wish, and to subscribe annually a sum not less than 2/6. Nothing simpler, nothing freer, yet how much depends on it."⁴⁵ So how could those attendees, often regular, be converted into members? For it was the members who were the life blood of the church. Exhortation alone did not seem to succeed. Other attempts were made to make the church inviting and to attract new people. Jellie formed a Literary Club for young adults in May 1911, which met on Friday evenings and was open to all. They studied Tennyson, Browning and Emerson and continued until May 1913. John Gammell offered to raise money with a series of evening lectures on the French Revolution which were open to the public.⁴⁶

The church received a great deal of encouragement from the visit, organised by the B&FUA, of the Rev. William Wooding (1840-1918), his wife Emily Evelyn (née Asquith, 1855-1937) and their daughter Lilian (1886-1949). (The Woodings' son was already living in New Zealand, and had a sheep station in Canterbury.) Emily Wooding was the only sister of Herbert Asquith (1852-1928), then Liberal Prime

Minister of the United Kingdom. The Asquiths were a Congregational family and indeed the Rev. Wooding had been Congregational before his "own enfranchisement [which] came with an acquaintance with the works of Darwin, Wallace and Lyell, whilst he was actually pursuing his ministry".[47] Wooding gave a series of sermons in Wellington which drew large attendances, before heading for Auckland.

Wellington, situated at the southern tip of the North Island, gave Jellie a base from which he could undertake work in the South Island. With Jellie's encouragement, the ex-Presbyterian minister James Chapple formed a Unitarian Society in Timaru and found substantial support for a liberal church. Chapple had finally resigned from the Presbyterian Church in 1910,[48] after he took the public platform to chair a meeting of the touring English Rationalist and ex-Catholic priest Joseph McCabe (1867-1955).[49] Any remaining doubt about his heterodoxy was extinguished when he visited the Auckland Unitarian Church and gave a sermon. When Jellie visited Timaru in July 1911 he found "a thoroughly live movement, an increasing congregation, a Sunday School with 50 on its roll, and a Discussion Society that meets during the week." At the evening service Jellie conducted there were 270 people; afterwards some 70 stayed behind to form a church. With characteristic foresight Jellie proposed that the three churches should form a "N.Z. Unitarian Association, to try to interest the many scattered Unitarians who live up and down the country, and to focus attention upon missionary efforts."[50]

When the Rev. William Fleming Kennedy (1864-1945)[51] arrived in Wellington in April 1912 en route for Dunedin and took a morning service, William Jellie hailed him as an old friend. Within a month they met up again, this time in Timaru, where they were joined by the Rev. Richard James Hall (1883-1930), Jellie's successor at the Auckland church, who had come from Auckland to celebrate the opening of the Unitarian Hall with James Chapple. Jellie declared the event a "glorious success" with some 120 people attending the afternoon dedication and 250 the evening social. The Sunday services had 75 in the morning and a crowd of at least 350 in the evening.[52]

The Rev. Kennedy meanwhile had founded his church in Dunedin, holding the first meeting on 12 May 1912 in the Trades Hall, Moray

Chapter 6

Place, attracting 80 people. From the beginning the Dunedin group seems to have had organisational problems and needed outside help. Jellie visited Kennedy that September and wrote a report to Richard Hall on the Dunedin prospects.[53] He found William Kennedy well supported by capable people: William Trimble, the Hocken Librarian; Mr Sidey[54] from the wealthy Dunedin family that built Corstorphine House and whose brother Thomas Sidey (1863-1933) was a local Member of Parliament; Mr Kendall, the Public Trustee and Official Assignee who had recently moved from Wellington, where he had been a member of the Unitarian Free Church; and a former member of the Auckland Unitarian Church, Mr Bonachie, a foreman painter at the Union Steamship Company. Kennedy was respected, but not seen as strong enough to carry out the work. He lacked good organisational abilities, and did not know how to form a committee, let alone work with one. William Jellie strongly advised him to stop acting as treasurer. He would need the support of the other three Unitarian ministers in the Colony if he was to succeed.[55]

Rev. William F. Kennedy, minister of the Dunedin Unitarian Church, and Mrs Kennedy

In New Zealand: Wellington

Rev. Richard Hall, Minister, Auckland Unitarian Church

On his way back to Wellington, Jellie stopped overnight at Timaru, where he delivered a lecture on the Bible in schools. It was a topic that was about to consume him. Ever since the passing of the Education Act in 1877, which made primary education free, compulsory and secular, there had been attempts to amend the law to allow religious instruction in schools.[56] Advocates of religious instruction believed that it was necessary for the preservation of Christian civilisation.[57] Opponents, which included the Unitarians, thought it would lead to the inculcation of religious superstition along sectarian lines.

It was a lecture of Joseph McCabe's that had spurred the formation of the Secular Education Defence League. John Gammell presided over a meeting at which he proclaimed: "Hands off! To all assailants of the secular system...no matter whether Catholic or Protestant religion prevailed, the clerical body in each had been the most bitter foe of every modern system of education. From 1877, the passing of the Act, the Churches of New Zealand had fought against it."[58]

Chapter 6

The meeting elected a fair number of Unitarians to its executive: John Gammell was elected President, Professor Mackenzie Treasurer, Henry Joosten one of the joint secretaries, and William Jellie a member of the executive committee. Following the campaign launched by the Bible in Schools League in 1911, Jellie actively used his pulpit to keep the issue before the congregation. He gave a series of sermons under the head "Against the Bible in Schools" and invited the Chief Inspector of Schools for the Hawkes Bay, Mr Hill, to give an address on his "Experiences of Bible-in-Schools in England, Australia and Elsewhere." Jellie publicly rebutted the "preservation of Christian civilisation argument" advanced by Bishop Cleary of the Catholic Church: "it is to escape from [the] pitiless logic [of the religious system] in the name of humanity, that the secular system has grown up out of the political and religious experiences of the last 400 years", he wrote. Furthermore, he claimed that the "work of the civil government is to administer justice, to guarantee civil and religious freedom, to secure the education of the children without trampling on the rights of any child or parent" and that now "religious affairs have been removed from political control to purely private management" because government was "now independent of the church."[59]

By 1913 a New Zealand National Schools Defence League had been formed, and once again Unitarians were prominent among the office holders. The president was Arthur Richmond Atkinson, who served on the Wellington City Council and the Victoria University College Council. The vice-presidents included Mrs A. R. Atkinson, Rev. W. F. Kennedy, Rev. W. Jellie, Mr John Gammell and Professor H. Mackenzie. The Honourable George Fowlds was also a vice-president. The list of office holders was long and included many academics and civic leaders.[60] The omission of the Rev. James Chapple was not on the grounds of any ideological difference; he was a supporter of secular education, but someone forgot to ask for his support. Earlier, the executive of the Wellington Secular Education Defence League had met in the schoolroom of the Wellington Unitarian Free Church to discuss alleged breaches of the Education Act in Timaru.[61]

At the same time Jellie was dealing with the threat to secular education and protecting the 1877 Act from the Bible-in-Schools campaign, he was aware that there were two fundamental problems within the Wellington church. One he had vanquished with his pleasant diplomatic manner; there was now an effective committee with an excellent working relationship with their minister. The second problem proved far more intractable. At a meeting of the congregation on the evening of 19 March 1913 there was only one item of business: the resignation of the minister. William Jellie's letter stated that he felt compelled to resign because of the financial state of the church. Many members rose to their feet to express their deep regret at the thought of losing Mr Jellie's services. The Treasurer then gave a financial report showing it would be impossible to continue with the present rate of expenditure. In short, the church could not afford its minister.[62]

Did Jellie have any idea how his departure was viewed amongst the wider public? Probably not. One newspaper opined about his loss to Wellington:

> Wellington will have to submit to a serious loss, from an educational, literary, and intellectual point of view, when the Rev. W. Jellie, B.A., head of the Unitarian Church, waves "good-bye" ... next month from the deck of the *Rotorua*. During his comparatively short stay, Mr. Jellie has left on the minds of his hearers and friends an impression for good that will not be quickly effaced. He is a man with the broadest outlook on the social and economic problems of the day, and *a firm friend of the people in their struggle for emancipation from wage-slavery* [emphasis added]. From his pulpit and in his private intercourse he has always advocated a brighter condition of things in this world.[63]

Judge's Chambers, Wanganui,

12th September 1913.

My Dear Mr Jellie,

I expected I would have been able to be in Wellington before your departure - but unexpectedly I have to go to Napier on circuit. I understand you are leaving next week and I am sending this care of Professor Mackenzie to be delivered to you. May I be allowed to express regret at your leaving. I know you have had an uphill battle - and this is always the case with those in advance of public opinion in the Colonies. Through the want of the strain and stress that is felt in the battle for freedom in the home country, Colonials do not realise what it means to maintain the liberty won for them. I feel sure, however, that you will carry with you the good wishes of all who have had the honour and the pleasure of meeting you. Your services for freedom in this colony have been great. May I convey my good wishes to Mrs Jellie as well as to yourself,

With kindest regards,

Believe me,

Yours very truly, Robert Stout

*Sir Robert Stout's farewell letter to William Jellie
September 1913*

7

Return to England

With the household furniture sold in September 1913, the Jellie family had to live in temporary accommodation for a month before sailing on the New Zealand Shipping Company's most modern vessel, SS *Rotorua*. Built in 1910, the *Rotorua* was a combined passenger and cargo ship. It accommodated 52 first class passengers, 72 in second class and 156 in third class, which could be increased by another 280 supplementary passengers as required. William and Ella Jellie and their two small children were most likely in second class, located on the upper deck towards the stern. William was able to use the time on the voyage to study Italian, as he wanted to read Dante in the original language. It must have seemed like an idyll for them both to be returning together to England. When Ella was there as a young single woman, studying at Royal Holloway College, she had seen some of Europe with her older brother Tom Macky, who was then working at the London office of Macky, Logan & Caldwell.[1] William Jellie was looking forward to visiting people and places with Ella and meeting old friends. He was at the peak of his profession, having over twenty years of successful ministry behind him, including the major achievement of building the Unitarian movement in New Zealand. For him return would surely bring recognition of his success. The future looked happy and bright. Perhaps they discussed whether they might settle in England permanently. Little did they know what fate had in store for them and for the world.

When they arrived in England they stayed in London for Christmas. William Jellie took the opportunity to attend the special meeting of the B&FUA held at Essex Hall, London, on 14 January 1914. The purpose of the meeting was to welcome home the secretary of the B&FUA, the Rev. W. Copeland Bowie, from his Canadian missionary tour. Mr.

Bowie spoke on his Canadian experiences; William Jellie described the New Zealand situation, while the Rev. Charles Hargrove talked about the world-wide movement in liberal religion.[2]

Arriving in England without organising a job in advance may have seemed a risk for a minister with a young family to support, but an opening soon presented itself in Southport, Lancashire, located on the coast of the Irish Sea, about sixteen miles north of Liverpool. The town of Southport had a population of 50,000 and within a year would be declared a county borough. The growth in the town was due to its proximity to centres of transportation and communication, initially the Leeds and Liverpool canal, followed by the incorporation of the district railway lines into the Lancashire and Yorkshire Railway. The Southport Unitarian congregation had opened the church building in 1867.

The incumbent minister, Rev. Robert Nichol Cross (1883-1970) had been appointed minister to the Mill Hill Chapel in Leeds the previous August.[3] Following his departure three months later, temporary supply was provided by some half dozen or so ministers, including William Jellie, who took services on 4 January and 11 January 1914. He was strongly recommended to the Southport Church Council by the Rev. W. Copeland Bowie, who also passed a favourable opinion about Ella Jellie as a minister's wife. At a Special Congregational Meeting on 3 February 1914 it was resolved: "That a cordial invitation be sent to the Rev. Jellie, B.A. to become the minister of the Congregation of this Church at a stipend of £300 per annum." In accepting the invitation Jellie especially asked to be able to attend the Church Council meetings, something he had done in New Zealand, but such a notion of democratic participation by the minister was novel in England. It was agreed he could either attend at his own request or at the invitation of the Council. Did this mean the Council could decline to allow him to attend? If so there is no record of this happening.

William Jellie took up his position in 1 March 1914. An official welcome for him and Ella was held in the Unitarian school room on 13 March 1914. A fellow minister from Liverpool, Rev. Joseph Crowther Hirst (1848-1919), told the gathering that "one of the glories of the Unitarian Church was that not only had the minister freedom of thought, but that every member of the church and congregation was equally free in that respect." William Jellie would have cause to reflect on that assertion towards the end of his ministry at Southport. Speaking for the congregation, Dr Robert Harris said he "thought the experience Mr. Jellie had in New Zealand should help him very much in Portland Street. It had no doubt encouraged in him a cosmopolitan spirit. Their congregation was somewhat cosmopolitan, and... judging by Mr. Jellie's tone in the pulpit ... that would appeal to them all."[4]

A member of the church, Thomas Holland, played an early part in the campaign for a public library, which was opened in Lord Street in 1878. A history of the library notes that, notwithstanding the "prevailing image of the town in terms of middle class values and services", the Southport Public Library "distinguished itself, after 1900, for its exceedingly eclectic resources, amply fulfilling its requirements to embrace, as far as possible, the literary relics of all classes in the community."[5] One of the town's literary figures, James Ashcroft Noble (1844-1896), whose works reside in the Library's collections of its famous sons, is "still commemorated in the Unitarian Church here".[6] William Jellie would have appreciated the literary and intellectual connection between the church and the public library and made full use of the facilities that the library afforded.

An important form of communication between the minister and the congregation in William Jellie's mind was the church *Calendar*. Wherever he went he ensured that they were produced on a monthly basis. This was not done at the Southport Church and he informed the Church Council he would produce them under his own management. Unfortunately a search has failed to find them.[7]

William, Ella, Hilary and Margaret settled into the Manse called "Laymore" at 7 Bickerton Road, Birkdale, within an easy walk to the sea front, the Unitarian church on Portland Road, and the Chapel Street railway station. As they were settling into their new town, making friends, gaining an understanding of the congregation and its expectations of William's work amongst them, they were overtaken by the outbreak of war between Britain and Germany on 4 August 1914, just five months after their arrival in Southport.

Events moved quickly as the pace of the war increased. Units of the East Lancashire Regiment were formed in August and September 1914 and moved to Southport by September 1914. Units of the Lancashire Fusiliers were being formed at Southport in the spring of 1915. The extensive beaches and vacant land made the Southport area attractive for

Chapter 7

training and many soldiers were billeted in the town. By October 1914 the church was responding to the needs of the soldiers. It was agreed that the school room would be used for recreation and would provide tea and coffee four nights a week. By November it was thought that more than four nights a week was needed and the church was asked if it could do more. William Jellie proposed that entertainment be organised. It was also decided to open the schoolroom for light refreshments every weekday evening and to invite soldiers to remain on Sunday evenings after service. A Soldiers Entertainment Committee, with William Jellie as chairman, was formed and began to meet weekly. It was decided to call on the ladies for help, to provide ashtrays, daily papers, games and writing materials. Advertisements were placed in the newspaper so the soldiers would know what was available. From time to time lectures were given, as were French language classes. It was arranged to sell postage stamps so soldiers could more easily write to their families. By December 1914 musical entertainment and lantern slides were introduced. A report of the Church's activities at this time said:

> Since the schoolroom was opened it has proved very popular – a piano has been installed, also bagatelle and ping-pong tables, and other games are played. There is a large selection of magazines and papers, men can write their letters with provided materials. Last evening young ladies presented a miscellaneous programme interspersed with items given by the soldiers. A warm welcome is extended by the church officers to the men to use the institute where everything will be done for their comfort.[8]

After June 1915 the activities of the Soldiers Entertainment Committee are only mentioned in the Church Council minutes. One decision was not to admit alcohol to the functions. By September it was noted that there were far fewer soldiers attending than previously, and in November it was decided not to open the schoolroom for entertainment. Tempting though it may be to see a direct connection between these events, a more likely explanation is that the number of soldiers transiting through the area dramatically declined. By May 1916 the Soldiers Entertainment Committee was disbanded. The church was still called upon, however, to allow use of the schoolroom. It provided an orderly room for the 10th Manchester Regiment, and the 4th East Lancashire Regiment used it for lectures on wet days.

Return to England

In the midst of organising social support for the soldiers Ella and William experienced an immense personal tragedy. Mary and Joseph Macky had decided to come to England, where they would visit the family and Joseph would conduct some business as well. They would be accompanied by their son Jack (John Macky, 1887-1977)[9] and a family friend, Sam Hannah, both of whom planned to enlist in the English forces. After travelling across Canada from Vancouver they intended reaching New York in time to embark on the Cunard Line's RMS *Lusitania* on 30 April 1915. When Joseph Macky wrote to his son Tom in New Zealand he was aware of the risks involved and appeared to be weighing them up:

Joseph and Mary Macky

...she should be as safe as any other boat, even an American. We get condensed wireless news on the steamer [RMS *Niagara*] every morning about 9 o'clock. There has been nothing very startling lately but the submarines appear to keep busy though apparently they only succeed with slow boats, mostly cargo boats. However we shall watch the news carefully from day to day till we get to N. York before finally deciding to cross or not.[10]

Unbeknownst to Mary and Joseph, Tom was at the same time trying to persuade Ella and William Jellie to return from England: "I don't think it will be a fair thing for you to necessitate him leaving us so much. You had better make up your minds to come back to N.Z. even if it is to Chch. [Christchurch] or Dunedin. Poor old Mother is really very much older, too".[11]

Upon reaching New York Jack and Sam decided to leave a week earlier on board the SS *Tuscania,* a decision which may have saved their lives. In an attempt to cross the Atlantic sooner with Jack and Sam, Joseph cancelled a planned visit to Montreal and Toronto, but still found it "impossible for me to get through my business here any quicker" than the following week, "while the boys are very eager to push on as they are afraid they are already too late to take advantage of the fresh recruiting movement" in England.

Joseph told Tom that Ella had written to her parents in New York. "She almost insists on our going on and indeed we have little fear." In fact the biggest problem Joseph Macky could see was in getting a berth on the *Lusitania*, as it was quite full. "Everybody is going on the fast steamer, no one by the slow, although the American steamers are all fairly full, as they expect that no German submarine will dare touch them."[12] Ever the businessman, Joseph Macky managed to get a first class cabin for the cost of second class, even if it meant that they used the second class dining room. He thought the £35 saved would otherwise have been an outrageous waste for a five and a half day trip! When the ship sailed on 1 May 1915 Joseph Macky was aware of the warning issued by the German government "published here this morning not to travel across the Atlantic, but we think we are safe in this good and fast ship. Anyway we are in God's hands and are content to leave with Him 'our going out and our coming in.'"[13]

Return to England

Sinking the Lusitania, 1915

Just after lunch on 7 May 1915 the *Lusitania* was torpedoed by a German submarine when it had reduced speed because of fog in the Irish Sea. It was a calamity which ranked next to the sinking of the *Titanic* for loss of life.

One of the survivors who had befriended the Mackys during the voyage and was with them when the ship was hit advertised in *The Times* for Jack Macky's address so she could tell him what happened.[14] William Jellie and Jack Macky went to meet her in Framlingham, a market town in Suffolk. William wrote an account of the meeting to Ella. "We are on the train returning to London after seeing Miss Manly", he wrote. Miss Manly had been at the Mackys' dining table and also had several talks on deck and got to know them. They were all at dinner when the shock came. They went to the life boat deck, which was two storeys up. There they found a great deal of confusion and difficulty in launching boats, but "father was working hard to right things. Miss Manly and her friend were pushed into the last boat that was left. They tried to persuade Mother to come but she refused, electing to stay with father." He went

Chapter 7

on to say that the memory he liked to hold on to was that of "father helping the others into the boats to the last & mother standing fast and smilingly refusing to follow the other ladies, partly because she chose to die with father & partly no doubt because the boat was already full."[15]

A public memorial service was held at the Auckland Town Hall on 20 May 1915 to acknowledge the deaths of Joseph and Mary Macky. About 3,000 people were present. Businesses were closed for two hours to allow staff to attend. The Mayor of Auckland expressed deep sympathy with the Macky family. The Rev. Robert Walker (1864-1956) led the service, speaking of the Macky family connection with St James Presbyterian Church and Joseph Macky's earlier association. The Rev. William Edward Williams (1877-1942),[16] who had arrived at the Auckland Unitarian Church the year before, offered the prayer. When the organist played Handel's dead march from *Saul* it was reported there was scarcely a dry eye in the place. A week later the Auckland Unitarian Church held its own memorial service.[17]

William and Ella Jellie now had to turn to their own family affairs, the demands of the Southport ministry and the effects of the war. Members of his old Auckland congregation who were stationed in England, some of them recovering from wounds, would turn up at Southport to visit. Margaret Jellie remembered, "All the young men from Auckland who were in the army flooded to our house as a second home."[18] And there were members of the Macky family in the armed forces who were in camp or convalescing, who would visit Southport or be visited by William and Ella Jellie. Ella's younger brother Jack Macky was wounded twice. After being severely wounded on the Somme, he was invalided to England at the end of 1916. Two of Ella's cousins were serving in the New Zealand forces, Thomas Roy Bayntun Macky (1885-1917) and his younger brother Neil Lloyd Macky (1891-1981), known as Polly. Thomas Macky went to England in 1916 before going on to France, where he was killed in action at Ypres.[19] Polly Macky was wounded in France on Christmas Day 1916 and returned to England for hospital care over a period of months.[20]

William, Hilary, Ella, and Margaret in England during World War I

The Jellies had another busy year in 1917. William Jellie continued with his duties as Chaplain to the Mayor of Southport, no doubt a reflection of his personal standing with the Mayor, which meant attending civic meetings and providing an opening prayer. Ella's brother Frank Macky (1891-1975) came to visit while stationed at Bulford Camp at Salisbury in Wilshire.[21] Ella and William Jellie decided that year they had to sort out Hilary's schooling needs. They found Terra Nova School very close to them. It had moved into new premises and offered an excellent schooling under the direction of the headmaster Edwin Owen. This meant Hilary could be a day boy. He started late in 1917 when in his seventh year and remained until they left England in 1921. He studied Latin, Greek, English, Mathematics and French.

In 1918 William took Hilary with him on a trip to Ireland.[22] They went by ship to Belfast and then to Farm Hill House at Carrickfergus where William's uncle John Jellie lived. This was probably the last time William Jellie saw the man who had been so influential in his life.

William Jellie was, in the words of his daughter Margaret, "Irish through and through."[23] This identification of his origins dovetailed into long standing Unitarian views on freedom for Catholics and Home

Chapter 7

Rule for Ireland. Motivated by the ideal of religious freedom, nineteenth-century Unitarians, although in no better position themselves, had spoken out for the emancipation of Catholics from civil disabilities.[24] Unitarian MPs introduced Bills into the House of Commons to grant Catholic freedom. Although the bills were unsuccessful, these activities culminated in the passing of the Catholic Emancipation Act in 1829.[25] The favour was returned when the Dissenters' Chapels Bill was before Parliament in 1844 with support forthcoming from leading Catholic MPs.[26] Furthermore the radical political outlook of Irish Unitarians in the late eighteenth and early nineteenth centuries was strongly motivated by the negative experiences of an enforced union with Great Britain.[27] This led to the support given by most Unitarians to the Liberal Party Home Rule policy in 1886. Those who disagreed went over to the Liberal Unionists.[28] Jellie's home rule views had also been reinforced during his time in New Zealand, where there was general expression in favour of such a measure and, within his circle, support from his close friend Sir Robert Stout.[29] When travelling back to England Jellie, like so many others, believed that the strenuous efforts being undertaken by the Liberal government would result in Home Rule. In July 1914, in the face of impending war, Winston Churchill would write: "Ireland I think is going to be settled."[30] The outbreak of war destroyed such hope just four days later.

By the end of the war William Jellie, who was normally a fit and healthy person, found himself unwell. To suffer from any malaise would have been something he was not used to, but this illness was far more significant. Could there have been two factors affecting him, an underlying physical illness worsened by depression? Throughout 1919 there had been concern within the church about his health. This came to a climax in 1920 with his resignation. In his letter to the Church Council he referred both to his health and to his concern over conditions in Ireland:[31]

> For the last year I have not felt entirely satisfied that I was giving the Church all that it ought to have. I have been much in the doctor's care. What I have done has been done with strain; it has been a whipping of a tired horse. I look forward to a prolonged holiday at the end of February. The circumstances of the time add much to this strain, and cannot but affect his work when the Minister is an Irishman who sympathises with the morally justifiable aspirations of his fellow countrymen.

During 1919 the political and military situation in Ireland deteriorated. Violence and repression went hand in hand. As Alan O'Day says, "With the formation of the Black and Tans, made up of ex-military personnel in January 1920, the scene was set for the nastiest phase of the conflict."[32] It was just this situation which must have appalled Jellie when he wrote with such intense feeling about the "morally justifiable aspirations" of home rule. In favouring the Irish independence movement Jellie had adopted an immensely controversial position. What he had not taken into account was that many Southport Unitarians, who shared similar views to other Protestants living along the west coast and the midlands, had gone over to the Unionist side.[33] These members may well have been a dominant bloc within his congregation. The minutes of the Church Annual General Meeting in 1921 recorded the resignation of William Jellie and noted there had been special difficulties during the preceding year. Several members had resigned their membership, including the chairman of the Church Council. The chairman's letter is not recorded in full but it seems to have been the result of politics from the pulpit.

After his ministerial duties finished at the end of February 1921 William, Ella and the children stayed at Southport for four more months. There were now four children: John Jellie (1920-2010)[34] had been born the same month his father wrote his resignation. Days before the family sailed on SS *Corinthic* on 28 July 1921, William Jellie wrote a letter to members of his former congregation.[35] He said he had planned a last home visit but to his great regret his illness made this impossible. And he went on: "I cannot say what affectionate regard and admiration I have for some among you of all classes, poor and rich. I call to mind lives and examples that have been my inspiration, and the memory of which will be an inspiration. How often have I blessed you in my heart for your splendid qualities." That "some among you" is telling; clearly he continued to feel a divide from some members of his former congregation even after his resignation. This could only have worsened the anguish he felt.

Part Three

Exchanging the Pulpit for the Lectern

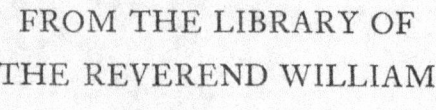

FROM THE LIBRARY OF
THE REVEREND WILLIAM
JELLIE
1865 to 1963
WHICH HE A SCHOLAR
AND EARLY TUTOR
IN ADULT EDUCATION
BEQUEATHED TO
THE UNIVERSITY

*Bookplate for the Jellie book collection
created by Prof. Paul Beadle, Dean of Fine Arts,
University of Auckland, 1964*

8

In New Zealand: Timaru

When the Jellie family arrived in Auckland in September 1921 it must have been a great relief to be back amongst family and friends. How differently things had turned out from the high hopes and expectations with which the family had left New Zealand seven years earlier. Having taken responsibility for organising the return and looking after the family, Ella had now become unwell during the voyage home. She also had to look after a sick husband with an uncertain prognosis. It was not known whether he would be able to return to work. The youngest child John was still a baby, not yet one year old. Mary[1] was not old enough to start school and stayed at home with her parents. The eldest daughter Margaret was asthmatic and it was hoped her condition would improve in the New Zealand climate. Decisions had to be made about continuing Hilary's education and finding schools for both him and Margaret. Hilary was sent to board at Waitaki Boys High School near Oamaru in the South Island. It is not known where Margaret, nearly ten years old at this time, was educated; if she boarded it was not at St Cuthbert's College, which she did not begin until 1925.

While money would not have been a particular concern, given Ella's inheritance following her parents' death, finding a suitable place to live, where William Jellie could recuperate, was a priority. The Jellies choose to go to a place they knew well and which had many happy associations from the past: Waiheke Island. There they could stay at Days Bay, next to Cowes Bay, owned jointly by the Macky and Wilson families. Fortunately the Mackys had built a second house on the property, so William, Ella and the children had the original holiday cottage for their use. Access was by boat; the environment was tranquil and allowed the

Chapter 8

recuperative process to gradually occur. William and Ella spent over fifteen months there between 1921 and 1923.

In the meantime arrangements would have to be made for the family's possessions. Over the seven years at Southport they had accumulated quite a lot, including furniture and William's books. It is unlikely they would have transported much if any furniture to the cottage, as it was already furnished and not big enough to hold much more. Their possessions could have been stored at one of the Macky, Logan, Caldwell Limited warehouses. William Jellie's books would have been another matter. With his well-known propensity for book collecting, it is likely that even by 1921 his collection would have been substantial and having some books around him to enjoy would have been paramount. What else was there to do at the island but walk, read, fish and appreciate the surroundings? Perhaps they had a gramophone and some records to listen to. William loved music and used to play the organ.[2] There were occasional visitors, such as Daisy Thornhill, whose stay "did her much good for which we are all grateful" according to her husband, the Rev. Albert Thornhill.[3]

Gradually taking up work again, William Jellie provided supply to the Wellington Unitarian Free Church in the last three weeks of November 1922, allowing the incumbent, Rev. Wyndham Heathcote[4] (1862-1955) to take leave. From there he went to Timaru where he preached at the Unitarian Church on 3 December 1922. This resulted in a unanimous invitation to accept their pulpit.

In many ways the Timaru Unitarian Church had the hallmarks of its founding minister, the Rev. James Chapple. The church had been built for Chapple by admirers in 1912. His style of ministry —a mixture of extreme theological modernism (some would say rationalism) and political radicalism — had achieved a significant following in this prosperous South Canterbury town.

There had been no settled minister at the Timaru church since Chapple left in 1915. After he departed for America the chairman of the church, Alexander McLean Paterson (1865-1949), conducted most of the services while he tried to find someone else to take over.[5] Paterson was a veterinary surgeon who had emigrated from Scotland to New Zealand in 1900. A keen supporter of the Labour Party (in 1931 he

In New Zealand: Timaru

Rev. James Chapple
Minister of the Timaru and Christchurch Unitarian Churches

stood in the Waitaki seat for Labour), he spent twenty years working as government veterinarian in South Canterbury.

An appeal to the B&FUA to find a minister had failed to elicit any response. By late 1915 Mr E. McDonnell, formerly associated with the Sydney Unitarian Church, had been appointed lay leader and continued in this role until he resigned in August 1916.[6] The church continued under a mixture of lay leadership, often provided by the chairman, and visiting Unitarian ministers, such as the month spent there by the Rev. Wyndham Heathcote from the Wellington Free Unitarian Church, or the visit during 1921 from the Rev. Rosalind Lee during her tour on behalf of the B&FUA. Occasionally the church returned to its radical roots, when an address would be delivered by a member of the Labour Party.[7]

It must have seemed like a godsend when the members of the Timaru church heard that William Jellie had accepted the appointment. How did it come about? His family and friends at the Auckland Unitarian Church would have seen that his health was improving and hoped that a full recovery would see him back at work. The idea of going to a smaller town with a dedicated congregation of around fifty people, which was the situation Rev. Rosalind Lee had found in Timaru two years earlier, would have been put to him as a good place to start. It had the additional attraction of being close to Hilary's school and to Craighead School for Girls, an excellent boarding school for Margaret, which made it easier for the family to come together during holidays and for William and Ella to make visits. William Jellie must have known that the time had come to leave the sanctuary of Waiheke Island and rejoin society at large once again. He had overcome the depression that had gripped him for so long. It never appeared again. Perhaps he was helped by the Anglo-Irish accord that led to the establishment of the Irish Free State under the 1922 constitution.[8] When his Timaru appointment was known in England *The Inquirer* noted that his "friends in this country will rejoice with New Zealanders in his restoration to health, and wish him success in his new work."[9] This tells us how widely his ill health had been known.

The family moved into 99 Wilson Street, Timaru, and William Jellie took his first service on 17 April 1923 at the Unitarian Hall.[10] The subject of his address "The Gospel of a Free Religion." Mr Paterson had decided that after many years of active service he could now step down as chairman and had given his farewell speech the previous Sunday. Two weeks later William Jellie took the subject of "Religion and Politics" for his sermon; unfortunately no record exists of this address. In July he responded to a request from the Labour Party by giving a sermon on "International Peace",[11] which would soon become a policy issue for the whole Unitarian movement. This was followed each Sunday in August with a sermon on the theme of "Utopias of the Past and Present", beginning with Plato's Republic and ending with H. G. Wells' *Men Like Gods* — "What Men are Dreaming".

Following the Japanese earthquake on 1 September 1923, which devastated Tokyo and Yokohama, killing over 100,000 people, the sermons for that month were taken up with various aspects of the disaster. The theme of human suffering begun with the Japanese tragedy continued when Jellie examined the "Hickson Mission." James Moore Hickson (1868-1933) was an Australian-born world-travelling Anglican faith healer who had recently turned up in New Zealand, attracting thousands to his mission at the Christchurch Cathedral. We can safely assume from Jellie's stance on science and religion that he would have come down on the side of those who thought psychological explanations accounted for the outcomes of Mr Hickson's endeavours.[12]

The end of the year saw a visit from the Rev. John Gillies Whait Ellis (1865-1941),[13] the new minister at the Wellington Unitarian Free Church. He delivered a sermon "An Outsider's View of Unitarianism". This must have been a subject that appealed to him, as it was the first sermon he gave to the Wellington Church, a few months before. He and Jellie had met at the conference of the Unitarian Association of New Zealand held in Wellington the previous month. The conference adopted a remit calling for international peace and the settlement of disputes by arbitration through the League of Nations. The issue of Bible reading in schools pitted the Auckland Unitarian Church, represented by the Rev. Albert Thornhill (1870-1938), who favoured readings under certain safeguards, against Timaru, where William Jellie was indefatigable in his opposition. The matter was dropped. Jellie gave a much-admired evening sermon to the conference, "The Unitarian Protest".

The year 1924 had a resounding start in Timaru when James Chapple arrived from Christchurch and gave a sermon on "Religious Liberalism versus Fundamentalism Superstitions", based on his observations in America. A month later Jellie followed this up with "Was Jesus a Communist?" which gave him wide opportunity to discuss how the teaching of Jesus could relate to the organisation of society. He took up the theme of influences on modern life over the next six weeks, examining money, fashion, sport, the church, and nature.

Now William Jellie made a decision that would greatly influence his future. He was invited to put his name forward for the position of President of the South Canterbury branch of the Workers Educational Association (WEA). How did this come about? It is likely that he was introduced by members of his own church committee who were already involved with the local WEA.[14] George Thurston Koller (1875-1951) served on the church committee for many years. A foundation member of the Labour Party in Timaru, he was a member of the Board of Governors of the Timaru Technical College and helped form the local WEA in 1918, serving on the Council and acting as librarian. Another Unitarian, Mr J. Seyb, the church secretary, was also a Council member of the WEA.

Chapter 8

In July 1924 while visiting England he attended the International WEA Conference at Oxford as the delegate for the local organisation.[15]

By May 1924 William Jellie was presiding over WEA lectures as President of the South Canterbury branch, a position he held until the April 1925 Council meeting, which recorded his resignation and expressed regret at his pending departure to live in Auckland.[16] Jellie was clear about the purpose of the WEA: it "aimed at enabling every man and woman to carry on education which would broaden the mind and develop the intellect throughout their whole life".[17] The Unitarian Hall was the venue for many of the WEA lectures, an alternative being the YMCA.

During his term as President, Jellie managed to deliver a lecture of his own as well as presiding over many others. In August 1924 his subject was "Some Aspects of Life in the Middle Ages". Not surprising, given his love of Dante, the impressions he gathered were from Dante's Divine Comedy, and the contemporary chronicles he referred to showed that "Dante did not in the least exaggerate [the Middle Ages] vileness."[18]

Horace Belshaw (1898-1962) was the resident tutor when William Jellie became President of the WEA. He and Jellie worked together, going on a visit to Waimate where a sub-council was set up. Belshaw had studied economics at Canterbury University College under John Bell Condliffe (1891-1981), gaining an M.A. with first class honours. He resigned in July 1924 when he received an award to study at Gonville and Caius College, University of Cambridge.[19] Professor Condliffe had attended the same College at Cambridge University at the end of the war, where he had become acquainted with leading figures of the English WEA, including Albert Mansbridge and R. H. Tawney.[20]

When Condliffe returned to New Zealand in 1920 to take up the chair in economics he became a driving force in the expansion of the WEA, being appointed Director of Tutorial Classes in 1923. He wrote to Timaru informing the WEA Council that there would be no problem finding a successor to Mr Belshaw in plenty of time to organise for next year and that he, Professor James Shelley (1884-1961)[21] and Mr Willis (Bill) Airey (1897-1968) would visit on 14 and 15 November 1924. The three men gave lectures on "The Art and Wit of Whistler," "War Drama since the War," "The Economic Outlook" and "The Empire and the

League of Nations". At the Timaru weekend school, which was under his control, Professor Shelley gave a special lecture on "Educational Tests."[22]

A Cambridge graduate, James Shelley arrived in New Zealand in 1920, after resigning as Professor of Education at Hartley University College, Southampton, to take up the chair of education at Canterbury University College where he was also appointed Director of Extension Work. (When John Condliffe left the College in 1926, sole control of the extension work was in James Shelley's hands, something he much preferred.) Now this was a man who would have immense appeal to William Jellie, in that "he brought to his adult teaching a lively mind, unique panache and a devotion to Shakespeare which included a willingness to undertake leading roles in stage presentations".[23] Besides his ebullient personality James Shelley was devoted to the same subjects that attracted William Jellie, Shakespeare and drama, so we can anticipate that they would have got on famously. Approaching his sixtieth year, by now Jellie could see that there were other possibilities for his future than continuing as a clergyman. The third visitor, Bill Airey, was another useful contact for William Jellie. He had gone to Merton College, Oxford on a Rhodes scholarship to read history, and would later return to Auckland University College to a lectureship in history.[24]

William Jellie and James Shelley met again the following February when the latter returned to introduce the new resident tutor for South Canterbury, Harold Gladstone Miller (1898-1989), at a meeting of the WEA in Timaru. This time James Shelley was accompanied by George Manning (1887-1976), the full-time organising secretary. William Jellie spoke on behalf of the Council and students:

> [He] extended a very cordial welcome to the new tutor and hoped that his stay with them would be so pleasant that it would always remain one of the happiest periods of his life ... he felt that New Zealand should be proud of a man of Mr. Miller's calibre, a man who had worked his way up through the various channels of education and through the Rhodes scholarship to the seat of the Empire's learning — Oxford University.[25]

Harold Gladstone Miller completed his M.A. with first class honours in philosophy at Victoria University College before going to Balliol College, Oxford where he read philosophy, politics and economics.[26] Returning in 1924, he continued the remarkable Oxbridge connection

Chapter 8

that had developed within the Canterbury WEA. George Manning, on the other hand, exemplified what a person could achieve through the educational opportunities presented by the WEA. He had left school at age 13 to do manual work and later was active in the trade union movement. In the first WEA economics class, his ability and determination impressed the tutor, John Condliffe, who in 1920 offered him the position of organising secretary.[27] Speaking to the meeting, George Manning made the point that the WEA "offered to the citizen the same course of study as was available at any of the Universities. A university did not represent brick walls only, but educational achievement, and it was the educational achievement that was brought to them by the WEA."[28]

Stimulating and demanding of his time as this new-found interest was, William Jellie was able to enjoy the fillip to the Unitarian cause with the visit of the Rev. William Priestly Phillips (1893-1972) in January 1925 as part of his tour of Australia and New Zealand, organised by the B&FUA. His Sunday sermon on a favourite Unitarian theme, the downfall of creeds, was followed by a public meeting during the week where he was joined by the Rev. Clyde Carr (1886-1962),[29] who supported the Christchurch Unitarian Church while James Chapple was away.

Rev Clyde Carr, MP
Minister of the Christchurch Unitarian Church

By now William Jellie was aware that it was unlikely that the Timaru church would be able to support him for a further year.[30] It seemed that the movement he had striven so hard to build in New Zealand before the war, which had four churches housed in three of its own buildings, had been seriously weakened. His departure meant that Unitarianism in the South Island was collapsing.[31] This must have given him great sadness but also cause to reflect. Religion generally since the war had entered into a critical state; membership and church attendances had fallen dramatically.[32] As voluntary associations in a secular society, churches were being deserted. The decline had begun around the turn of the century and since then had continued, particularly in the main centres of Auckland, Wellington, Christchurch and Dunedin. The Great War had accelerated this trend, as many were unable to reconcile the God of love with the suffering they had experienced and seen on the battlefield.[33] As William Jellie reflected on the changes he saw around him, he must have wondered what the future would offer to a minister approaching his final working years.

9

The Poor Person's University

When William Jellie decided on a new career it was not surprising that he turned to education. The Unitarians, especially in the nineteenth century, had a long history of involvement in adult education.[1] Jellie would have been aware of the tradition of Mechanics Institutes, which were founded in Britain during the first part of the nineteenth century, and readily transported to New Zealand with the English settlers.[2] And he would also have known about — possibly had some experience of — Working Men's Colleges, which, as we have already seen, were promoted by the Rev. Henry Solly. One of the most successful of these colleges was situated at Ipswich when William Jellie had his ministry there and was working for the university extension movement.[3] He would have also seen the important difference between England and New Zealand in this area: whereas university extension originated under the aegis of Cambridge University in 1873 and Oxford University in 1878,[4] it had simply not got off the ground in New Zealand. Instead, New Zealanders aspiring to further education had to rely on voluntary associations, including the Adult Schools run by the Quakers,[5] which some members of Jellie's Auckland congregation had attended.[6]

In New Zealand William Jellie's old friend Sir Robert Stout had been instrumental in ensuring that the new movement for working-class education got off to the right start. When the Wellington Workers Educational Association was being formed, Sir Robert urged that it should be connected "with existing educational institutions, otherwise there would be the risk of failure."[7] He was shown to be right, when a joint venture was formed between the WEA and university colleges, through which funding for the WEA programme flowed, and academic staff could be either appointed directly as WEA tutors or drawn from the university college. The affiliation of trade unions with the WEA ensured that the needs of their members were addressed in the courses taught.[8]

William Jellie would have found this new profession attractive for a variety of reasons. First he was eminently qualified academically to teach in a number of subject areas. He was knowledgeable in English literature and its place in Western Civilization, and familiar with a number of languages (French, Italian, Greek and Latin), as well as being a Dante scholar. And, as we shall see, over the years he had continued to acquire knowledge in other areas, which he was capable of passing on to students. Secondly, he could see that in doing so he was providing an important contribution to society: the development of an educated democracy. In a sense this was a continuing expression of the social ethic he had imbibed through the teaching of Philip Wicksteed. Thirdly, he could contribute to individual self-improvement. This was a view that was of special importance to his Unitarian beliefs. As John Hollings had said to the Boston Mechanics Institute in 1852, the "true dignity of man consisted in his intellectual capacity", and all that was "precious in literature, or ennobling in knowledge, or graceful in art" should be as widely available as possible to uplift the human condition.[9] Above all, his new work allowed Jellie to express his empathy for the needs of working men and women in a practical manner without requiring overt political action on his part.[10]

When Jellie's letter of appointment came early in 1926 from the Director of Tutorial Classes for the WEA in Auckland, it was more by way of inquiry. "I should have looked you up long before this", wrote Mr L. A. Mander, M.A.[11] He went on: "The Tutorial Class Committee wishes to know if you are free to conduct a W.E.A. Literature Class in the city during the coming winter." He then commented that he "should be glad to have an opportunity of talking matters over with you", which indicated that the two had yet to meet. Clearly the inquiry was coming from the committee and not the other way round, so who might have put Jellie's name forward? It could have been Jellie's close friend Sir George Fowlds, at whose home Albert Mansbridge, founder of the WEA in Britain, had stayed during his tour in 1913.[12] Fowlds was President of the College at the time, a position he held until 1933. He had been on

Chapter 9

the foundation executive of the WEA and supported a move to broaden the range of subjects taught, saying that the WEA must "cultivate also the deeper feelings and richer powers of appreciation, and develop the finer susceptibilities. It must widen the interests of many whose lives through their work are narrow."[13] Equally likely, the suggestion to contact William Jellie could have come from Nellie Ferner (1869-1930),[14] a prominent member of the Auckland Unitarian Church. She was a member of the Council of the WEA and the Auckland Education Board, amongst many other public roles. She knew both William Jellie and Sir George Fowlds well.

By now the Jellie family, with the exception of Hilary who remained at Waitaki Boys High for the next two years, were all back in Auckland. Mary and John started at the local Three Kings primary school and Margaret went to St Cuthbert's College. Ella had bought the land at 14 Warren Avenue, Three Kings, in July 1925, just two months after they returned from Timaru. It was a sizeable piece of land, close to three quarters of an acre, which allowed the construction of a substantial home for the family, with three bedrooms and a porch off the main bedroom where William Jellie liked to sleep in summer. His study was a book-lined annex at one end of the dining room; he had also filled the hallway with bookcases. Soon his books appeared nearly everywhere in the house. There was a long driveway from the road which became circular in front of the house, where later a white cherry tree was planted. A grass tennis court was laid out and nearby a chicken run built and a vegetable garden prepared, both activities on which Jellie enjoyed spending his time. This was the first permanent home of the Jellie family. They had moved into the new house in 1926, so beginning to teach for the WEA that April fitted in very well.

After a year spent concentrating on family affairs, Jellie was now back at work, organising a whole programme of study for an adult class. Although the work only occupied him part time, it was mentally stimulating. Little did he realise he would continue to teach for the next fourteen years. It is likely that both the pleasure he derived from teaching and the settled state of his family, not to mention his mature years, made it easy for him to reject the overture from the Sydney Unitarian Church when their pulpit became vacant a few years later.[15]

Jellie started his teaching career with English Literature, which proved to be the course he taught most frequently. The range he covered was vast, from eighteenth- and nineteenth-century poets and writers to the moderns, both poetry and prose. His course usually comprised 24 two-hour sessions, each consisting of a one-hour lecture and a one-hour tutorial. Within his courses he drew out reflections of political and social change, such as the struggle for constitutional and religious liberty in England seen through the works of Milton.

A series of three courses between 1934 and 1936 discussed social and political change mediated through literature. In one course he examined the sufferings of the common people of eighteenth-century France, which led to the revolution in that country, and traced its impact on the reforms in Britain and the later Russian revolution. Here he looked at writers ranging from Voltaire and Rousseau to Wollstonecraft, Paine, Byron and Shelley. He delivered a two-part course over the last two years, covering political and social ideas of the early Victorian period — the Utilitarians, Socialists and Chartists — through the writings of Carlyle, Ruskin, Trollope, Clough, Arnold and others. This was followed by a course on the Age of Liberalism, 1860-1900: the revolutions in thinking in politics, economics, science and religion; the dominance of political Liberalism and the emergence of socialism, including William Morris, Matthew Arnold, Tennyson and Browning. There was ample opportunity in his teaching for Jellie to show the relevance of these writers to the working classes. The Chartists had shown a preference for the works of Bunyan, Burns, Milton and Shelley, as these were writers who had raised the struggle for reform.

In addition to these, Jellie taught an appreciation of Shakespeare. Shakespeare was popular with working-class radicals from the mid nineteenth century onward. There was a Shakespearean Chartist Association, and his plays were studied by the poet Gerald Massey and the secularist George W. Foote. Working-class people often learnt to read from his plays and would recite from them. "In their eyes, Shakespeare, like Milton and Chaucer, appeared as a defiantly plebeian figure."[16]

Another frequent subject for Jellie's courses, second only to his course on general English literature, was the works of Dante.[17] Dante Alighieri (1265-1321) was a Florentine poet and philosopher writing at the end of the medieval period and beginning of the Renaissance. Jellie's love of Dante had been inspired by his mentor Philip Wicksteed. The Victorians had adopted Dante with great gusto as part of their revival of interest in Italian literature and culture. In nineteenth-century England Dante was seen as the opponent of tyranny, which was mirrored in contemporary English thought. This idea was reflected in such English poets as Milton, Henry Hallam, and Samuel Taylor Coleridge.[18]

Dante's *Divine Comedy,* written in Italian rather than Latin, marked a momentous change in literary style. Notwithstanding the subject matter of its three volumes — Hell, Purgatory and Heaven — it took human individuality and happiness seriously. This earthly life was not seen as mere preparation for the afterlife, but as a place where people could find happiness. This was a major break with medieval theology — arguably the point at which the Middle Ages began to dissolve and Renaissance humanism emerged.[19] This had immense appeal to the Unitarians, given their desire to remove suffering and enable humanity to achieve happiness in this life. When William Jellie gave his first sermons in Auckland, "Our Aims" and "The Principles and Doctrines of Unitarians", he was at pains to make this very point.

Dante's *De Monarchia* provided an equally radical treatment, for the time, of the relationship between church and state. Although Dante

*William Jellie's bust of Dante
in the foyer of the University of Auckland Main Library*

believed that peace required a single or universal monarch, he argued that neither the Pope nor the Emperor should reign supreme over both temporal and spiritual areas; they should have separate jurisdictions. This view conflicted with that of Pope Boniface VIII, and the work was condemned as heretical. When the Index of forbidden books was drawn up under the Papacy of Paul IV, *De Monarchia* was included and was not removed until 1881. Once again, the idea of separation between church and state was one which Unitarians believed in and advocated throughout their history. It was a concept that William Jellie would have been only too pleased to expound upon.

William Jellie kept a substantial workbook to record items of interest.[20] In it are reviews, dating from 1910, many about new Dante titles, as well as philosophy by A. N. Whitehead, poems by Gordon Bottomley, a biography of the Sitwells, prose by Walter de la Mare, and a biography of Thomas Hardy. The discovery of the earliest portrait of Dante is recorded in a four-page article with five other portraits, concluding with drawings of his supposed skull. Obituaries are to be found: the notation on one says it is from the Editorial Office of the *Auckland Star* and this is on a clipping from the *Christchurch Star*; the article concerned is a D. H. Lawrence obituary reprinted from the *New Statesman*. Who did Jellie know in the *Auckland Star* to provide him with clippings? Virtually all the items, although not often sourced and dated, appear to be from overseas newspapers. There was a clipping on the annual dinner of Morley College for Working Men and Women where Sir Herbert Samuel spoke about the ideas of the age, including "The long struggle to establish political liberty in Ireland, the question of religious education in schools and public control..." — matters dear to the heart of William Jellie. This was the college where Amber Blanco White (1887-1981), daughter of Maud and William Pember Reeves, taught for thirty-seven years.

Starting from 1928, many articles are from *The New Statesman*, founded in 1913 by Sidney and Beatrice Webb, George Bernard Shaw and other members of the Fabian Society. William Jellie would have appreciated the excellent book reviews and reports on dramatic performances. Articles on "The Unitarians" and "American University

Chapter 9

Presses" were collected from the *American Mercury*. *The Queen* contained delightful reports on English homes (the Sitwells' for example) and country regions with literary associations, while C.E.M. Joad wrote about the philosophy of food and the "humiliating English indifference to expert cooking".

By 1930 there is a change in the clippings; more political items start to appear, as do articles about international affairs. An item from *The Times* points out the similarities in the Nazi German and Soviet Russian dictatorships. Many articles are from the English WEA magazine *The Highway*; among them are numerous political commentaries. While book reviews continue to dominate, by now many are of political publications about Germany, Russia and the League of Nations. By 1934 a heading in *Time and Tide* says it all quite well: "New Deal or Dictatorship". The book reviewed is *Reconstruction, a Plea for a National Policy* by Harold Macmillan, and has the reviewer saying "this is in substance, the most important book of the year." With the appearance of the stark alternatives of fascism and communism to democracy the comments now take on a prophetic air. The reviews allowed Jellie to follow up, reading the titles of interest to keep his courses up to date.

Articles from the *Illustrated London News* tend to be about archaeology and science. *The Spectator* provides reports on political topics. A review of four books about Ireland has some marginalia indicating Jellie's interest. *The Manchester Guardian* can now be identified along with *The Observer*. Complete articles are kept from *The Book Society News*: "Whistler", "Eight Victorian Poets", and "The Mysterious Universe" to name but a few. One review from *The Observer* would have fascinated Jellie: William Rothenstein's *Men and Memories,* a memoir which includes mention of William Jellie when they were both students at University Hall.

How did Jellie come to assemble this collection from such a range of sources? He may have subscribed to some of them, such as *The Book Society News*. *The Highway* would have been available from the Auckland WEA. Is it possible the article from the *Auckland Star* Editorial Office provides a clue? Could he have had a friend who gave him access to overseas papers? In any event the workbook shows how he kept abreast of new publications and developments around the world. His information was not limited to western countries; there were reports on the Japanese invasion of China, and events in other parts of the world.

The Poor Person's University

Awareness of the changed international political and economic system is reflected in the four lectures Jellie gave to the Hamilton WEA in 1939 on "What communism means today". Here he distinguished between communism, which he called revolution by violence, and socialism, which he saw as evolutionary change, presumably in a lawful and constitutional sense. Then he examined the role of scientific thought in the development of humanitarian legislation and social utopias and discussed how revolutionary change can result in dictatorships, which destroy any hope for democracy. In this lecture he referred to the *History of the Freedom of Thought* by John Bagnell Bury (1861-1927),[21] the classical scholar and historian. This book is full of sentiments that chimed with William Jellie's Unitarian views, such as: "In what we may call the earliest justification of liberty of thought we have two significant claims affirmed: the indefeasible right of the conscience of the individual — a claim on which later struggles for liberty were to turn; and the social importance of discussion and criticism"[22] and "If the history of civilisation has any lesson to teach us it is this: there is one supreme condition of mental and moral progress which it is completely within the power of man himself to secure, and that is perfect liberty of thought and discussion. The establishment of this liberty may be considered the most valuable achievement of modern civilisation, and as a condition of social progress it should be deemed fundamental."[23] Jellie agreed with Bury that freedom of thought was just as important for the individual as it is for society as a whole.

Jellie gave a lecture on "The Philosophy of Modern Pacifism" probably about the same time as his lectures on communism.[24] This is noteworthy because there is no record of him raising the subject at the time of the First World War. In this lecture he referred to the works of C. E. M. Joad (1891-1953).[25] After examining the role of nationalism in war he advocated the necessity of an international authority to control arms, and specifically war planes.[26] He also advocated an international arbitration system to maintain peace. Strangely, this lecture does not appear to place any emphasis on the claims of the individual pacifist to his or her conscience. Rather, the emphasis is on the maintenance of international peace. However, the notes are not long, and the question of individual conscience may have been covered in his extempore presentation or in material from Joad's works.

One of the most interesting courses Jellie delivered was "Utopias through the Ages", his last for the Auckland WEA, given from April to September 1939.[27] (By now the former 24 lectures and tutorial programme had been reduced to 22.) The course was a survey of Utopian models from a wide variety of times and places. Jellie did not focus on New Zealand as the Utopian Paradise, although it had often been portrayed as such from the nineteenth century onward.[28] This course covers a sweeping array of utopian thought including Plato's *Republic*, Plutarch's *Sparta* and *Lives of Lycurgus,* Dante's *De Monarchia*, Thomas More's *Utopia*, Karl Marx's *Communist Manifesto,* Robert Pemberton's *Happy Colony,* Edward Bellamy's *Looking Backward*, William Morris' *News from Nowhere,* H. G. Wells' *A Modern Utopia* and Aldous Huxley's *Brave New World.*

Two of these utopian works have a particular New Zealand flavour. One was Edward Bellamy's *Looking Backward,* the work that William Jellie had first encountered as a student in Philip Wicksteed's course on Sociology, Economics and Social Problems at Manchester New College. By the time Jellie taught his course, *Looking Backward* was already influential in New Zealand. In the 1890s it had been praised by William Pember Reeves as "the book of the day" and sold in its tens of thousands.[29] The depression of the 1930s gave birth to a resurgence of interest in the work of Edward Bellamy and, in particular, *Looking Backward.* The riots of unemployed workers in Dunedin, Auckland and Wellington in 1932 and the banning of another of Bellamy's books, *The Parable of the Water Tank,* that same year, helped reignite working-class interest. The Edward Bellamy Society of New Zealand was formed in Wellington in 1936 after the broadcast of a radio talk on Edward Bellamy as part of a series on "Modern Utopias"; a branch was set up in Auckland in 1937. The Society's influence was expanded through its weekly column in the Labour party newspaper *The Standard.*

The views of this American socialist had an important influence on social policies and legislation in New Zealand.[30] Two members of Parliament joined the Bellamy Society initially, and there were an additional seven Labour MP supporters in the government: J. Thorn,

Rev. Clyde Carr, E. J. Howard, C. M. Williams, W. Lee Martin, A. S. Richards and Dr D. G. McMillan; later Mrs Catherine Stewart joined. With this parliamentary support the Bellamy Society representatives put proposals before the Parliamentary National Health and Superannuation Committee and a Select Committee of the House of Representatives. Even the Prime Minister, Michael Savage, agreed with their proposals for universal state benefits.[31] Not only did the Bellamy Society influence the Social Security Scheme, it helped introduce principles such as full employment, home ownership by working-class people, free education and health service, motherhood endowment, universal superannuation and other State-supplied benefits.[32] So by the time William Jellie was teaching this course he could point to the adoption of many Bellamy Society ideas by the first Labour government in New Zealand.

The other decidedly New Zealand utopian topic was *The Happy Colony*.[33] This was a plan to achieve the utopian ideal in New Zealand, promulgated in 1854 by Robert Pemberton (1788-1879),[34] a follower of Robert Owen (1771-1858).[35] Pemberton proposed that 200,000 acres should be bought in Taranaki, probably at New Plymouth, to build ten towns housing 10,000 people each. However, as the Taranaki war broke out soon afterward, Pemberton could not advance the scheme. Instead he took a job with the government service and subsequently was appointed surveyor for the Ashley district in Canterbury.

A surprising omission in William Jellie's course was the Rochdale Pioneers. Jellie was surely familiar with the Rochdale Equitable Society, the co-operative movement that started in 1844 and spread around the world, including New Zealand.[36] Before World War I consumer co-ops were formed in Christchurch, Westport and Wellington. After the war they spread to other centres and increased in number, although price competition from chain stores in the 1920s saw some co-ops shut down. However the depression years saw a resurgence of co-ops and later they appeared in state house areas developed under the first Labour government.

As John Colquhoun noted, one of the "most important of the experiments that the New Zealand WEA movement produced was the summer school."[37] William Jellie was an enthusiastic participant in these schools. At Pukekohe in 1926 the first summer school was held in the local technical high school over ten days during Christmas and

Chapter 9

New Year. Camp life consisted of lectures, walks, sporting activities such as tennis and cricket, community singing and a concert put on by lady campers. William Jellie spoke on "Literature of the Elizabethan Period" and on the Sunday morning "Religious Trends of the Elizabethan Period" and gave the final lecture on "Shakespeare" on the morning before camp was broken. The camp was seen as a great success and stimulus to the Auckland WEA: "To see a university graduate peeling potatoes and discussing foreign affairs with a carpenter by trade, also doing his share in preparing the meals, was one illustration of our motto 'Labor et scientia'!"[38] "Work and knowledge" was a good motto for the WEA, combining its ideals of bringing knowledge to the working man and woman. The second summer school was held at Hamilton Technical High School. The format was similar to that established by the first school: lectures, tennis, swimming, music and play reading in the evenings. William Jellie gave a lecture on the life and times of Dante.

Much of the success of the school was due to the work of Norman Macdonald Richmond (1897-1971), the new director of the Auckland WEA who followed Linden Mander. Richmond gave lectures on "The Challenge of Fascism" and "The Challenge of Sovietism" which by all accounts were found to be quite striking.[39] With his flair and organisational drive he brought a committed Marxist view to his work which was reflected in his belief that the WEA should be an agent of social change.[40]

Norman Richmond's Unitarian antecedents ran deep: he was the grandson of James Crowe Richmond (1822-1898), the younger brother of Judge Christopher Richmond; his mother Flora Hursthouse Macdonald Richmond (1862-1928) was the granddaughter of Helen Hursthouse (1803-1895), first of the extended Hursthouse-Atkinson-Richmond families who came to New Plymouth in 1843. His father Maurice Richmond had been active in the Forward Movement while practicing law in Wellington, and was appointed to a chair in law at Victoria University College, which he gave up in 1910. Norman Richmond had completed a B.A. at Canterbury University College before serving in the in the New Zealand Expeditionary Force in 1918. His wartime experience turned him towards pacifism. He was awarded a Rhodes scholarship and took a B.A. in modern history and politics at University College, at Oxford University.[41]

It was not long before Richmond was joined by another former Wellington Unitarian, John Cawte Beaglehole (1901-1971), who had returned to New Zealand in 1929 after completing a Ph.D. at the London School of Economics. Like Richmond, his family had also been involved in the Forward Movement and the Wellington Unitarian Free Church, where John had been church organist. He became Tutor-Organiser for the Waikato WEA in 1931 under the direction of Norman Richmond. In Hamilton John and Elsie Beaglehole were welcomed by the chairman of the WEA committee, Fred de la Mare, a former Forward Movement and Wellington Unitarian Free Church member, who had more recently joined the Rationalist Association.[42] These were friendly faces to William Jellie, people he had known along with their families, during his time in Wellington. And there were other Auckland Unitarian friends involved with the WEA, some no doubt introduced at his own behest.

One of the Auckland Unitarians had an involvement that predated Jellie's own: John Guy's interest in adult education began in England and through this he developed a friendship with John Ruskin and joined one of his utopian agrarian communities. Ruskin referred to John Guy as a "brave and gentle Companion".[43] Following his work with the Adult Schools John Guy became a foundation member of the Auckland WEA in 1915, studying music and economics, and in 1926 was made an honorary life member. The Russian Revolution in 1919 saw John Guy subsequently become a self-confessed Bolshevist.[44] When he died in 1929, aged 84, his funeral service was taken by William Jellie.[45]

The third summer school, from 26 December 1928 to 3 January 1929, was held at Hunua Falls at the "up-to-date camp site of the Presbyterian Bible Class Union".[46] It was claimed to be the best held yet, despite the three days of rain at the start. William Jellie took a literary role as usual, giving lectures on the "Great Writers of America" as part of the main study programme, with "Some Modern Poets" in the additional courses. There were two lectures each day: all students attended those from the main course but they could choose amongst the offering from the additional lectures.

Sir George Fowlds' desire to see the cultivation of "finer susceptibilities" and "powers of appreciation" amongst WEA students was certainly realised in the teaching of drama and art and music appreciation. In

Auckland the drama class with over 400 students was taken over by the Rev. William Abbott Constable (1889-1968), who arrived in 1929 to replace Rev. Albert Thornhill at the Auckland Unitarian Church. That year William Constable also helped found the WEA Dramatic Club. During its second season three plays were produced for the annual concert, including choral work by the music class, and presented to an audience of 700. The Dramatic Club soon became one of Auckland's leading amateur dramatic societies.[47] William Jellie also took part in the Club's productions, his acting ability and bonhomie endearing him to the students: "Nearly all of them, becoming warmly attached to a tutor in the play, joined his class in Dante the following year and spent 30 [sic] weeks on that poet."[48]

The Dramatic Club was part of left wing theatre that developed in Auckland during the depression years, staging politically radical productions. The WEA director Norman Richmond engaged R. A. K. Mason (1905-1971), the well-known Marxist poet and dramatist, to organise trade union audiences for its production of *Waiting for Lefty* by the American playwright Clifford Odets in October 1936. The result was so successful that within a month the trade unions and WEA inaugurated the People's Theatre to produce plays with a special working class interest; William Jellie's close friend Arthur Sewell (1903-1972), Professor of English at Auckland University College, became President, and Ron Mason became Organiser. By 1939 Ron Mason was elected vice-president. The teacher and writer Joseph Denis Coyne (1905-1973), a member of the Auckland Unitarian Church, became secretary.[49]

William Constable was vice-president of the Auckland WEA during 1932 and 1933 and briefly president before leaving New Zealand in 1934. He was also active in the Little Theatre Society, which had been formed in 1925 and closed in 1938, their last production being Noel Coward's *Private Lives*. The fate of the Little Theatre had been sealed by "prosperity and snobbishness" when some of its members formed the Auckland Repertory Theatre.[50] But in 1934 the Society was at its peak.

William Constable taught WEA drama classes throughout the four years of his joint ministry with his wife, Rev. Wilna Livingstone Constable (née Smart, 1888-1966).[51] In 1929, a meeting of the Auckland Unitarian Church presided over by William Jellie decided unani-

The Poor Person's University

*Revs. William and Wilna Constable
joint ministers of the Auckland Unitarian Church*

mously to appoint Wilna and William Constable, thus making history by inviting New Zealand's first clergywoman. The Unitarians were well ahead of other denominations in accepting women ministers. In the latter part of the nineteenth century there was growing involvement amongst women in Unitarian colleges and ministries. The first woman Unitarian minister, Celia Burleigh, was ordained in America in 1871, and there was a steady growth in numbers throughout the remainder of the century. The first woman minister in the British Empire was ordained in 1873 at the Melbourne Unitarian Church. In 1876 the trustees of Manchester New College voted to admit women students. Gertrude von Petzold (1876-1952) was the first woman accepted for training for the ministry at Manchester College, Oxford, in 1901, qualifying and becoming ordained in 1904.

We can gain some insight into the nature of the students attending William Jellie's classes from the annual reports between 1926 and 1939.[52] In his first year there were 59 enrolments, although the average number attending class was 36 (61 percent). By 1929 his class had increased to 105, his highest number, with an average attendance of 52 (50 percent). Thereafter it ranged from a low of 32 in 1936, of whom 21 attended on average (68 percent), to 59 in 1938 with an average attendance of 35 (59 percent).

Students were predominately female. In 1931, the first year for which we have an analysis by gender and occupation, 84 percent of the students were women, of whom 61 percent were unmarried and 42 percent did not work. Clerks and teachers accounted for nearly all those women who worked. Men, on the other hand, were all working; they included a clerk, a porter, a teacher, an engineer, a hotel manager and a printer. By 1939 the proportion of men had increased to 22 percent. Women made up 78 percent, and unmarried women had declined to 55 percent. However nearly the same proportion of women were not working, 41 percent. Working women were employed as typists, clerks, an importer, a bookkeeper, a domestic, a masseuse, a librarian and a teacher; a wider range of occupations than previously reported. Men's jobs included cabinet maker, civil servant, minister of religion, linotype operator, waterside worker and drafting clerk. While the spread of occupations for men in both 1931 and 1939 indicates that manual labour and trades were common, there were members of office, teaching and professional groups.

William Jellie was vice-president of the Auckland WEA from 1936 to 1938 and on the executive until he retired in 1939. The annual report for 1937 contained the following observation, which clearly indicates the standing of his teaching amongst his peers.[53] One of them ventured the opinion that the literature course offered by William Jellie, "starting with one of the two great poems of Greece which mark the beginning of European literature and finishing with the two books of the later end of the 19th century [Darwin's *Origin of Species* and Marx's *Capital*] which probably have done most to make the mental atmosphere in which we live and work to-day" was an outstanding piece of work.

10

The Epilogue

When he retired from the WEA on 31 October 1939 William Jellie was seventy-four years old. He could have been forgiven for imagining that his contribution to society had been well and truly fulfilled. Just five years earlier he had shouldered the additional responsibility of returning to the pulpit of the Auckland Unitarian Church. This was the interregnum between the departure of the Constables in February 1934 and the arrival of the Rev. Dr Cyprus Richard Mitchell (1881-1955) in March 1936. It was during his temporary ministry that awareness of the serious effects of the Depression grew.[1] The Church set up a register of unemployed for anyone connected with it.[2] Ella Jellie worked most afternoons at an old house on the Three Kings Reserve, helping to organise relief work for unemployed men. The nearby Three Kings School grounds were constructed this way. The year 1935 proved to be a difficult one for the Jellie family; Ella went into hospital for an operation and was "under medical orders to abstain from all kinds of work outside the home for the next six months."[3] It was a relief when Dr Mitchell arrived to take charge of the church.[4]

Dr Mitchell's departure just before William Jellie's retirement coincided with the outbreak of war in September 1939. The church found it impossible to arrange a replacement minister and turned to Ken Thomas (1903-1978) to provide lay direction. He would serve the church in this capacity for ten years until the arrival of the Rev Ellis Henry Morris (1897-1973) in 1948. As an elocutionist with formal qualifications, experienced in debating and public speaking, he was confident in the pulpit. He shared the work with William Jellie and James Chapple, then living in West Auckland.

Chapter 10

Rev. Dr Cyprus Mitchell

The first service in October 1939 was unique in the history of the Church: the premiere production of a play by R. A. K. Mason. "BMA: A Sketch on Social Security" was performed in place of a sermon, the service being led by Joseph Denis Coyne.[5] The first Labour Government wished to introduce a free and universal health service, which put it on a collision course with the leaders of the New Zealand branch of the British Medical Association (BMA) who thought it their duty to save the profession from socialism. Ron Mason's play, written in support of socialised medicine under the Social Security Act of 1938, revolves around the conflict experienced by a doctor called upon to treat the child of a poor worker in a public works camp and the issues arising from the profession's opposition to the government-funded scheme. It ends with the doctor deciding he has to do the "right" thing and treat the child, which his wife has been urging him to do all along.[6] The following three services in October 1939 were taken by James Chapple, William Jellie and Ken Thomas respectively. The service on 29 October was another

The Epilogue

play, this time put on by the children from the Sunday school and although Joseph Coyne had given up his regular teaching at the Sunday school he helped with the production of this play.[7]

William Jellie had long accommodated rationalism in his religious philosophy. The application of rational thought to Unitarian principles was well understood. "By Rationalism we mean that man has no other criterion of truth and goodness than those intellectual and moral faculties which, in different degrees of potency, are common to the race",[8] wrote fellow Unitarian minister the Rev. Frank Walters (1845-1908). Developing the theme that Unitarians were religious rationalists, he went on:

> Our chief objection to authoritative religion is that it detracts from the validity of a man's immediate conviction of truth, deflects the mind from its own tendency, and weakens the sense of personal responsibility. As rationalists we uphold freedom of thought, and the solemn duty of every man to prove all things, and hold fast that which is good.[9]

It was on this basis that William Jellie found it easy to develop such a close working relationship with individual rationalists and their organisation. His greatest friend in this regard had been Sir Robert Stout. "I remember my first interview with him, shortly after I came to New Zealand", Jellie wrote. "He said in a challenging way, as if he expected to shock me, 'My religion is based on evolution,' and when I said straight out, 'So is mine, and without a but,' we became friends at once." He went on to describe the common features of rationalist and Unitarian thought each exemplified:

> He wanted, above all things, freedom of thought for the attainment of truth. In what other way can truth be attained? Can truth be found by any other than the Freethinker? And when a Unitarian Church was established in Wellington on the basis of freedom of thought Sir Robert became a member, after preaching for it and in it, and of late years was its president. He was a rationalist. But Rationalism and Unitarianism are not incompatible. I also claim to be a Rationalist repudiating any authority for truth outside of the human spirit and the final court of appeal within myself. I am a Rationalist in religion and not so very far removed from many supporters of the rationalist movement.[10]

Chapter 10

When William Jellie rejoined the fight against his old foes who wanted to introduce religion in state schools, he aligned himself with those with a similar outlook to his own. The Rationalist Association and Sunday Freedom League, which was affiliated with the Auckland WEA, took an uncompromising stand on the issue. Even before his retirement Jellie appeared with Fred de la Mare at an Auckland meeting discussing the promotion of the Religious Instruction in Primary Schools Enabling Bill by the Bible in Schools League and the Roman Catholic Church. (No doubt he was provoked by the change of heart by the Catholic Church, which had thrown its lot in with the League.) A year later he returned to the same topic when speaking at the Rationalist Association Sunday evening at the Majestic Theatre.[11]

By now Jellie was playing a much more prominent role in the campaign to defend the status quo: in 1931 he was sent to Wellington as a delegate for the State Education Defence League where he gave evidence to the Education Committee of Parliament.[12] In 1937 he supported the Rationalist Association delegation to the Minister of Education Peter Fraser (1884-1950),[13] who told the delegation that the use of legal loopholes by the Bible in Schools League to introduce religion into State Schools was "discreditable".[14] In his address to the Minister, Jellie said, "At the heart of the defence of the present system lay the fact that it was part of the world-wide struggle to liberate the State from ecclesiastical control and interference, and the secular system was a logical and integral part of our secular state."[15]

The secular state in New Zealand was not anti-religious. It was not even indifferent to the promotion of religion; in fact, it supported all forms of religion. Its policy was one of impartiality towards all forms and activities of religion, and it also threw a necessary cloak of protection over those who objected to all forms of religion.

Meanwhile the three-way shared responsibility at the Auckland Unitarian Church was not working well. James Chapple was determined to follow the political line espoused by the local Communist Party in support of the Soviet Union.[16] So long as the Molotov-Ribbentrop Pact held and Germany only waged war in Western Europe, he was content to disparage

The Epilogue

the Allied war effort, which he portrayed as aggression by imperialist powers. This he did at the Auckland Unitarian Church while waving the *People's Voice*, the paper of the New Zealand Communist Party, from the pulpit (before the paper was banned in June 1940). This did not endear him to most of his congregation. While he did a *volte face* when Germany invaded the Soviet Union in June 1941, the incongruity of the situation did not escape him, and he decided not to continue delivering sermons. A church member reflected, "Somehow, we were sorry to lose him; exasperating as he was, we were beginning to develop an affection for him."[17]

Chapple's departure meant that church work now had to be undertaken by William Jellie and Ken Thomas. By 1942 William Jellie was referred to as Minister Emeritus and Ken Thomas as Lay Officer-in-Charge.

There was still one last battle for William Jellie to fight over religion in schools. The Minister of Education, Rex Mason (1885-1975),[18] convened an educational conference in Christchurch in October 1944 and "Religion in Education" was on the agenda.[19] For this item speakers were chosen to lead the debate: those from the Rationalist Association, the Sunday Freedom League and the New Zealand Educational Institute opposed any change to the secular system, while speakers from the Catholic Church and National Council of Churches were in favour of introducing religion into schools. The Auckland Unitarian Church made a written submission on behalf of its "Ministers, Congregation and Committee", one of ten published in the Conference papers on this topic, strongly supporting the principle of separation of Church and State. It said in summary:

> We believe that it would injure our schools, impair the structure and administration of democracy, curtail our liberties—and, furthermore, that it would, in the long run, injure the cause of true religion—if the State decided to impose upon our State schools the important but delicate duties of religious worship and instruction. We believe that New Zealand will best be served in the future as it has been in the past by faithful maintenance of the policy of free, secular, and compulsory education in State schools.[20]

Chapter 10

Faced with an impasse, the Conference appointed a committee to examine the issue, which reported back that it was unable to make any recommendations. This was taken as a win by those opposed to the introduction of religion into State schools.[21]

In August 1945 the war ended with the surrender of Japan. William Jellie led the Thanksgiving Service at the Auckland Unitarian Church on Wednesday, 15 August 1945, "on a day of joy", he said, "the like of which, it is to be hoped and prayed for, none of us will live to see again." His sermon continued to rejoice at the salvation shared by all the peoples of the United Nations and observed the terrible fate that New Zealand had been delivered from, but that had been experienced by so many others. In his view there had been no alternative than to fight: "Resistance to evil rose before us as a duty, the most sacred imaginable." As he expressed thanks to God "that the awful and cruel struggle is over", he also saw grounds for hope that once again humanity could look forward to a

John Jellie (second from right) on the HMS Emperor, *1944 after attacking the German battleship* Tirpitz

The Epilogue

better world that "may open itself to the Brotherhood of Man". It was a sermon for the times, giving thanks for the end of a terrible era for the nation and the world; few, if any, appreciated the implications that the dropping of the atomic bombs on Japan meant for humankind.

As time went by, Jellie's thoughts turned once more to those Unitarians who had travelled to New Zealand before him, names of families he had recognised on his arrival and their descendants whom he met or had corresponded with. He had written about the development of New Zealand Unitarianism after being in the country for just over a decade; then he was able to survey matters with some satisfaction. Following the establishment of the Auckland Church, other Unitarian churches were established in Wellington, Timaru and Dunedin. New Zealand, he thought, had a great future and was a "Unitarian field that must never be abandoned".[22] When, forty-five years later, he assisted in writing an article that once again looked at the history of Unitarianism in New Zealand, it was a different story. Now there was only one church left, in Auckland. The New Zealand Unitarian Association formed in 1912 to support four churches and their missionary work had lapsed, he wrote, because of the "effects upon the national community of the major wars".[23] Elsewhere he recognised the attrition of Unitarian descendants "largely absorbed into other churches" as cause for regret.[24] The reasons for the decline received no detailed examination, although the contrast with fifty years earlier would have been painfully obvious.

One of the early families who stayed true to the church was the Gribbles. William Jellie had nurtured the ambitions of Lincoln Gribble to attend Manchester College at Oxford to study for the Unitarian ministry. When Gribble left in 1952 William Jellie wrote him a long letter of encouragement. Telling him that as a young New Zealander in England he would meet many sorts of people, he warned that "In matters of belief many are somewhat conservative, and they may meet your forthright, radical opinions, many of which must naturally be expressed negatively, with chilling silence." But he cautioned him to have patience and tact, for on the other hand:

> [M]ost of our Unitarian people are Liberal at heart. They were reared in the Liberal School of thought, religious and political of which they were leaders when I was young. And while many have become Labourites,

Chapter 10

Rev. Lincoln Gribble

Socialists, perhaps even Communists, they have not lost the Liberal tradition of freedom for themselves and for others. I have always found that with patience and tact I could steer my way through the different grades of belief and criticism in any congregation because of the fundamental liberal tradition.[25]

This simple rule of patience and tact would, he believed, allow Lincoln Gribble to hold and cherish his most radical opinions. And he also saw him as being able to make an important contribution to broadening the world view of people he met in Oxford and Manchester through what he would bring as a New Zealander. Lincoln Gribble completed an M.A. with honours in English at Auckland University College before entering Manchester College on an Exhibition (scholarship) in October 1952.[26]

When Lincoln Gribble returned to New Zealand in 1960 their friendship resumed. But in the eight years Gribble had been away, Jellie had aged significantly.[27] When Gribble joined *Motive* as an associate editor in 1961, he wrote suggesting that Jellie might write an article. The reply was disheartening: "My friends I fear must learn to put no dependence on me. I am realising that the years have taken their toll. I am a spent force." Jellie went on to talk about how he was now unable to pursue his favourite pastime, gardening: "In the garden when I attempt anything I fall back physically and have to be assisted to rise or actually

The Epilogue

to be lifted up. It is like that mentally. There seems no remedy."[28] He was in his ninety-seventh year.

Lincoln Gribble conducted the funeral service for William Jellie at the Auckland Unitarian Church on 20 April 1963.

An important theme running through this book has been the relationship between Unitarianism, which "stood at the left pole of the theological spectrum",[29] and the political left. The Auckland Unitarian Church drew support from those who held left wing sympathies and attracted working class men and women from its inception. It did this while enjoying support from middle class members who also welcomed social reform. While William Jellie's skill as a minister meant that he never let overt party politics become entangled with the church's religious mission, that did not stop him from being a voice for the working classes and later devoting himself to their educational cause.

As the twentieth century unfolded, Unitarianism became the victim of the growing liberalisation of mainstream Protestant theology. Theological liberalism spread to other dissenting denominations: the Quakers rapidly turned liberal; the Congregationalists followed and later still the Presbyterians. The Unitarians began to lose their distinction as a solitary theological outpost. This trend was reinforced by the growing tendency within Protestantism for dogmatic and especially denominationally based thinking to become marginalised. The academic teaching of theology at overseas universities, notably Oxford and Cambridge in England and Harvard in America, served to strengthen this direction. Much later this trend would reach New Zealand, but only after the Second World War. From the outset William Jellie's views were congruent with the liberal and ecumenical Protestant thinking which would later emerge internationally. In this, as in so many other things, he was ahead of his time.

William Jellie in his study

Appendixes

Appendix 1

William Jellie's Synopsis of Philip Wicksteed's Lectures on Social Problems in the Light of Economic Theory

There are two notebooks stuck together containing notes of Philip Wicksteed's lectures, entitled *Social Problems in the Light of Economic Theory*, at Manchester New College, 1888-89. Jellie has signed the outside of one notebook and both are written in his hand. See also Dennis Porter, *A Catalogue of Manuscripts in Harris Manchester College Oxford* (1998), p. 302.

Elements of Sociology: The Structure, Institutions & Vital Processes of Human Societies

Lecture I: The Human Environment, n.d.

The social element is the most important in the environment of each man, but not with animals where the social element is comparatively insignificant. Workers exchange their products and services with many others; by comparison a single worker would be able to create very little for himself. Cf. Henry George, *Progress and Poverty*. Social interaction is even more important for mental and intellectual life. Our emotions are part of our social life. Our contact with divine things comes through our fellow men. The moral sphere is also part of the social sphere. The action of society creates our social environment in which human relations occur. From this arises continuity of successive generations and solidarity i.e. pairing, bonding, families. Read [Auguste] Comte and also [Herbert] Spencer, but make personal observations.

Appendix 1

Lecture II: [Instruments and Organs of Continuity and Solidarity], n.d.

Man can exert power on nature and society greater than the individual. Material wealth is any substance that supplies a want or furthers a purpose; or "utility fixed in a material substance" which [John] Ruskin is down upon as a definition of wealth. ["There is no wealth but life..."] We will only look at wealth that has human effort expended on it to make it supply a want. Cf. J. S. Mill [*Principles of Political Economy*], Book 1, Chapter 1, paragraph 2. According to this definition animals have wealth, e.g. birds' nests, burrows and ant hills. Civilized man uses wealth to obtain more wealth. The surplus of production over consumption is the main instrument which makes possible the physical continuity and solidarity of mankind. [Henry] Sidgwick says that most of a country's savings must go into tools to enable them to make things they want rapidly. Language is the chief way humans combine forces. Comte gives an interesting account of the origin of language. The language of signs is more natural than that of sounds and we always revert to it when we can't use conventional language. The power of language is that it gives existence to ideas and allows thought to occur. It also allows people to act in solidarity and allows reason to occur (Sayce, *Science of Language*). The Hebrews and other Semites with the same language characteristics have similar reasoning and logical concepts. We depend on language for development of our emotional life. Religious beliefs are built up around certain statements and beliefs. Language can also hold us bondage by its concepts and limitations.

Lecture III: [Society as an Organism], 26 October 1888

The material universe acts on man through society in a way it could not otherwise act upon him. Men can act on the environment in a way impossible to individuals. Society has its own actions which man does not have in isolation; and it has its own laws. Society has the attributes of an organism; we sometimes look on humanity or some particular society as an organism. Society consists of members who are mutually dependent on each other. Spencer has said that in social insects the difference of function follows the lines of sex. In man this division of labour is carried to a great extent. All books on Political Economy discuss in detail the question of division of labour. Even St Paul urges men to cultivate some special function. Dante is right to be mentioned here as doubtful. In the beginning of *De Monarchia* he says that society as a whole has functions, aims and goals that individuals do not. Part of human destiny is only to be realized in society, cf. with the mediaeval aim of men and angels. Hobbes says that "Sovereignty is an artificial soul." All of Comte's works are relevant to the question of man in society.

Spencer has worked with great ingenuity in the comparison of human function with that of society. Specialization of function equals division of labour; so too with intellectual actions. As soon as knowledge is acquired the imparting of it makes for human intercourse. However it is only with the individual that the result of collective action can be governed.

Lecture IV: [The Goal of Society and the Problem of Civilisation (i)], 2 November 1888

To speak of society as an organism is to use a metaphor. Altruistic impulses are assumed part of human nature; the happiness of others is an object we pursue. Egotistical impulses may be strongest in some individuals but altruism is strong in society. The goal of society must be found in each individual; society must impartially pursue the good of each member. This must include the feeling of communion with others, including the divine. Religion is any kind of communion, including a religion of nature. Communion may have great variety and led to the poets Schiller and Wordsworth to regret the passing of old polytheistic beliefs. We may also have a scientific communion with nature. It is less necessary to dwell on the religion of humanity. We might conceive of a religion of humanity parallel to our religion of nature which should glorify and transfigure humanity. The good of each individual comes in the raising of his intercourse with nature, man and god, into communion. It is idle to talk of Sociology and Political Economy without that good for which men should toil. The problem of civilization is to subordinate nature to man and coordinate men with each other. History shows great success with the first but much less with the second. Self sacrifice is required, not a surrendering of the inner self. This seems capable in the family and sometimes town and country.

Lecture V: [The Goal of Society and the Problem of Civilisation (ii)], 9 November 1888

Frequently, a certain class recognizes its claims superseding the claims of others, including the family and have no consideration beyond their class; e.g. the sense of community among wage earners leads them not to compete with each other, but they may look on those outside their class as enemies. This spirit can be shown in national life when statesmen and even divines hold that selfishness is right and a self-sacrificing nation is weak. It can be found when one nation looks on another as chattel slaves. Slavery in early times was defended as necessary to maintain leisure; Greek art would have been impossible without slave labour. Humanity at large reaped great benefits from the martyrdom of slaves. There is an ideal balance when a worker enjoys the advantage from his work just to

Appendix 1

the point where the disadvantage is struck. When this balance is disturbed the principle of slavery enters. The power of social tyranny, implying slavery, increases with the increasing poor of society. The division of labour is the mechanism whereby the individual is thrown upon the cooperation of others. It would be good to keep the option open of returning to previous primitive arrangements, especially on the land. The lot of the Lancashire mechanic is better than that of the London poor.

Lecture VI: [Property], 16 November 1888

The institutions of society are instruments for furthering the good of society. I cannot give such an institution as property any intrinsic value. I cannot attribute inherent absolute sanctity to it. Property, does it rest on a natural basis of right? If it is a good institution a good man will not violate it. If property is a satisfactory social instrument it must claim ethical sanction. In which case the commandment not to steal depends on property's social purpose. The claim for a natural basis is the belief that man has an absolute right to what he has made. This also means he has a right to his own person. Individualists and socialists accept this. Socialists used to say that capitalism took away from a man what was his own and demand the full enjoyment of what he had made. They differed in their methods of finding what he had made. Gradually the idea of contract was substituted for mere procession, that is a socially directed right to property. It changes the definition from what a man has made to what he is entitled to under certain conditions. Highest in the list of advantages of property is the sense of personal connection with material things, e.g. a house. The sense of fitness that applies to all relations, not just property, at times challenges the results of existing system of property, e.g. when there is a strong feeling that it is unjust that a large number of people live on interest, in itself constitute a moral weakness and social danger. Again chattel slavery rested on the principle of property as then understood. When it offended the sense of fitness it was challenged and had to be removed.

Lecture VII: [The Family], 23 November 1888

The family is the primitive type of organisation and rests on the permanent facts of sex and maternity. Maternity furnishes the citadel of altruism. This is the dominant factor of human and family life. Family life is general among the higher animals, i.e. the vertebrates. (Which Darwin has proved.) The maternal instinct may be impaired and infanticide occurs, often among savages; it may even become the norm in highly developed societies e.g. China, Greece and Rome. Family life impaired can recover with the development of human intelligence. The continuity and permanence of paternity came to be recognised as much as maternity. Brotherhood is the weakest of the ties and an addition to established family relations. The primal connection of male and female is the test of real progress toward civilization. Spencer tells of an island [populated] by Indians with higher and lower races on it, in which the lower treat their [wives] better than the higher. Efficiency of civilization is gauged by its power of transforming the sexual life. It is an instance of how the spiritual life of man is built upon a lower material physical basis. So literature, romance, poetry, which stirs feelings is built upon the relationship of the sexes. Dr Elizabeth Blackwell among others, attempts to direct this passion in positive ways. The most awful form of human tyranny is when men are carried away to subjugating women. The greatest oppression is done when the sexual instinct is allowed to become the tyrant, instead of being the central fire of the human family. The Monastic Ideal deserves attention. Those who think social life can only come through the family are disproved by monastic life. The ideas expressed in Romantic literature are based on the notion of property: woman is the property of the father, next given to the husband. No claim of chastity is laid on the man, only the woman as a breach of property rights. However these ideas of property do not satisfy modern people. The most beautiful ideal of family life is the Teutonic. The family is the natural unit of society. The family keeps alive the ideal of contributing according to means and receiving according to needs. Spencer defines Justice as "the right to get for work what competition of the market determines as the market value." This is inadequate. Justice demands that everyone should give according to his power and should receive according to his needs. The state i.e. industry should make a contribution as favourable as possible to individual needs. The public ethic is survival of the fittest, the family ethic care for the weakest, sacrifice by the strong. The religious sanction controls the flesh more than any other. In its decay the institution of family may be threatened. The family is also threatened by Individualism and Socialism. My hope for humanity depends on the institution of the family, "the cement of society" as Dr Martineau calls it.

Lecture VIII: Government, n.d.

Government primarily is any organizing power in society with command of adequate physical force. Law is the system of principles that regulate members of society and it rests ultimately on force. Ideal law is force completely moralized, force that has put itself at the service of the moral sense. The ideal government is completely socialized cf. with Professor [T. H.] Green's work, volume 2, on relation of Government to the morals of the people. There is universal agreement the government must secure the protection of the person and property. Many think this exhausts its function. It may include acts that Spencer protests against e.g. laws against adulteration of food; compulsory vaccination, a striking case of interference with personal liberty; regulations about mines. Spencer on the other hand would extend no protection to persons except from physical violence; he would allow a man to mutilate himself if he contracted to do so. The protection of property opens the question of contracts and what constitutes property. But there are other functions of government: what of the protection of helpless members of society: the recent land Laws in Ireland affected tenants who were helpless. Previously the Factory Acts only interfered with employment of women and children, adult men made their own contracts. Now there is a change in principle — a step toward state socialism. Enforcing conduct deemed to be for the public good such as closing businesses on Sundays. These are acts of prohibition, protection and prevention. Then there are socialistic acts; collective action taken for the public good. There is no reason why government should not exercise an industrial function, the only question is would the state do it better than the private sector? Is government to protect the moral sense from outrage? If the state is to perform the development of the moral sense its course is accompanied by extreme danger. It is one of its most desirable functions and yet it commits to a theory of moral censorship which in extreme becomes enslaving and tyrannical. It has recently become the suppression of anti-religious polemics; see the prosecution of [George W.] Foote. The socialistic ideal of government abandons the idea of it being a check on anti-social behavior; its concept is for government to give direction for the collective action of society. The danger of socialism is in this contraction of the scope, initiative and enterprise of individuals. See [William] Stanley Jevons *Methods of Social Reform*.

Lecture IX: Education and the Spiritual Power, n.d.

Education is closely connected with the higher organizing power of society. Education involves "learning the acts and acquiring the powers required for living." There is a growing importance of education which increases with the growth of things to be learnt. Human beings are only human in society. Learning is required in order to associate with other human beings. The first requirement of education is language, which allows for the passing on of material and spiritual efforts. Then a man has to be able to earn a living to obtain his wants. Technical education in making something that others want, or doing something that others want. The artist or literary man performs in the higher life for himself and others. Machiavelli says in *The Prince*, about political changes, that there is an advantage in governing a state which has not had many changes, and every revolution leaves a basis for further revolution. So every change in education should leave the way to further change. There is a special interest in economic education as it contributes to deeper knowledge over the conditions of life. In a narrow sense education should be aimed at getting power over one's own will. The question of the separation of church and state is really a question of the separation of spiritual and temporal power.

Lecture X: The Place of Economics in Sociology, n.d.

The higher spiritual life depends on material life. Property rests on wealth; government on organized physical force; family on the physical facts of animal nature. Industrial organisations bring men into fellowship with each other. The study of wealth, i.e. accumulation and disposal of human effort to secure changes in material substance, is doing well and occupies a great place in the study of society. But it is not the study of wealth but of life itself that is the study of sociology. Wealth is a means of human life; economics is the study of human effort upon material things. Dante in *De Monarchia* says "Some studies we can contemplate and cannot modify (as Astronomy and Mathematics); others we can contemplate and modify, and in them speculation exists for the sake of action." The orthodox view holds that economics is a speculative study; the most outspoken exponent of this is [Nassau W.] Senior. He separates government and political economy: the former is the welfare of mankind, the later the study of wealth. We cannot study wealth without coming into contact with other things: wealth has a living element to it, wealth is only of value if it ministers to human want. If want changes wealth may also change. "How is the wealth of a community to be increased?" Mill in his *Essays on Political Economy* describes economic man as only seeking wealth, averse to labour and liking expensive luxuries. [Francis Amasa] Walker, *Political Economy*, p. 16, opposes this idea. See also *On Wages* and female labour. The fallacy in regarding economic man as being solely actuated by wealth; if all were millionaires we should all live in cottages. Under the present system the desire for wealth is permanent and universal among those engaged in industry. It is a habit of the business mind to strive for wealth. We must avoid the idea that the economic man is the normal one or that in him we study the actual action of human behavior. The Political Economists have not succeeded in gaining public favour because their science is seen as only speculative. Jevons in his primer takes up a position nearer my own, saying that political economy "deals with wealth of nations and aims at teaching what should be done that the poor may be as few as possible and that all should be as well paid for their work as possible. Various social sciences are needed in addition e.g. jurisprudence. But Political Economy treats of what wealth is, how best to get it and how best to consume it when got." Read *The Alphabet of Economic Theory* by P. H. Wicksteed, MacMillan & Co., 2/6.

Appendix 1

Social Problems in the Light of Economic Theory

Introduction: Mathematical Elements, 21 December 1888

Description of mathematical applications used to solve problems in economics; use of algebra; representing data on a curve; increase and decrease in rates for data plotted on a curve.

Lecture I: Value — The Problem, 11 January 1889

The theory of value — John Stuart Mill [*A System of Logic*] Book III says "almost every speculation of the economic interests of society implies the theory of value"; still more true of Jevons; the connection between value in use and value in exchange.

Lecture II: Value — The Solution (i), 18 January 1889

The theory of utility; value in exchange is determined by utility; Jevons and final utility i.e. marginal utility; [Carl] Menger and the Austrian School of Economics (see article in the *American Quarterly Journal of Economics*, October 1888) demonstrate how to determine the exchange value of any article.

Lecture III: Value — The Solution (ii), 25 January 1889

Distinguish the total effect from marginal effectiveness; marginal effectiveness [utility] which is the measure of value in exchange; importance in understanding diagrammatic explanations, especially measuring rates of change.

Lecture IV: The Test of the Solution, 1 February 1889

When a good is produced for sale we find who wants it relative to other things — its marginal usefulness. Only two things modify the marginal desirousness for an item: [supply] and [demand]. Laws of diminishing and increasing returns.

Lecture V: Exchange, 1 March 1889

Law of increasing returns, the advantage gained from producing articles in larger amounts. Law of diminishing returns occurs when all the best opportunities are taken up first. The development of exchange secures the additional advantage of division of labour. Each man is best employed on the tasks he does best relative to the tasks of others. International trade — restrictions on free trade are analogous to domestic restrictions on divisions of labour.

Lecture VI: Free Trade and Fair Trade, n.d.

The British example of adopting free trade has not been followed, not even in the colonies. Fair trade is advocated as a step toward free trade. Free traders believe that closer commercial relations between countries help maintain peace. Free trade is conditional on reciprocity.

Lecture VII: Population and Immigration, n.d.

These questions are connected to free trade. If there is universal peace and free trade there is no reason why England should not manufacture for the world, if that is advantageous. Will a multiplication of workers result in diminished per capita return to workers? Will two men working with the same "natural powers" get more or less if there are 10 working? Competition is a law of nature; the law of self-preservation conflicts with the desire of cooperation. The fittest to survive are not those swayed by altruism but those with the power to secure enough for them. A man with 8 or 10 children causes increased struggle. If Malthusianism is true a man with a large family sins against the family and is a social malefactor, for he has intensified the struggle and caused the deaths of others. Malthus' argument that doubling the population does not result in a doubling of production, especially food, rests on the law of decreasing returns. Regarding the facts in England see [John Elliott] Cairnes, *Some Leading Principles of Political Economy Newly Expounded*. The truth or falsity of the Malthusian theory cannot be found in abstract argument; it must be demonstrated in experience. Free growth of population implies readiness to immigrate. Socialists object to emigration because it is an outlet rather than dealing with change at home.

Lecture VIII: Low Wages, n.d.

The right distribution of workers amongst occupations is as important as the right geographical distribution. Wrong distribution of labour causes overproduction and trade depression. Relative overproduction in some localities is the cause of low wages in those occupations. When this happens the wage earner is at a disadvantage to the capitalist because capital is perpetually replacing itself. Business ability can shift with ease, but Adam Smith said "Of all kinds of luggage man is the least removable". The results of long term overproduction fall on wage earners almost exclusively, which results in degrading labour. See Walker, *The Wages Question*. Survival of the "fittest" is for them to live in the most degraded and de-humanised circumstances. Cairnes pointed out that the trades open to the humbler classes are very few and they are obliged to keep within a narrow group. Walker says in most cases there is no choice at all. A person who works hard ought to secure a minimum comfort. Who is to pay it? Not employers, they can't or else they would be making a gift of their capital. When we decide what a fair wage is? The unanswerable question follows – who is to pay it? The ultimate cause of low wages is the fact that poor workers have no

Appendix 1

alternative and compete with each other in a trade already over supplied with labour. Public opinion does not accept the idea that firms should take a greater interest in worker welfare. By providing an asylum for refugees London also suffers from imported cheap labour. There is less foundation for the idea that Jewish clothing firms are the worst. English firms that cannot compete with cheap foreign labour will leave the trade entirely. The only way to escape from low wages is to leave low paid trades. Women and children are paid worst of all and their employment often deprives men of work. We should be getting the employers to compete for labour as much as labour to compete for employment.

Lecture IX: Land Nationalisation — The Case for It, n.d.

Agriculture is the natural equilibrating industry. It is important to keep agriculture open, by various ways to many people e.g. by allotments, which teach men to farm at home or abroad. Or by succession [? inheritance] of land. Competent men have found agricultural work to be the nearest possible to the ideal state, compared with the dens of London. Without idealizing the peasant life, e.g. Mill and the French peasant proprietor, it must be admitted that the life got from the soil is desirable. Why is land going out of production and people swarming into London? The reason is in private ownership of land. There must be a surplus, however small, so that the landlord is able to let part of the land to the labourer.

Lecture IX continued, 29 March 1889

Another problem is land being acquired for building resulting in greater rents. When agricultural values are falling, the fact that land is held in private ownership is an obstacle to its proper use, because owners demand a rent that is not payable by users. Thus the question of land nationalization arises from the position of municipal ownership. This leads to the question of whether private ownership of land is on the same footing as private property in general. The first question is that of "economic rent". By this the political economist includes what is paid for the "prairie value" of the land, the primitive inalienable proprietor of the soil. If land were in unlimited supply there would be no economic rent because everyone could get as much as they wanted. But it is not clear that the rent should go to the "owner"; who is the primitive proprietor of the soil? A Land premium is paid for the advantage one kind of land has over another. The greater part of the premium is due to the position of the land and it is the community that gives the value to the land. In our country the Crown holds [i.e. owns] the whole country and allows land to be held to certain tenants in return for service. Spencer condemns the individual holding of land and advocates nationalisation. The arguments for land nationalisation are: [1] the land premium belongs by right to the people for it is owing to the community; [2] the restoration of public ownership would ultimately abolish the necessity of taxation so make free trade possible; [3] it would remove the need for public debt; [4] it would tend to keep agriculture in small holdings as an alternative to larger industries; [5] it would provide clear spaces in large towns for parks, railway stations, markets and improvements generally without expense, except for the cost of buildings destroyed.

Lecture X: Land Nationalisation — The Case Against, 5 April 1889

Objections to private ownership of land have been admitted by writers such as Walker in *Land and its Rent* and *Political Economy* and many opponents admit that private property in land should never have been allowed to occur. [Economic historian Arnold] Toynbee said in his lecture on Henry George's *Progress and Poverty*: "I agree with George that it has been a mistake to sell land to private individuals instead of keeping it for the use of the people." [Alfred] Marshall also complained of the mistake in allowing private ownership of land to become absolute. However if it is later found to be a mistake to buy out the landlords this could not be rectified without inflicting injustice and the expense involved may be greater than the wrong righted. The annual amount of the "land premium" is a "trivial fraction of the total resources of the country". Toynbee thought £60 m p.a. compared with £1300 m p.a. income. Also land values may not continue to rise. Transport has reduced the advantage of corn fields in England to the market. Buying out the landlords would put too heavy a burden on the nation. To restore the land to the people without adequate compensation would undermine public confidence in the government and invite the devil into the crusade. Land nationalization is now adopted by the socialists "on the grounds that land is exactly the same as other property." It could be seen as the preliminary step to seizing other forms of property. The government would have to administer a huge land department. Henry George's proposal to tax the land would only secure the revenue and not meet all the objections to private ownership. Charles Wicksteed [Philip's brother] in *The Land for the People* proposed full compensation, expecting the value of land to increase. Philip Wicksteed proposed borrowing against the security of the land and paying the current interest until the principal is paid in full. Or a substantial land tax could raise the funds to gradually purchase land. Both methods could be used together.

Appendix 1

Lecture XI: Socialism and Business Profits, n.d.

If land should be public property, what about other forms of property? "We are all socialists to some extent nowadays" says [Liberal politician Sir William] Harcourt. This is a change in the last 30 years. Part of a desire to secure equal opportunities for all. Jevons defined socialism as the desire to give equal rewards to unequal sacrifices. Hardships are seen as the result of the general working of society and this must be corrected by collective regulation. Connected with this is distrust of economic motives and the principle of laissez faire. The basis of capitalism is competition, with the goal of unqualified victory or defeat of the competitors. Socialism would substitute co-operation for competition so all will get a share. To date society has been organized by the commercial and professional classes: "England is the heaven of the rich, the hell of the poor and the purgatory of the wise and seeing" (Parker).* The notion of class interests has largely superseded patriotic motives; workers feel greater sympathy for fellow workers in other countries than their fellow countrymen. Real socialists are impatient with "drawing room socialists". Co-operation they see as a bribe to the worker. They want to change the present system so that all instruments of production, i.e. land and capital, are national property and then interest and business profits will become extinct. The most intelligent of the labour system in the future is found in [Edward Bellamy's] *Looking Backward 2000-1887*. Marx's theory of surplus value is very subtle, but when stripped of its hard logic is inadequate. Marx accepts the Ricardian theory of value and says that the exchange value of anything is determined by its labour content. There is no such thing as the exchange value of labour. Marx admits the facts do not agree with the theory. Walker's theory of profits in *Political Economy* begins with the no-profit employer at the lowest scale of the system and by analogy with rent increases according to personal ability. What prospect is there of socializing profit? Ultimately the best option for the socialist is income tax to redistribute, but this is merely tinkering with the present inequitable capitalist system.

Lecture XII: Socialism and Interest, 3 May 1889

Aristotle says a coin does not breed and therefore interest is contrary to nature; Dante puts usurers among those guilty of unnatural offences. Interest is a species of hire; it represents the cost of capital. The function of capital is to render human labour more efficient. Men will take from the industry that gives less interest and

---

* "England is the richest country in the world, perhaps, but that in which there is the most misery. It is the paradise of the rich, the purgatory of the wise, and the hell of the poor." Theodore Parker, letter to Dr [Convers] Francis, 18 March 1844.

invest their capital in businesses that gives more. Public debt prevents the interest falling low. Prudent people are changing industrial investments for mortgages or property. If there were no public debt there would be no public security. The land-premium or "economic rent" is admitted to be a public fund as a matter of abstract right. Interest is a fund that tends to extinguish itself in favour of earnings. Profit is a differential personal fund that can only be attacked in open defiance of the individualistic theory of competition.

Ethical and Theological Aspects of Sociology

Lecture I: Economics and Ethics, n.d.

The theory of the economic man says he wants to get the maximum wealth with the minimum effort; but we have dealt with the normal man who might have more wealth than he desires. There are moral and emotional reasons why people desire wealth. What the motives are and what they should be takes us into the study of economics from the sociological, philosophical and ethical areas. The true function of economics is to analyse and formulate the facts of industry with a view to bringing out the moral and vital significance of our industrial actions and industrial machinery. There is no political economy which stands for the entire world; this is especially true for the English school of economics. We can measure how much of one unit is worth in terms of another i.e. equivalence of worth at the margins. This will change with the quantity processed. This applies to the law of indifference, and is key to much of economics. Economics says under certain conditions what will follow: it states [1] universal underlying facts and laws [2] the particular form in which these manifest themselves in any society. Re-examines exchange value, a relative scale of equivalence of marginal worth. If people cease to desire something it ceases to have value. The introduction of the Drink Bill indicates that the desire for intoxicating drink is diminishing; which can be attributed to moral feeling. The desire to have a mortgage on those supplying drink is increasing, although the breweries don't seem to be aware of this moral objection to them. "My utopia would be a state of [affairs] ... where we should know we were doing best for the world where we got most for our labours." But different wants and privations mean different amounts of suffering. As ministers we are gravely responsible in this matter. "We must have purity, simplicity and directness of life or we shall not be a transforming influence on others. cf. Jacobs blessing in Dante." If we feel that wealth is only a means toward life that conviction will stamp itself on those we come into contact with and lead them to make wealth a means in support of life. We must have some material well-being to build a higher life on.

Appendix 1

Lecture II: The Social Sense and the Devotional Life, n.d.

Extra ecclesiam nulla salus or the social and spiritual relation between man and God in the Roman Catholic church, which involves social collective relations between human society and God. The Protestant reaction against abuses in the church has gone too far in ignoring what this expression stood for and thinking that religious life is a matter for each individual. Protestantism is in harmony with modern ideas of industry; there is an affinity between its maxims and morals and individualistic capitalism, which is accepted in Protestant countries. The only protests to it are to accidents and not its principles. This means that individualistic theory has gone too far in ethics as in religion. The wants of others are an important factor in our daily lives; and unless they are pure and perfect contamination enters our lives. Some wants are illegitimate: love of beauty degenerating into slavery for fashion; a doctor with evil patients asks him to assist with gross immorality and sin; a shop girl ministering to frivolity and vanity. There is collective responsibility and guilt regarding the products of civilization. Abstinence may not help, such as abstaining from sugar because it is slave grown. To change conditions the only possibility may be collective action: for free education, or sanitary housing. Therefore there is no use striving for personal perfection. There is a growing sense of solidarity in our devotional life, to find unity with our fellow man. There is a great danger in substituting social furor for moral furor.

Lecture III: Social Studies and Theology, n.d.

Imagine theology constructed on a dualism between two different principles in the universe; or of Evolution, with no conflict between the different principles. The theology of dualism where the purposes of human life are permanently thwarted by the conditions of human life; but evolutionary theology allows the conditions of life to be made into a support for the purposes of life. The dualistic contradiction is the battle between two hostile systems, but the evolutionary is the growing pains, the strain arising from unequal progress anticipating the next stage. Should the creator be regarded as essentially one being or should we accept that self-existent matter is alien to the spiritual being? It is practically impossible to regard Ethical Idealism as a byproduct of evolution. It is an error to confound the evolution of the fittest and the evolution of the best; which is the best ethically depends on the circumstances. The idea that happy and pure homes are purchased by the degradation of other homes and pushing competitors over the edge is a contradiction. In evolution the ethical element must be the leading principle. The goals of life are fixed by our moral and spiritual nature. To achieve our goals requires harmony amongst ourselves and the Supreme (cf. Dante). It is in investigating the contradiction and harmony issue that Sociology and Economics bear on Theology. The material life is necessary for the

William Jellie's Synopsis of Philip Wicksteed's Lectures

spiritual life as lived on earth. Issues: Is there enough room on the planet for all the humans, what of human reproduction? Will we require the sacrifice of the many for the benefit of the few? Is there antagonism between the public good and private wants? Spencer points out that well disposed individuals have motives which if followed by the majority would be destructive. Can selfish motives be socialized? If our ministry is to be helpful we must take up these problems, which have a real and vital connection with everyone. (Read Dr [Philip] Herbert Carpenter's article "Evolution and the Existence of Satan" in the *Christian Reformer*, May 1886, no. 5.)

Bibliography for Wicksteed's Lectures

Bellamy, Edward. *Looking Backward 2000-1887*. New York: Houghton Mifflin, 1888.

Blackwell, Elizabeth. *The Human Element in Sex: Being a Medical Enquiry into the Relation of Sexual Physiology to Christian Morality*. London: J & A Churchill, 1884.

Bonar, James. "The Austrian Economists and their View of Value". *Quarterly Journal of Economics* 3:1 (1888), pp. 1-31.

Cairnes, John Elliott. *Some Leading Principles of Political Economy Newly Expounded*. London: Macmillan, 1874.

Carpenter, Philip Herbert. "Evolution and the Existence of Satan, II". *Christian Reformer*, May 1886, pp. 269-276.

Comte, Auguste. *A General View of Positivism*. London: Trubner, 1865.

Dante Alighieri. *La Vita Nuova di Dante Alighieri; I trattati: De vulgari eloquentia, De Monarchia, e La questione de aqua et terra, con traduzione italiana delle opere scritte latinamente, a note e illustrazioni di Pietro Fraticelli*. Firenze: G. Barbera, 3rd edition, 1887.[*]

———. *The Divina Commedia of Dante Alighieri, translated line for line in the terza rima of the original with notes, by Frederick K. Haselfoot*. London: Kegan Paul, 1887.[†]

Darwin, Charles. *On the Origin of Species by Means of Natural Selection*. London: John Murray, 1859.

———. *The Descent of Man, and Selection in Relation to Sex*. 2 vols. London: John Murray, 1871.

———. *The Expression of the Emotions in Man and Animals*. London: John Murray, 1872.

George, Henry. *Progress and Poverty*. Garden City, NY: Doubleday, Page, 1879.

---

[*] This edition of *De Monarchia* is in Latin with Italian on opposite pages. It was one of the books in the Dante Collection given by Jellie to the University of Auckland.

[†] This edition of *Commedia* is one of the books in the Dante Collection given by Jellie to the University of Auckland.

Appendix 1

Green, Thomas Hill. *Prolegomena to Ethics*, ed. A. C. Bradley. Oxford: Clarendon, 1883.

———. *Works of T. H. Green*, ed. R. L. Nettleship. 3 vols. London: Longmans, Green, 1885-88.

Jevons, William Stanley. *Methods of Social Reform and Other Papers*. London: Macmillan, 1883.

———. *The Theory of Political Economy*. London: Macmillan, 1871.

Machiavelli, Nicolo. *The Prince*. 1513-1515.*

Malthus, Thomas Robert. *An Essay on the Principle of Population, as it Affects the Future Improvement of Society, with Remarks on the Speculations of Mr. Godwin, M. Condorcet, and Other Writers*. London: J. Johnson, 1798.

Marshall, Alfred. "The Present Position of Economics". Inaugural lecture upon election to the Chair of Political Economy, University of Cambridge, 24 February 1885.

Marshall, Alfred and Mary Paley Marshall. *The Economics of Industry*. London: Macmillan, 1879.

Marx, Karl. *Capital*, vol. 1: *The Process of Production of Capital*, ed. F. Engels, trans. Samuel Moore and Edward Aveling. London: Swan Sonnenschein, 1887.

Mill, John Stuart. *On Liberty*. London: John W. Parker and Son, 1859.

———. *Principles of Political Economy*. London: Longmans, Green, 1848.

———. *A System of Logic*. New York: Harper & Brothers, 1874.

Ruskin, John. *Unto This Last: Four Essays on the First Principles of Political Economy*. London: Smith Elder, 1862.

Sayce, Archibald Henry. *Introduction to the Science of Language*. 2 vols. London: Kegan Paul, 1880.

Senior, Nassau William. *An Outline of the Science of Political Economy*. London: W. Clowes and Sons, 1836.

Sidgwick, Henry. *The Principles of Political Economy*. London: Macmillan, 1883.

Smith, Adam. *An Inquiry into the Nature and Causes of the Wealth of Nations*. London: W. Strahan and T. Cadell, 1776.

Spencer, Herbert. *First Principles of a New System of Philosophy*. New York: D. Appleton, 1865.

———. *The Principles of Sociology*. 3 vols. New York: D. Appleton, 1876-96.

Walker, Francis Amasa. *Land and its Rent*. Boston: Little, Brown, 1883.

---

* The publication year is variously given as 1513 and 1515, a few years after Machiavelli's death. The publication details are not readily found. It is difficult to know which edition Wicksteed would have used.

———. *Political Economy*. New York: Vol. V of the American Science Series, 1883.

———. *The Wages Question: A Treatise on Wages and the Wages Class*. London: Macmillan, 1876.

Wicksteed, Charles. *The Land for the People: How to obtain it: How to manage it*. London: William Reeves, 1885.

Wicksteed, Philip Henry. *The Alphabet of Economic Science*. Part 1: Elements of the Theory of Value or Worth. London: Macmillan, 1888.

———. *Dante: Six Sermons*. London: Elkin Mathew & John Lane, 1879.

APPENDIX 2

Forward Movement Literary Society Lectures

An Introduction to the Study of Literature of the Nineteenth Century, 17 April 1895
Lecture by Rev. W. A. Evans, Rechabite Hall.
Source: *Evening Post*, 17 April 1895, p. 2.

A Night with a Novelist, 8 May 1895
Lecture by Sir Robert Stout, Ballance Hall.
Source: *Evening Post*, 8 May 1895, p. 3.

The Life of John Bright, 22 May 1895
Lecture by Mr C. W. Benbow, Ballance Hall.
Source: *Evening Post*, 23 May 1895, p. 2.

George Eliot, 5 June 1895
Lecture by Mrs W. A. Evans, Ballance Hall.
Source: *Evening Post*, 8 May 1895, p. 3.

Two Pictures of Women Past and Present, 19 June 1895
Lecture by Mrs J. S. Fleming, Ballance Hall.
Source: *Evening Post*, 20 June 1895, p. 2.

Extracts from the works of Alice Meynell and Professor Fairbairn,* 26 June 1895
Lecture by Messrs D. E. Beaglehole and D. Gain
Source: *Evening Post*, 27 June 1895, p. 2.

---

* Alice Meynell was a poet, editor, and suffragist. Rev H. M. Fairbairn was Principal of Mansfield College (Congregational) at Oxford.

Forward Movement Literary Society Lectures

John Ruskin, 3 July 1895
Lecture by Dr Findlay, Ballance Hall.
Source: *Evening Post*, 8 May 1895, p. 3.

Arnold Toynbee, 19 July 1895
Lecture by Mr J. H. Holliwell, Ballance Hall.
Source: *Evening Post*, 11 July 1895, p. 2.

Robert Browning, 31 July 1895
Lecture by Mr Justice Richmond, Ballance Hall.
Source: *Evening Post*, 8 May 1895, p. 3.

The Higher Education of Women, 21 August 1895
Lecture by Mrs Fleming, Ballance Hall.
Source: *Evening Post*, 22 August 1895, p. 2.

Thomas Carlyle, 28 August 1895
Lecture by Mr T. W. Rowe, M.A., Forward Movement Hall.
Source: *Evening Post*, 8 May 1895, p. 3.

The Life of J. G. Whittier, 11 September 1895
Lecture by Mr D. Gain, Forward Movement Hall.
Source: *Evening Post*, 12 September 1895, p. 2.

Tolstoy, 25 September 1895
Lecture by Rev. J. R. Glasson, Forward Movement Hall.
Source: *Evening Post*, 8 May 1895, p. 3.

[John Ruskin's] Sesame and Lilies, 16 October 1895
Lecture by Miss Kirk, Forward Movement Hall.
Source: *Evening Post*, 17 October 1895, p. 2

Study of the Eighteenth Century Literature, 25 March 1896
Lecture by Mr W. A. Evans, Forward Movement Hall.
Source: *Evening Post*, 20 March 1896, p. 3.

[Joseph] Addison, 29 April 1896
Lecture by Sir Robert Stout, Forward Movement Hall.
Source: *Evening Post*, 20 March 1896, p. 3.

Appendix 2

A Night with Defoe, 13 May 1896
Lecture by Mr C. Wilson, Forward Movement Hall.
Source: *Evening Post*, 14 May 1896, p. 2.

[Alexander] Pope, 27 May 1896
Lecture by Rev. J. Reed Glasson, Forward Movement Hall.
Source: *Evening Post*, 20 March 1896, p. 3.

[Thomas] Gray, 17 June 1896
Lecture by Mr W. R. Haselden, Forward Movement Hall.
Source: *Evening Post*, 18 June 1896, p. 5.

The Novel of the 18th Century, 1 July 1896
Lecture by Mr T. W. Rowe, Forward Movement Hall.
Source: *Evening Post*, 30 June 1896, p. 5.

The Songstresses of Scotland, 8 July 1896
Lecture by Mrs Fleming, Forward Movement Hall.
Source: *Evening Post*, 2 July 1896, p. 5.

Dr Johnson's "Rasselas", 5 August 1896
Lecture by Mr Alfred W. Duncan, Forward Movement Hall.
Source: *Evening Post*, 6 August 1896, p. 5

Dr Johnson, 12 August 1896
Lecture by Dr Findlay, Forward Movement Hall.
Source: *Evening Post*, 11 August 1896, p. 6

[Oliver] Goldsmith, 26 August 1896
Lecture by Mr C. W. Benbow, Forward Movement Hall.
Source: *Evening Post*, 26 August 1896, p. 6.

[Edmund] Burke, 23 September 1896
Lecture by Mr A. R. Atkinson, Forward Movement Hall.
Source: *Evening Post*, 24 September 1896, p. 4.

Elizabethan Literature, 18 May 1897
Lecture by Mr T. W. Rowe, Forward Movement Hall.
Source: *Evening Post*, 19 May 1897, p. 4.

Appendix 3

William Jellie's Public Education Courses

Unless otherwise noted, the source for all information in this Appendix is: William Jellie MSS 91/4, University of Auckland Special Collections (UASC).

Wellington Unitarian Free Church Literary Club

Emerson Readings. 1913. 10 weekly lectures and tutorials.

Lectures by Jellie, essay presentations from class members and poetry readings. Club open to the public, not just church members.

Source: Wellington Unitarian Free Church *Calendar*, August 1912, September 1912, April 1913, May 1913. Literary Club, Unitarian Free Church, Wellington, Emerson Readings. William Jellie MSS A-70, UASC.

South Canterbury Workers Educational Association

Some Aspects of Life in the Middle Ages. 1924. 1 lecture.

Lecture given at Timaru.

Source: *Timaru Herald*, 20 August 1924, p. 1.

Auckland Workers Educational Association

Dante and the Divine Commedia. 1921 [?]. 1 lecture and tutorial.

Includes biographical sketch of Dante.

Source: William Jellie MSS A-70, UASC. The date of 26 January 1921, given in the A-70 inventory, is incorrect; William Jellie was still in Southport at that date.

Appendix 3

The Appreciation of Poetry. 1926. 12 lectures and tutorials.
Illustrated from Wordsworth, Byron, Shelly and Keats. (1) How shall we read Poetry? (2) The Growth of the Poet's Mind: The Prelude. (3) The Influence of the French Revolution. (4) The Moral Influences of Nature. (5) The Still Sad Music of Humanity. (6) Politics and Patriotism. (7 and 8) Byron, Aristocrat and Revolutionary. (9) The Spirit of Revolt in Shelley. (10) Prometheus Unbound. (11 and 12) The Enchantment of Keats.

Tennyson and Browning. 1926. 12 lectures and tutorials.
(1) The sweet Singer of Musical Verse. (2) Early Victorianism. (3) The Vision of Sin and the Palace of Art. (4) In Memoriam. (5 and 6) Idylls of the King. (7, 8 and 9) Some Shorter Poems of Browning; Autobiographical; Heroism and Adventure; the Conduct of Life; Love. (10) Pippa Passes. (11 and 12) The Ring and the Book.

Shakespeare. 1927. 11 weekly lectures and tutorials.
Spirit of the Age. Shakespeare's life. Midsummer's Night's Dream. The Elizabethan Playhouse. Richard III. Beginnings of English Drama. Merchant of Venice. The Lady of Belmont.

English Literature — Milton and his Age. 1928. 24 weekly lectures and tutorials.
The Study of Literature for Workers. The Dedicated Poet. His Early Poems. England's Struggle for Constitutional and Religious Liberty. Milton, the Champion of Human Liberty. His Prose Works. The Great Spirit in Defeat. His Triumph in Paradise Lost. The Great Epics of the World. Milton and Classical Mythology. Cavalier and Puritan in Life and Song. Bunyan, the true expression of Puritan England. Pepys' Diary. Samson Agonistes and Greek Drama.
Source: WEA Auckland University District City Classes for 1928.

Modern Poets. 1929. Given at WEA Summer Camp, Hunua.
Thomas Hardy, Roy Campbell, Laurence Binyon, Humbert Wolfe, Edith Sitwell, John Masefield. American literature.

English Literature — Development of the Novel. 1929. 24 weekly lectures and tutorials.
A study in the historical order of twelve representative works of fiction in the light of the author's life, and the time (its events, movements, manners) in which each was written. The Novel — its popularity, influence, what to look for in a Novel, the Novel as a work of art. Cervantes and Don Quixote. Fielding and

Tom Jones. Goldsmith and The Vicar of Wakefield. Jane Austen and Emma. Sir Walter Scott and The Heart of Midlothian. Dickens and David Copperfield. Thackeray and Esmond. George Eliot and Adam Bede. Melville and Moby Dick. Meredith and The Egoist. Hardy and Tess of the D'Urbervilles. Galsworthy and The Forsyte Saga.
Source: WEA Auckland University District City Classes for 1929.

Modern Poetry. 1930. 24 weekly lectures and tutorials.
A study of some modern poets (1) as a means of adding to life's enjoyment the peculiar pleasure that poetry affords, and (2) as an aid to the understanding of our own age. Among the subjects will be: Thomas Hardy, A. E. Houseman, John Masefield, Ralph Hodgson, [Walter] de la Mare, W. H. Davies, Gordon Bottomley, Humbert Wolfe, John Freeman, Laurence Binyon, Siegfried Sassoon, Charles Williams, Robert Bridges, Alice Meynell, Herbert Read, D. H. Lawrence, War Poetry, National Poetry, Humour, and Satire.
Source: WEA Auckland University District City Classes for 1930.

Contemporary Poetry. 1931. 24 weekly lectures and tutorials.
An attempt to understand our own age — the stream of life in which we move and have our being — as its moods, thoughts and tendencies, revolt, pain and despair, satire, sources of hope, relief of fancy and of humour, etc, are reflected in one branch of its art, viz., poetry. The course will deal with some poets dealt with last year, but will mainly take notice of others, such as H. Wolfe, Roy Campbell, Lascelles Abercrombie, Gordon Bottomley, Sturge Moore. Note will also be taken of contemporary American, Scottish and New Zealand poetry.
Source: WEA Auckland University District, 1931 Tutorial Classes.

Landmarks in Western Literature. 1932. 20 weekly lectures and tutorials.
Studies in a series of classical works which at once draw to a focus the ideas of a previous age and transmit them in artistic form to the ages that follow. An attempt to survey the process of Western Civilisation as recorded in great literature. Homer's Iliad and Odyssey (c. 950 BC). Vergil's Aeneid (19 BC). St. Augustine's City of God (413-426). Shakespeare's Plays (1591-1611). The English Bible (1611).Milton's Paradise Lost (1658-65). Goethe's Faust (1775-1832). Emerson's Essays (1840-70). Browning's Ring and the Book (1868-69). Translations, where necessary, will be provided in the class library; and an attempt is being made to procure screen-pictures illustrative of each age.
Source: WEA Auckland University District 1932 Tutorial Classes.

Appendix 3

Dante's Divine Comedy — A Reflection of the Middle Ages. 1933. 24 weekly lectures and tutorials.

Dante was one of the few supreme geniuses of the race — poet, prophet and teacher. His age was most important in the development of European history, preparing for changes which produced the modes of life of the present day. His poem, in the form of a voyage through Hell, Purgatory and Paradise, sums up the knowledge and practice, the politics and religion, philosophy and science of the Middle Ages. Its crimes and tragedies, its struggles after reform, its hopes and aspirations, the highest ideals of its men and communities pass over its pages. The poem is human and dramatic.

Source: WEA Auckland University District 1933 Tutorial Classes.

Landmarks in Literature. 1933-34. Given at WEA Summer School.

Dante — spirit of the Middle Ages. Shakespeare — spirit of Romanticism. English Bible — spirit of the Reformation. Milton — spirit of Puritanism. Goethe — spirit of Modern Science. Browning — spirit of the 19th Century. Eliot — spirit of Modernism.

Literature of the French Revolution. 1934. 22 weekly lectures and tutorials.

In these days of revolutions, Russian, German, Spanish, a study of their great forerunner in France, parent of them all, should be of interest and value. The study here projected will be neither political nor economic, but literary. The subject will be, generally, the movement of thought and feeling in the 18th century which, reacting on the sufferings of the common people throughout Europe, gave impulse and form, in France, to the Revolution and in England to reform. More specifically this subject will be the expression of that movement of the spirit of Literature.

Beginning with sketches of the Russian and French Revolutions, the course will proceed to deal with some of the work of such writers as Voltaire, Condorcet, Rousseau, Goethe, Schiller, Cowper, Burns, Wordsworth, Godwin, Mary Wollstonecraft, Burke, Paine, Byron and Shelley.

Source: WEA Auckland University District City Programme 1934.

The French Revolution in English Literature. 1934.

The second in a series of four WEA weekly Radio Broadcasts on 1YA.

Source: WEA Auckland University District City Programme 1934.

Early Victorianism, 1830-1865. 1935. 22 weekly lectures and tutorials.

England 100 years ago, recovering from 20 years' war and moving to prosperity. A period of decisive transformation, now passing out of memory and

maligned, but holding within itself the roots from which our present world has grown by reaction and expansion. How the great writers illustrate the manners and customs and social organisation, the political and social ideas and other movements of the spirit, which went to mould the modern mind. The course will include: Roots in Eighteenth Century. The Age of Creevey. The Utilitarians. The Oxford Movement. The Liberal Movement in Religion. Science and Doubt. The Socialists. Chartism. Carlyle. Ruskin. Disraeli. Thackeray. Trollope. The Brontes. George Eliot. Clough. Arnold. Tennyson and Browning.
Source: WEA Auckland University District City Programme 1935.

Literature: The Age of Liberalism, 1860-1900. 1936. 24 weekly lectures and tutorials.

The Age between the ancient race of real Victorians and that race of yesterday — The Georgians.

A direct continuance of last year's course, tracing the transformation and gradual working out of those Revolutions in Politics, Economics, Science and Religion from which flowed the manifold changes in man's ways of life in the 19th century; changes which were to be followed by further changes after the Boer War. Britain is in the main orderly, rich, expanding in commerce, consolidating her position in the world; Liberalism victorious and passing over into Socialism; Victorian conventions and orthodoxies breaking up; but the main stream of movement crossed by many divergent currents. The age of us, our parents and grandparents.

The course will include: the historical background. Currents and cross currents. Tennyson, Browning and Matthew Arnold in their later phases. George Meredith, poet and novelist. Rossetti and the Pre-Raphaelites. Walter Pater and Art for Art's sake. Oscar Wilde and Aestheticism run to seed. William Morris and the Socialist Movement. Swinburne and Paganism. The victory of Evolution. Fitzgerald. Some Pessimists. Thomas Hardy. Samuel Butler. Stevenson and Romance. Kipling and Imperialism. The Celtic Movement and Yeats. Robert Bridges and Normality. The class will be invited to discuss the value of these movements for to-day.
Source: WEA Auckland University District City Programme 1936.

Literature: Stages in the Progress of the Human Spirit as revealed in Great Books. 1937. 22 weekly lectures and tutorials.

Books, said Milton, are not dead things: they have a potency of life in them as active as the soul from which they sprang. "Good books are the precious life-blood of master-spirits." What has flowed from one such heart and mind may be relied on to reach others. Some books, we may add, contain the life-blood of

Appendix 3

the age in which they were written: in them we have the "articulate, audible voice of the Past": they are historical documents, yet alive. Some books have moulded the thought and nourished and strengthened the feelings of millions, century after century. Some have made revolutions, pulling down and building up social and religious systems, exercising an influence mightier than armies, overleaping the barriers of race and language and time. Some books are among the greatest achievements of the human spirit, and stand out as landmarks on its progressive march. The course is designed as an introduction to a few such books, for pleasure and for instruction.

Homer's Iliad (c. 850 BC). Aeschylus' Oresteia (525-456). Plato's Republic (428-348). The Book of Job (c. 400). Virgil's Aeneid (70-19). The Revelation of St. John (c. 95 AD). Marcus Aurelius' Thoughts (121-180). Boethius' Consolation of Philosophy (470-524). Nibelungenlied (c. 1200). Dante's Divine Comedy (1265-1321). Chaucer's Canterbury Pilgrims (1340-1400). Thomas à Kempis' Imitation of Christ (1380-1471). Machiavelli's Prince (1469-1527). Calvin's Institution of the Christian Religion (1509 -1564). Shakespeare's Hamlet (1565-1615). Milton's Paradise Lost (1608-1764). Swift's Gulliver's Travels (1667-1745). Boswell's Life of Dr. Johnson (1709-1784). Wordsworth's Prelude (1770-1850). Darwin's Origin of Species (1809-1882). Marx's Capital (1818-1883).

Source: WEA Auckland University District City Programme 1937.

Literature: The Works of Shakespeare. 1938. 22 weekly lectures and tutorials.

The course will be a challenge to our students to read through the poems and plays during the winter. How many have made the acquaintance of more than the one or two plays studied at school, and how many have been put off from further explanation by school methods? Yet surely it behoves all lovers of literature to know our supreme poet and dramatist, who is acknowledged in all countries to be one of the world's supreme poets and dramatists. It would shame us to learn of plays like King Lear being performed in Russia before popular audiences and have to confess that we know nothing but the name. We shall avoid school methods, and try to re-discover his magic for ourselves. As the plays were written for the stage we shall make some effort to combine class reading with general understanding; and we shall direct attention, where possible, to the political and social conditions of the time.

(1) Introductory. (2-5) Early histories — Henry VI, Richard III, Richard II, King John, Henry IV and Henry V. (6-7) Early Comedies — Comedy of Errors, Taming of the Shrew, Two Gentlemen of Verona, Love's Labour's Lost. (8) Romeo and Juliet. (9) Midsummer Night's Dream. (10) Merchant of

Venice. (11) Poems and Sonnets. (12-13) The Supreme Comedies — Much Ado About Nothing, As You Like It, Twelfth Night, Merry Wives of Windsor. (14-16) The Roman and Greek Plays — Julius Caesar, Troilus and Cressida, Antony and Cleopatra, Coriolanus, Timon of Athens. (17) Hamlet. (18) Othello and Measure for Measure. (19) King Lear. (20) Macbeth. (21) Cymbeline and Winter's Tale. (22) Tempest and Henry VIII.
Source: WEA Auckland University District City Programme 1938.

Literature: Utopias through the Ages. 1939. 22 weekly lectures and tutorials.

Studies in the literature of political and social discontent and change, aspiration and prophecy; the literature of the forward look and the work of men who dreamed of reorganising human life in better ways: from the time when Europe began to think about the social order till the present age of confused and conflicting answers to the questions: What is the ideal goal of human effort? And how are we going to reach it?

The course will deal with books such as Plato's Republic (c. 400 BC), St Augustine's City of God (c. 400 AD), Dante's De Monarchia (1309), More's Utopia (1516), Bacon's New Atlantis (1623), Harrington's Oceania (1656), Fourier's Le Monde Nouveau Industriel (1829), Marx's Communist Manifesto (1848), Pemberton's Happy Colony (1854), Utopia in New Zealand, Bellamy's Looking Backward (1888), Morris' News from Nowhere (1891), Wells' Modern Utopia (1905), Huxley's Brave New World (1932) and others. Were they the work of mere amiable visionaries? Have they done any good for the world? and if so, what? Has such a survey of a long line of social dreams any lesson for us of to-day?
Source: WEA Auckland University District City Programme 1939.

What Communism Means Today. 1939. 4 lectures.

Defining socialism and communism; social science, humanitarian legislation and happiness; dictatorship.

Women's Institute

Shakespeare. 1927. 1 lecture.

Lecture given at Swanson.

Enjoying Shakespeare. 1927. 1 lecture.

Illustrated from the Merchant of Venice. Lecture given at Henderson.

Appendix 3

Dante — The National Poet of Italy. 1944. 1 lecture.
Lecture given at Titirangi.
Source: William Jellie MSS A-70, UASC.

Dante. 1950. 1 lecture.
Impossible to understand & appreciate T. S. Eliot, the major poet of our time, without a good working acquaintance with Dante.
Source: William Jellie MSS A-70, UASC.

Academic Club

1929. 1 lecture.
Beauty and Property — Forsyte Saga. Osbert Sitwell.

British Empire Shakespeare Society

Shakespeare. 1932. 1 lecture.
The universal genius; His Life; The man and his Age — Elizabethan England; His private view of Life; Anti-Shakespearean influences.

Some Questions on Art. 1936. 1 lecture.
The Art Movement in the latter half of the 19th Century; The Pendulum of Taste; What is Beauty?

Jewish Literary Society; Fabian Club

Dante's Divine Comedy. 1937. 1 lecture.
A study in Medievalism.

Association of Teachers of English, Auckland University College

The Teaching of English. 1938. 1 lecture.
T.S. Eliot and the "Waste Land" Literature

Penwomen's Club

Dante's Divine Comedy. 1952. 1 lecture.
Lecture given at Auckland.
Source: William Jellie MSS A-70, UASC.

Appendix 4

Addresses by Rev. James Chapple at the Rationalist Association Sunday Evening Public Meetings

Each meeting consisted of a lecture followed by a film. The meetings were held at the 1200-seat Strand Theatre in Auckland.

Robert Green Ingersoll — Champion of Freethought, 30 September 1934
Film: unknown

Why the Bible Should be Kept Out of Schools, 14 April 1935
Film: unknown

Fascism a Menace to Freedom: New Zealand at the Crossroads, 1 September 1935
Film: *Love's Old Sweet Song*

Evolution: Its Implications regarding the State, 27 October 1935
Film: *His Wife's Mother*

Humanism and the Gospel of Reason, 1 December 1935
Film: *Oh What a Night!*

Mark Twain: His Philosophy, 12 January 1936
Film: *Sleepless Nights*

Samuel Butler of *Erewhon* Fame — Wanted: A Modern Satirist, 8 March 1936
Film: *The Flame of Love*

Appendix 4

Kindness to Animals; Justice to Sub-humans, 5 April 1936
Film: *Children of Chance*

Voltaire: The Champion of Tolerance, 9 August 1936
Film: *A Lucky Girl*

The Menace of Empire, 8 November 1936
Film: *Invitation to the Waltz*

The Bible: A Stumbling Block to Progress, 10 January 1937
Film: *Reunion*

Thomas Paine, 31 January 1937
Film: *Radio Pirate*

Godless Russia vs. Godly (?) New Zealand, 30 May 1937
Film: *Ex-Flame*

The Martyrdom of Ferrer, the Great Spanish Patriot,* 11 July 1937
Film: *The Scotland Yard Mystery*

Why Reactionaries Want the Bible in our Schools, 15 August 1937
Film: *The Awful Truth*

Make Way for Tomorrow, 7 November 1937
Film: *My Song Goes Around the World*

Freethought's Call to Youth, 5 December 1937
Film: *The Rosary*

Orthodox Christianity: Will it drift left or right politically?, 30 January 1938
Film: *For the Love of Mike*

[Giordano] Bruno — Freethought Martyr, 27 February 1938
Film: *The Lottery Bride*

---

* Francisco Ferrer y Guardia / Francesc Ferrer i Guàrdia (1859-1909) was a Catalan freethinker and anarchist. He was the founder of the Modern School, an experimental school designed to draw out the students' ideas rather than to cram them with the ideas of others, which became the model for many others worldwide. In 1909, during an uprising in the city of Barcelona, Ferrer was sentenced to death by a miliary tribunal and executed by a firing squad.

Addresses by Rev. James Chapple

The Devil: Are churchgoers ashamed of him?, 27 March 1938
Film: *Blossom Fair*

The Crusade for Peace, 15 May 1938
Film: *Love at Second Sight*

The Bible in Schools: Is it a book to put in the hands of children?, 22 May 1938
Film: *The Joy Ride*

New Zealand as a Peace-Loving Commonwealth, 14 August 1938
Film: *The Rampant Age*

The Freethought Congress, 11 September 1938
Film: *Laburnum Grove*

Great Thinkers and their Ideals, 1 January 1939
Film: unknown

A New Zealand Renaissance, 19 February 1939
Film: *The Dominant Sex*

Ingersoll, 7 April 1940
Film: *Sing While You're Able*

Robert Burns, 4 August 1940
Film: *Sins of Children*

Appendix 5

Office Holders of the First and Second Unitarian Congregations and the Auckland Unitarian Church

Names for the first congregation are contained in an undated handwritten document "Unitarian Movement in Auckland." Those for the second congregation are taken from the Secretary's Report appended to the minutes of the Annual Meeting of the Auckland Unitarian Congregation held 26 March 1900. Names for the Auckland Unitarian Church officers and committee members are taken from minutes of annual meetings and committee meetings.

First Congregation 1863-66

Mr R. Ridings, *Chairman*
Mr J. Utting, *Secretary*
Mr John Leech, *Treasurer*
Committee: Messrs Cox, Probert, Springall, A. Bradley, Ellen, Montgomery, A. E. Smith, C. Corbett, Burns, Eastwood and Morris

Second Congregation 1898-1900

Meeting, 3 March 1898
Mr Shawcross, *Chairman*
Mr Hugh C. McCready, *Secretary and Treasurer*
Committee: Miss Leech, Mrs Shawcross, Captain Lamb, Mr and Mrs Robert Corbett-Cook, Mr and Mrs Slack

Office Holders of Auckland Unitarian Congregations

Auckland Unitarian Church

Annual Meeting of the Congregation, 26 March 1900

Mr H. Tindale, *Chairman* [resigned September 1900]

Mr C. Newland, *Treasurer*

Mr A. Orr Polley, *Secretary*

Committee: Messrs T. Read senior, G. Read, R. Murray, F. E. Leith, T. H. White, Mrs St John and Miss Leech

Mr McCready and Mr Moore, *Wardens*

Mr McCready, *Librarian*

Messrs C. Carter and T. Read junior, *Auditors*

Annual Meeting of the Congregation, 27 March 1901

Mr Thomas Henry White, *Chairman*

Mr Robert Young, *Secretary*

Mr Charles Newland, *Treasurer*

Committee: Messrs Frank Castle senior, George Carter, Thomas Read senior, George Edward Read, Harry Sherriff, George Healy, Hugh C. McCready [resigned 2 October 1901], William Moore, William Frederick Cheshire [resigned 11 December 1901], R. C. Foster [resigned 2 October 1901], James Ferner, Robert Murray; Joseph Cochrane Macky [co-opted to the committee 20 October 1901]

Messrs T. Read and C. Carter, *Auditors*

Miss Leech, *Treasurer to Sunday school*

Mrs Lepine, *Flower Secretary*

Messrs McCready and Foster, *Wardens* [appointed committee meeting 3 April 1901]

Special Meeting of the Congregation, 4 September 1901

Trustees, Messrs R. Murray, J. C. Macky, T. H. White, R. C. Foster, George Healey, George Read, T. Read junior, Charles Newland, Robert Young, Captain Adamson, Captain Lamb, J. Ferner

Annual Meeting of the Congregation, 12 March 1902

Mr Joseph Cochrane Macky, *Chairman*

Mr Robert Young, *Secretary*

Mr Charles Newland, *Treasurer*

Committee: Messrs J. Ferner, R. Murray, T. H. White, George Carter, B. C. Blakey, R. C. Foster, Captain Adamson

Appendix 5

Miss J. Leech, *Treasurer to Sunday School*
Miss Verrall, *Secretary to Sunday School*
Miss Macky, *Flower Secretary*
Messrs J. Ferner and R.C. Foster, *Wardens* [appointed committee meeting 2 April 1902]
Mr G. Healy, *Librarian*

Annual Meeting of the Congregation, 11 March 1903

Mr Robert C. Foster, *Chairman*
Mr R. Young, *Secretary*
Mr C. Newland, *Treasurer*
Committee: Messrs J. Ferner, R. Murray, T. H. White, George Carter, B. C. Blakely, J. C. Macky, Captain Adamson
G. Carter and T. Read, *Auditors*

Annual Meeting of the Congregation, 9 March 1904

Mr Thomas Read snr., *Chairman*
Mr C. Newland, *Treasurer*
Mr R. Young, *Secretary*
Committee: Messrs J. Ferner, R. C. Foster, R. Murray, T. H. White, Captain Adamson, George Read, B. C. Blakey, W. A. Chitham, George Carter, J. B. Guy, George Healy

Annual Meeting of the Congregation, 8 March 1905

Mr James Ferner, *Chairman*
Mr C. Newland, *Treasurer*
Mr Robert Young, *Secretary*
Committee: Messrs J. C. Macky, R. Murray, T. Read snr., George Read, J. B. Guy, B. C. Blakey, George Carter, W. A. Chitham, F. Lepine, G. Richardson, Watson

Annual Meeting of the Congregation, 14 March 1906

Mr George E. Read, *Chairman*
Mr C. Newland, *Treasurer*
Mr R. Young, *Secretary*
Committee: Messrs B. C. Blakey, A. Chitham, J. B. Elliot, J. Ferner, W. Fossey, R. C. Foster, J. B. Guy, F. Lepine, J. C. Macky, G. Read, G. Richardson, Watson

Office Holders of Auckland Unitarian Congregations

Annual Meeting of the Congregation, 13 March 1907

Mr B. C. Blakey, *Chairman*

Mr C. Newland, *Treasurer*

Mr R. Young, *Secretary*

Committee: Messrs A. Chitham, J. B. Elliot, J. Ferner, W. Fossey, R. Murray, F. C. Munro, J. B. Guy, J. C. Macky, George Read, R. C. Foster, G. Richardson, A. Chilham.

Annual Meeting of the Congregation, 1908

There are no minutes in the Minute Book, but a list of committee members is recorded. The Minutes of the General Committee Meeting 1 April 1908 records that "minutes of the annual meeting were read" and elections were held to fill vacancies on the Committee.

Mr R. Young, *Chairman*

Mr C. Newland, *Treasurer*

Mr W. A. Chitham, *Secretary*

Committee: Messrs J. C. Macky, George E. Read, J. B. Guy, R. C. Foster, B. C. Blakey, J. Ferner, J. B. Elliott, F. C. Munro, G. Richardson, Ben Hobson, George Carter

Annual Meeting of the Congregation, 10 March 1909

Mr J. C. Macky, *Chairman*

Mr Robert Young, *Vice-Chairman*

Mr C. Newland, *Treasurer*

Mr W. Alfred Chitham, *Secretary*

Committee: Messrs B. C. Blakey, R. C. Foster [resigned], B. Hobson, R. Briffault, J. M. Melville, F. C. Munro, J. B. Elliott, George E. Read, George Carter, J. B. Guy [co-opted to vacancy].

Auditors: Messrs T. Read and T. Macky

Glossary

Agnosticism	The view that nothing can be known one way or the other about God.
Antitrinitarianism	Denial or disbelief in the Christian doctrine of the **trinity**. Unitarians believed this was added to Christian belief in the centuries after Christ.
Atheism	Denial or disbelief in the existence of God.
Blasphemy	Insulting and/or disparagement of God or religion.
Broad Church	A nineteenth-century movement within the Church of England that did not insist upon a strict adherence to Anglican doctrine. There was an affinity between Unitarians and Broad Churchmen as they dealt with common religious problems, and many Unitarians felt they ought to be part of the National Church.
Dissenter	One who dissents from the teachings of the Church of England; Protestants who from 1662 rejected the 39 Articles of the Church of England, including Presbyterians, Congregationalists, Baptists, Quakers, Methodists and Unitarians.
Freethinker	Anyone who refuses to accept unquestioningly received opinion, custom, and beliefs, especially in regard to religion. The outlook adopted by those who hold these views is known as freethought.
Heresy	A heretic is one who holds an opinion contrary to the approved doctrine of the Church.
Historiography	The writing of history and the study of history writing, especially the critical examination of sources and the selec-

Glossary

	tion of particular details and synthesis of those details into a narrative that withstands critical examination; an awareness of different ways of doing history.
Humanism	(1) Renaissance humanism emphasised Classical education and involved a mode of inquiry that developed in Italy in the thirteenth and fourteenth centuries. (2) Modern humanism is the philosophy that places central emphasis on the human realm, believing that meaning and purpose must be arrived at in the context of human life here and now.
Humanitarianism	*Humanitarian* is a portmanteau of "humanity" and "Unitarian", coined in 1794 to describe the Christian philosophical position of one who affirms the humanity of Christ and denies his pre-existence and divinity. It took on its current meaning of "ethical benevolence" in 1838. The meaning of "philanthropist" or "one who advocates or practices human action to solve social problems" came into use in 1842.
Modernism	A movement usually associated with the late nineteenth and early twentieth century and with a repudiation of settled, traditional, approaches, especially in literature, music, architecture, and art. In religious belief, tradition is subordinated to modern thought.
Myth	(1) Stories often involving supernatural persons. (2) Actions or events that have special significance to a society or group, and deal with issues such as its origins, leadership, or destiny. (3) A fictional account. (4) A view that is deeply ingrained and resistant to contradictory evidence.
Mythicists	A group of mainly rationalist scholars active in the first half of the twentieth century who argued that Jesus Christ was not a historical person.
Nonconformist	One who does not conform to doctrine or discipline of an established church, especially a member of a Protestant sect dissenting from the Anglican church. See **Dissenter**.
Owenism	Socialist co-operative movement established by Robert Owen, who was known as the Father of English Co-operation; also seen as communitarian. Owen was an advocate of **secularism**.

Glossary

Positivism	The philosophy of August Comte, which recognises only positive facts and observable phenomena and rejects theism and metaphysics.
Rational Dissent	Those **nonconformist** traditions, especially the English Presbyterians and Unitarians, who held that religion was primarily to be determined by reason.
Rationalism	A branch of **freethought** which seeks to examine religious and other claims by the standard of reason and evidence rather than faith.
Secularism	The belief that society is better when church and state are separate.
Test and Corporation Acts	Acts from the time of Charles II that prevented **dissenters** from holding public office because they would not take Anglican sacraments. They were repealed in 1828.
Trinity	The Christian doctrine that God comprises the Father, Son, and Holy Spirit, all united in the Godhead.
Universalism	The belief that all human beings will attain salvation, regardless of religious beliefs.
Universities Tests Act 1871	At the beginning of the nineteenth century, Oxford and Cambridge Universities discriminated against those who did not subscribe to the 39 Articles of the Church of England. Religious groups including Catholics, Methodists, Unitarians, and Quakers campaigned for a change in the law. In 1871 Parliament passed the Universities Tests Act, which allowed **dissenters** to be conferred with M.A. degrees at Oxford and Cambridge.
World View	A particular philosophy or view of life held by an individual or group; the framework of ideas and ethics which form the belief system through which the individual and/or group interprets the world and interacts with it.

Notes and Bibliography

Notes

Abbreviations

The following abbreviations are used throughout the Notes.

ADB	Australian Dictionary of Biography
AUCMB	Auckland Unitarian Church Minute Book
B&FUA	British & Foreign Unitarian Association
DNZB	Dictionary of New Zealand Biography
DUUB	Dictionary of Unitarian and Universalist Biography
HMC	Harris Manchester College
ODNB	Oxford Dictionary of National Biography
TUHS	Transactions of the Unitarian Historical Society
WEA	Workers Educational Association

Note

Sources cited in notes are identified by author, title, publication date and, in the case of articles, the publication in which they appear. Complete bibliographical details, including location of unpublished documents, may be found in the Bibliography.

Notes

Introduction

1   "What we need now is a book entitled 'Queen Victoria: by a Personal acquaintance who dislikes her' ... The proper person for the work would be some politically indifferent devil's advocate who considers the Queen an over-rated woman and who would take a conscientious delight in disparaging her." George Bernard Shaw quoted by Michael Holroyd, "On the Border-line between the New and the Old: Bloomsbury, Biography, and Gerald Brenan" in Joe Law and Linda K. Hughes, eds., *Biographical Passages: Essays in Victorian and Modernist Biography* (Columbia, MO: University of Missouri Press, 2000), p. 34.

2   Dietrich Bonhoeffer, letter, 2 March 1944, in Eberhard Bethge, ed., *Dietrich Bonhoeffer Letters and Papers from Prison*, trans. Reginald Fuller (London: SCM Press, 3rd ed., 1967), p. 79.

3   Stephen E. Koss, "British Political Biography", *Political Science Quarterly* (1973), pp. 713-724. A similar point is made by Shirley A. Leckie, "Biography Matters: Why Historians Need Well-Crafted Biographies More than Ever" in Lloyd E. Ambrosius, ed., *Writing Biography: Historians & Their Craft* (Lincoln & London: University of Nebraska Press, 2004), p. 12.

4   The Dunkin endowment enabled a lectureship in social economy to be established at the College, which was held more than once by Philip Wicksteed. Other prominent lecturers followed him. V. D. Davis, *A History of Manchester College* (1932), pp. 173, 183. J. Estlin Carpenter, when Principal of the College, said that the reasons for teaching sociology included sensitivity to the "deep sores of poverty, suffering and degradation" and "the conviction that all economic questions have also a moral side" which requires that "the distribution of wealth shall be brought into some closer relation with acknowledged Christian ideals." He went on to say that, following the reports of the Poor Law Commission in 1907, Mrs Beatrice Webb's lectures at the College filled the Library to overflowing and many had to be turned away. *The Inquirer*, 27 November 1909, p. 797.

5   William Jellie, *Our Aims* and *The Principles and Doctrines of Unitarians* (1900), pp. 8-9.

6   When attacked by an opponent over his views on religion during the debate on temperance, Sir Robert Stout replied that he was supported as a Unitarian by the Women's Christian Temperance Union and that "in America the people did not say that a Unitarian was not a Christian". *Evening Post*, 28 November 1896, p. 5.

7   William Jellie was not alone in doing this; a study found that by the early twentieth century the use of secular literature in the Sunday lesson was part of

an overall trend in Unitarian practice. R. K. Webb, "Views of Unitarianism from Halley's Comet", *TUHS* (1986), pp. 180-195.

8   Michael Holroyd, *Works on Paper: The Craft of Biography and Autobiography* (London: Abacus, 2003), pp. 10-11.

9   William Jellie, letter to Mary Richmond, 18 January 1943.

10   Winston Rhodes wrote to Ella Jellie on 10 July 1969 seeking information about Frederick Sinclaire. Ella replied on 23 July 1969 saying she felt upset "because only a year or two ago I had burnt some letters from him to my husband written while he was in Melbourne — Mr Jellie had filed so many hundreds of letters dating back from 1890 & I went through them & distributed the ones I thought might be valuable — some from well known early ministers I sent to Manchester College. I pondered over Fred's letters dealing almost entirely with the Melbourne Church but could think of no one who might be interested." Rhodes replied on 6 August 1969, "I am sorry that his letters to your husband are no longer available ... Your few remarks and memories are quite useful to me." The Winston Rhodes letters and draft of Ella's reply are held by the author. The biography by Winston Rhodes, *Frederick Sinclaire* (Christchurch: University of Canterbury/Caxton Press, 1984), p. 43, refers to "the unfortunately destroyed correspondence between Sinclaire and Jellie".

11   James Chapple's books, *A Rebel's Vision Splendid* and *The Divine Need of the Rebel: Addresses from texts from the wider Bible of literature*, were both published in 1924 by C. W. Daniel Co., London. Chapple was the real life counterpart of the character Plumb in the novel of that name by Chapple's grandson, Maurice Gee. The first volume in a trilogy, *Plumb* was published in 1978 and has remained in print ever since.

Chapter 1: From Carrickfergus to London and Oxford

1   Birth entry registered in the District of Comber in the Union of Newtownards, County Down.

2   Marriage entry in the Parish of Comber, County Down.

3   Arthur B. Jellie, letter to his extended family in New Zealand including a Jellie family tree, 20 August 1982.

4   Mary Kok (née Jellie) thought her grandfather Robert may have been an alcoholic and that he died in America. Conversation with the author 18 December 2007. There is some support for this view as a search of the Northern Ireland Wills Calendars 1865-1877 and the Index of Wills for the period 1878-1900 found no will for Robert Jellie. Historical Research Associates report to the author, 22 April 2005.

Notes

[5] Public Records Office of Northern Ireland, Royal Belfast Academical Institution, Sch 524/1A/4.

[6] Public Records Office of Northern Ireland, Royal Belfast Academical Institution, Sch 524.

[7] *Belfast News-Letter*, 6 October 1881.

[8] Public Records Office of Northern Ireland, Royal Belfast Academical Institution, Sch 24/1A/7-Registers 1838-1848-Collegiate.

[9] John Jamieson, *The History of the Royal Belfast Academical Institution 1810-1960* (1959), p. 251 nn.1-2.

[10] William McMillan, *A History of the Moneyreagh Congregation* (1969), p. 38.

[11] *The Disciple*, May 1883, p. 184.

[12] Manchester New College was founded as Manchester Academy in 1786 to replace the Warrington Academy. It was known as Manchester College while at York, 1803-1840; Manchester New College while at Manchester, 1840-1853 and London, 1853-1889; and Manchester College when it moved to Oxford in 1889. It changed its name to Harris Manchester College in 1996 when it became a chartered college of Oxford University.

[13] William Jellie, letter to James Martineau, 5 April 1884, enclosing letters from James C. Street and others; W. A. Adamson; and John McDowell.

[14] John Jellie, letter to the Secretary to the College, Rev. H. Enfield Dowson, 8 April 1884.

[15] James Martineau, letter to Rev. H. Enfield Dowson, 12 May 1884.

[16] Lester Burney, *Cross Street Chapel Manchester and its College* (1983), p. 48.

[17] William George Tarrant and Joseph Worthington, "University Hall, London", *TUHS* (1927-30), pp. 1-15.

[18] *Report of Manchester New College, Ninety-Ninth Annual Meeting, 1885*, p. 16.

[19] *Report of Manchester New College, Ninety-Ninth Annual Meeting, 1885*, p. 66.

[20] *Manchester New College (In Connection With The University of London, and University College London), University Hall, Gordon Square, London. Regulations as to Admission of Students, Course of Study & Exhibitions. University Hall Conditions of Residence* (1884), pp. 59-61.

[21] *Report of Manchester New College, Ninety-Ninth Annual Meeting, 1885*, p. 13.

[22] *Report of Manchester New College, One Hundredth Annual Meeting, 1886*, p. 8.

[23] *Report of Manchester New College, One Hundred and First Annual Meeting, 1887*, p. 9.

24 *Report of Manchester New College, One Hundred and Second Annual Meeting, 1888*, p. 6.

25 *Report of Manchester New College, One Hundred and Second Annual Meeting, 1888*, pp. 8-10.

26 William Rothenstein, *Men and Memories: Recollections of William Rothenstein 1872-1900* (1931), pp. 26-27, 31. Rothenstein's interest in paintings by the French-born British painter Alphonse Legros (1837-1911) led him to meet a prominent Unitarian clergyman, Dr Stopford Brooke. He particularly admired a drawing by Rossetti which Brooke left him in his will.

27 "Almost every day for five years I listened to the bell of that church, as I lived in that brick building in Gordon Square which is now Dr Williams' Library." William Jellie, Journal, June 9, 1903.

28 Two notebooks containing notes of lectures on sociology given by P. H. Wicksteed at Manchester New College. One of the notebooks is signed by William Jellie. Jellie's synopsis of Wicksteed's lectures is found in Appendix 1.

29 *Report of Manchester New College, One Hundred and Fourth Annual Meeting, 1890*, pp. 3, 9, 10.

30 Ian Steedman, "Rationality, Economic Man and Altruism in Philip H. Wicksteed's *Commonsense of Political Economy*" in Barbara Smith (ed.), *Truth, Liberty, Religion: Essays Celebrating Two Hundred Years of Manchester College* (1986), pp. 293-294.

31 Israel M. Kirzner, "Philip Wicksteed: The 'Austrian' Economist", Ludwig von Mises Institute, 23 June 2007.

32 C. H. Herford, *Philip Henry Wicksteed: His Life and Work* (1931), pp. 89, 347-355.

33 Replying to Jellie's letter of condolence on the death of his wife, Wicksteed wrote, "... how much I was impressed by your eager receptiveness, and it is a true solace to me in my old age to know the fullness of the life to which I was then privileged to introduce you." P. H. Wicksteed, letter to William Jellie, 31 May 1924.

34 *Report of Manchester New College, One Hundred and Fourth Annual Meeting, 1890*, pp. 8-10.

35 The College site in Mansfield Road was bought from Merton College. Mansfield College is located at the other end of the road. The name was changed to Manchester College, Oxford in 1894.

36 In 1901 Manchester College was recognised as a Permanent Private Hall of Oxford University. The next step did not occur until 1965, when Manchester

Notes

College was granted the status of an Institution for Higher Study by Oxford. This meant that Manchester College students could attend University lectures and could study for an Oxford B.A. in Theology and Diplomas in Education and Social and Administrative Studies. In 1967 Manchester College students could take the University's special Diploma in Social Studies. In 1996 a new Royal Charter granted full College status within the University of Oxford. Barbara Smith (ed.), *Truth, Liberty, Religion*, pp. xxiii-xxiv; and Susan Killoran, Librarian HMC, personal communication, 13 January 2009.

[37] Burney, *Cross Street Chapel*, p. 73.

[38] Burney, *Cross Street Chapel*, p. 73.

[39] These points are discussed by Arthur J. Long, "The Life and Work of J. Estlin Carpenter" in Barbara Smith (ed.), *Truth, Liberty, Religion*, pp. 274-275; and Burney, *Cross Street Chapel*, p. 77.

[40] The certificate Jellie received dated June 1890 is inscribed "Manchester New College, London. Removed to Oxford 1889". However, when Jellie's Dante book collection was given to the University of Auckland, the commemorative booklet (*Dante and His Times: The Jellie Collection*, University of Auckland Bibliographical Bulletin, 1964) recorded that Jellie "was educated at the Universities of London and Oxford". This is not correct, but it indicates how powerful the early association of Manchester College, Oxford became in people's minds with the University of Oxford.

Chapter 2: A New World Vision

[1] A. J. Long, "Carpenter, (Joseph) Estlin (1844-1927)", ODNB. Wicksteed commemorated their life-long companionship in the dedication of his *The Reactions Between Dogma & Theology Illustrated from the Works of S. Thomas Aquinas* (1926): "To Joseph Estlin Carpenter, most dear and constant friend, as a young man you dedicated to me the first fruits of your genius. Now I, as an old man, have offered back to you after forty years these fragments of a book. You always used to expect more of me than I was capable of. May you nevertheless graciously accept what is so much less, alas, than you hoped for." Translated from the Latin by Arthur J. Long, "The Life and Work of J. Estlin Carpenter" in Barbara Smith, ed., *Truth, Liberty, Religion: Essays Celebrating Two Hundred Years of Manchester College* (1986), p. 277.

[2] C. H. Herford, *Philip Henry Wicksteed: His Life and Work*, (1931), p. 190.

[3] The British and Foreign Unitarian Association (B&FUA) was formed in 1825 for the promotion of Unitarian Christianity in Great Britain and overseas

Notes

by assisting poor congregations, providing missionary preachers and protecting and extending the civil rights of Unitarians. Member congregations nominated two representatives to the general meetings. Sydney Herbert Mellone, *Liberty and Religion: The First Century of the British & Foreign Unitarian Association* (1925), pp. 31-36.

In 1881 the B&FUA helped establish the National Conference of Unitarian, Liberal Christian, Free Christian, Presbyterian and other Non-Subscribing and Kindred Congregations, which held triennial meetings. In 1928 the National Conference and B&FUA amalgamated and became the General Assembly of Unitarian and Free Christian Churches. Mortimer Rowe, *The Story of Essex Hall* (1959), pp. 50-51.

4 The advantage of this system is seen in comparison to the failure experienced by the Methodists: in 1899, some eleven years after Wicksteed's course began at Manchester College, a motion was introduced at the Methodist Conference to include the study of social problems in the training of theological students. The motion stalled in committee. It was not until 1909 that the Methodists approved a course in social training for theological students. The Congregationalists on the other hand fared much better: just five years after the introduction of Wicksteed's course they were able to respond with a similar educational programme. See K. S. Inglis, "English Nonconformity and Social Reform, 1880-1900", *Past & Present* (1958), pp. 73-88; and K. S. Inglis, *Churches and the Working Classes in Victorian England* (1963), p. 295 n.2.

5 In 1854 religious tests were abolished for bachelor's degrees other than divinity at the universities of Oxford and Cambridge. Tests for taking M.A. degrees were abolished in 1871 and for divinity degrees in 1919. Raymond V. Holt, *The Unitarian Contribution to Social Progress in England* (1952), pp. 242-243. However the University of London, established in 1836, could enrol students and confer degrees without doctrinal subscription.

6 Jean Raymond and John V. Pickstone, "The Natural Sciences and the Learning of English Unitarians: An exploration of the roles of Manchester College" in Barbara Smith, ed., *Truth, Liberty, Religion: Essays Celebrating Two Hundred Years of Manchester College* (1986), p. 155. Nineteenth-century Unitarianism has been characterized as "a more rational minority against the religious dogmas of eternal punishment, inherited guilt, vicarious atonement, the Trinity and hell-fire." Peter d'A. Jones, *The Christian Socialist Revival 1877-1914* (1968), p. 394. This rational style extended to their method of persuasion: "a Unitarian Evangelical is unthinkable, a sort of *lusus naturae* [freak of nature], for the Unitarians were and always had been since the days of Joseph Priestly and Richard Price and Mrs Barbauld of

Notes

the Warrington Academy, an enlightened intellectual minority." Donald Davie, *Essays in Dissent: Church, Chapel, and the Unitarian Conspiracy* (1995), p. 55.

[7] The course was paid for by an anonymous donation of £100. Wicksteed was later appointed to the staff of the College as a Lecturer in Social Economy, the first such appointment from outside the College staff of Professors. See *Report of Manchester New College, One Hundred and Third Annual Meeting, 1889*, p. 9; and P. H. Wicksteed, "The Place of Sociology in the Circle of Theological Studies" in J. Estlin Carpenter and P. H. Wicksteed, *Studies in Theology* (1903), pp. 284-300.

[8] Wicksteed, "The Place of Sociology", pp. 286-287, 289.

[9] Wicksteed, "The Place of Sociology", pp. 290-291.

[10] Wicksteed, "The Place of Sociology", pp. 293-294.

[11] Wicksteed, "The Place of Sociology", p. 295.

[12] Wicksteed, "The Place of Sociology", p. 299.

[13] *Report of Manchester New College, One Hundred and Third Annual Meeting, 1889*, p. 9.

[14] Jose Harris, "Spencer, Herbert (1820-1903)", ODNB. Spencer's father was a dissenter but from an early age Spencer was a sceptic, later identifying with agnosticism after T. H. Huxley invented the term in 1869. His education was undertaken by an uncle, a clergyman who was a radical reformer. Spencer initially worked as an apprenticed railway engineer. He wrote occasionally to newspapers and considered immigrating to New Zealand, until he found work as a sub-editor on the *Economist*. London provided the opportunity to meet prominent scientists and reformers and Spencer's thoughts turned to a literary career. He was interested in discovering natural laws that governed society and led to human progress. Eventually this would result in a synthesis of scientific and philosophical thought. Spencer's project to produce *A System of Synthetic Philosophy* would last 40 years and be published in five volumes. He incorporated Darwin's discoveries and coined the phrase "survival of the fittest". His concept of society as an organism whose parts adopted a self-regulating function, comparable to biological organisms, was seen by Wicksteed as a strong explanatory model. Wicksteed referred to Spencer in four lectures and used various aspects of Spencer's *Synthetic Philosophy*, which incorporated evolutionary biology, psychology, sociology and ethics. It is interesting to note the apparent lack of critique of Spencer's philosophy on Wicksteed's part.

[15] Sam Addison, "Archibald Henry Sayce 1845-1933, Professor of Assyriology, Oxford", biographical introduction to Sayce's Gifford Lectures.

16 Victor Grassian, *Moral Reasoning: Ethical Theory and Some Contemporary Moral Problems* (1981), p. 47. Bentham invented the utility concept in economics and "the greatest happiness for the greatest number" as a social maxim. As a moral principle this may well not have found favour with Wicksteed.

17 Robert Wuthnow, "Altruism and Sociological Theory", *Social Service Review* (1993), pp. 344-357.

18 M.A. Elston, "Blackwell, Elizabeth (1821-1910)", ODNB. When she was eleven Elizabeth Blackwell left England with her family to settle in New York. In 1849 she graduated M.D. from Geneva Medical College, New York, the first woman doctor in America. She organised a hospital for poor women and children in New York. In 1858 she visited London and was registered with the General Medical Council under a clause that recognised doctors with foreign medical degrees practicing in Britain. Thus she became the first woman doctor in Britain. During the American Civil War she worked on the provision of nursing services for the Union army. At home again in England she advocated the case for women doctors, public health and preventive health care through hygiene, but her rejection of aspects of modern medicine put her at odds with the medical establishment.

19 P. H. Wicksteed, "Elements of Sociology", Lecture VIII. See Appendix 1.

20 Andrew Vincent, "Green, Thomas Hill (1836-1882)", ODNB. Green had been a student of Benjamin Jowett's at Balliol College, Oxford. He had dissenting views and only signed the Thirty-nine Articles after much doubt, probably in order to gain his degree. He became Whyte's Professor of Moral Philosophy at Balliol College. He supported the university extension movement and university education for poor students and working men. He developed an ethical and political philosophy in response to the complexities of industrial society. His ideals of citizenship, freedom and social duty were still influential in the twentieth century.

21 This idea is discussed in Mark Bevir, "Welfarism, Socialism and Religion: On T. H. Green and Others", *The Review of Politics* (1993), pp. 639-661.

22 Matt Carter, *T. H. Green and the Development of Ethical Socialism* (2003), p. 50.

23 Denys P. Leighton, "T. H. Green and the Dissidence of Dissent: On Religion and National Character in Nineteenth-Century England", *Parliamentary History* (2008), pp. 43-56.

24 Edward Royle, "Foote, George William (1850-1915)", ODNB. George William Foote left the Anglican church of his mother and became Unitarian as a teenager. When he went to work in London he joined the Young Men's Secular Association. After rising to prominence in the secular movement he followed

Notes

Charles Bradlaugh as President of the National Secular Society. He published under the Pioneer Press imprint.

25   Edward Royle, "Bradlaugh, Charles (1833-1891)", ODNB. Charles Bradlaugh was an articled solicitor's clerk in London, although he practiced as a solicitor. A noted radical who supported extension of the franchise and republican causes, he published the *National Reformer* and was founder and President of the National Secular Society. Together with Annie Besant, he published Charles Knowlton's pamphlet on birth control. This resulted in an obscenity prosecution and a sentence of six months imprisonment, which was later quashed. Bradlaugh was elected MP for Northampton in 1880 and after being ejected from parliament was re-elected in 1881, 1882, 1884 and 1885. He took his seat in 1886, but it was not until 1888 that a law change permitted parliamentary affirmations.

26   Warren Sylvester Smith, *The London Heretics 1870-1914* (1967), p. 63.

27   G. W. Foote, *Prisoner for Blasphemy* (1886).

28   Smith, *The London Heretics*, pp. 65-66.

29   The ruling was highly controversial. "A blasphemy law so interpreted was unworkable, as the failure to reach a verdict in the third *Freethinker* trial implicitly suggests. Even commentators who approved the ruling could not find the chain of precedents convincing." Joss Marsh, *Word Crimes: Blasphemy, Culture, and Literature in Nineteenth-Century England* (1998), pp. 160-161. For the full judgement see John Duke Coleridge (Lord Chief Justice of England), *The Law of Blasphemous Libel: The Summing Up in the Case of Regina v. Foote & Others* (1883).

30   David Tribe, *100 Years of Freethought* (1967), p. 157; Foote, *Prisoner for Blasphemy*. The B&FUA general meeting called for a change in the law so that no one could be prosecuted for publishing any opinion about religion and notified the Home Secretary that Foote should be released from prison. It also supported moves to allow affirmations instead of oaths in Parliament. *The Times*, 18 May 1883, p. 3.

31   A. L. Goodhart, "Kenny, Courtney Stanhope (1847-1930)," rev. Richard A. Cosgrove, ODNB. Educated at Cambridge University, where he became a Fellow of Downing College, Kenny was an MP from 1885 to 1888. He then retired to become a Reader in English Law at Cambridge. He was appointed Downing Professor of English Law in 1907. See also D. W. Bebbington, "Unitarian Members of Parliament in the Nineteenth Century: A Catalogue", *TUHS* (2009).

32   P. H. Wicksteed, "Elements of Sociology", Lecture IX. See Appendix 1.

Notes

[33] This summary of the *Alphabet of Economics* is based on Paul Flatau, "Jevons's One Great Disciple: Wicksteed and the Jevonian Revolution in the Second Generation", *History of Economics Review* (2004), pp. 69-107.

[34] James Bonar, "The Austrian Economists and their View of Value," *Quarterly Journal of Economics* (1888), pp. 1-31.

[35] P. H. Wicksteed, "Social Problems in the Light of Economic Theory", Lectures IV and V. See Appendix 1.

[36] P. H. Wicksteed, "Social Problems in the Light of Economic Theory", Lecture VI. See Appendix 1.

[37] P. H. Wicksteed, "Social Problems in the Light of Economic Theory", Lecture VII. See Appendix 1.

[38] Adrian Desmond and James Moore, *Darwin* (1991), pp. 264-265. "The 'surplus' workers shipped to the colonies rose exponentially. Malthus sanctioned such an escape in his sixth edition, which differed strikingly from the unrelentingly bleak first edition." Malthus's theory was also instrumental in helping Charles Darwin formulate his ideas about natural selection. Unitarian Harriet Martineau, a close friend of Charles' brother Erasmus, is credited with bringing it to his attention.

[39] P. H. Wicksteed, "Social Problems in the Light of Economic Theory", Lecture VIII. See Appendix 1.

[40] P. H. Wicksteed, "Social Problems in the Light of Economic Theory", Lectures IX, IX continued and X. See Appendix 1.

[41] Alan Kadish, "Toynbee, Arnold (1852-1883)," ODNB. Arnold Toynbee, a Tutor at Balliol College, Oxford, was a disciple of T. H. Green, active in the co-operative movement and adult education, and advocated trade unions, friendly societies and state welfare to improve the standard of living for the working classes. His important work, *The Industrial Revolution*, was published posthumously in 1884.

[42] Charles Wicksteed, *The Land for the People: How to Obtain It, How to Manage It* (1885). He continued campaigning for land nationalization; see Charles Wicksteed, *Our Mother Earth: A Short Statement of the Case for Land Nationalization* (1892).

[43] Kirk Willis, "The Introduction and Critical Reception of Marxist Thought in Britain, 1850-1900", *The Historical Journal* (1977), pp. 417-459.

[44] *Looking Backward* sold over 100,000 copies in America in 1888, its first year of publication, and went on to sell over a million copies worldwide. It was the third best-selling fiction book in the nineteenth century.

Notes

⁴⁵ P. H. Wicksteed, "Ethical and Theological Aspects of Sociology", Lectures I, II and III. See Appendix 1.

⁴⁶ Students were referred to an article by Dr Philip Herbert Carpenter (1852-1891), a brother of J. Estlin Carpenter. Philip Carpenter's article "Evolution and the Existence of Satan II", *The Christian Reformer*, May 1886, pp. 269-276, was a reply to an anonymous article by an Anglican clergyman, "Evolution and the Existence of Satan", *The Christian Reformer*, April 1886, pp. 223-235. The Anglican's principal argument against evolution appears to be the question of how evil could arise without a deity. Carpenter demonstrated the eons involved in laying down rocks and limestone, the waste in animal and plant kingdoms throughout time, and how pointless it was to attribute such natural phenomena to the agency of a good or bad deity. The same issue had a further article on this topic (pp. 277-282) by a Unitarian minister, the Rev. Dr Charles Hargrove (1840-1918), exploring a theological question: why is there sin, sorrow and suffering if there is a good God? It is noteworthy that Wicksteed directed his students not to the theological controversy but to the scientific description of evolution by Philip Carpenter.

⁴⁷ *Report of Manchester New College, One Hundred and Fourth Annual Meeting, 1890*, p. 6.

⁴⁸ Fox and Evans have been identified through the B&FUA's *Essex Hall Year Book for 1904*, pp. 13-14. Richard Thomas Nicholson is identified in Alan Ruston, "Obituaries of Unitarian Ministers 1900-1999: Additions, Corrections and Extended to the end of 2004", *TUHS* (2005).

⁴⁹ Frank Parnell is not found in the collections of obituaries of Unitarian Ministers 1850-1899 or 1900-1999; the *Essex Hall Year Books* for 1903, 1904 and 1905; or the Index of Obituaries of Unitarians at Harris Manchester College.

⁵⁰ *Report of Manchester New College, One Hundred and Fifth Annual Meeting, 1891*, p. 8.

⁵¹ Ruston, "Obituaries of Unitarian Ministers 1900-1999", *TUHS* (2000), p. 219.

⁵² R. K. Webb, "Trevor, John (1855-1930)", ODNB.

⁵³ The Labour Church was opened on 4 October 1891 and Trevor left Upper Brook Street a month later. Trevor wrote, "I have so many causes to feel grateful to him [Philip Wicksteed] — perhaps this the chief — that, from the first, he understood what I meant by the Labour Church. Long before anyone else understood, the knowledge of his sympathy with my work cheered and sustained me through many a dark hour." John Trevor, *My Quest for God* (1897), pp. 219, 244-245.

⁵⁴ Herford, *Philip Henry Wicksteed*, p. 99.

Notes

Chapter 3: Religious Socialism and Social Change

1   For example, the social gospel of the Wesleyan Methodist minister Hugh Price Hughes (1847-1902) arguably had little influence among Unitarians, especially those seeking a more radical reconstruction of society. In *The Christian Socialist Revival 1877-1914: Religion, Class, and Social Conscience in Late-Victorian England* (1968), Peter d'A. Jones wrote: "[Hughes] did not involve himself with secular or religious socialist organisations. Instead, he used the vocabulary of the socialist and the policy of the social-mission worker" (p. 408). Nor would his well-known loathing of Unitarians and his efforts, largely successful, to exclude them from Free Church Councils, have endeared him to Unitarians. See D. W. Bebbington, *The Nonconformist Conscience: Chapel and Politics, 1870-1914* (1982), p. 72.

Often overlooked is the episode, extending over five years, that mired Hughes' reputation. In 1890 he published *The Atheist Shoemaker: A Page in the History of a West London Mission*, which purported to be a deathbed conversion story. George W. Foote exposed it as a fake, identified the anonymous "shoemaker" and his family as lifelong believers, and pointed out that Hughes' West London Mission had financial problems which were helped with publication of this story. The damaging controversy surrounding the affair led the Baptist divine Charles Spurgeon, among others, to urge Hughes to reveal the source of his story, which Hughes never did. Diane Lee Grosso, *Hugh Price Hughes: Late Victorian Nonconformity and the Kingdom of God* (2004), pp. 146-156.

2   Thomas Percival was a staunch Unitarian active in the antislavery campaign. Audrey Burrell, "Dr Thomas Percival, MD: Eighteenth Century Pioneer in Medical and Social Reform", *TUHS* (2006), pp. 649-662.

3   John V. Pickstone, "Ferriar's Fever to Kay's Cholera: Disease and Social Structure in Cottonopolis", *History of Science* (1984), pp. 401-419.

4   In later life Ferriar and Kay attended Anglican churches. Dr Thomas Percival was a member of the Cross Street Chapel, which from 1839, together with the Mosley Street Chapel, moved to a new building on Upper Brook Street. See John Seed, "Unitarianism, Political Economy and the Antinomies of Liberal Culture in Manchester, 1830-50", *Social History* (1982), pp.1-25.

5   Edward Ryle, *Annual Reports of the Manchester Domestic Missionary Society, 1833-1908.*

6   "In view of the criticism [Elizabeth] Gaskell incurred on the publication of *Mary Barton* for having drawn an exaggerated picture of the problems harassing industrial Manchester, her anxiety to give a truthful account is noteworthy." Monica Correa Frykstedt, "*Mary Barton* and the Reports of the Ministry to the Poor: A New Source", *Studia Neophilologica* (1980), pp. 333-336.

Notes

[7] V. D. Davis, *The London Domestic Missionary Society: Record of a Hundred Years 1835-1935* (1935); Alan Ruston, "London's East End Domestic Mission – Spicer Street, Buxton Street and Mansford Street", *TUHS* (1996), pp. 117-135; Brian A. Packer, "The Founding of the Liverpool Domestic Mission and its Development under the Ministry of John Johns", *TUHS* (1984), pp. 39-53; E.A. Elton, "A Victorian City Mission: The Unitarian Contribution to Social Progress in Holbeck and New Whortley, 1844-78", *Publications of the Thoresby Society* (1977), pp. 316-332; H. G. Wilson, "One Hundred Years of Religious and Social Work in Birmingham", *TUHS* (1945), pp. 113-121; Jack Simmons, "A Victorian Social Worker: Joseph Dare and the Leicester Domestic Mission", *Leicestershire Archaeological and Historical Society Transactions* (1970-71), pp. 65-80.

[8] A detailed account of the origins of the Unitarian domestic missions is provided by David Steers, "The Origins and Development of the Domestic Mission Movement Especially in Liverpool and Manchester", *TUHS* (1996), pp. 79-103.

[9] H. W. Schuff, "Education for the Neglected: Ragged Schools in Nineteenth-Century England", *History of Education Quarterly* (1972), pp. 162-183.

[10] Alison Twells, *The Civilising Mission and the English Middle Class, 1792-1850* (2009), pp. 172-173.

[11] From the first annual report of the Unitarian Home Missionary Board, quoted in David L. Wykes, " 'Training Ministers suited to the wants of the less educated Classes'; The Establishment of the Unitarian Home Missionary Board", *TUHS*, (2005), pp. 615-624. Founded in 1854 as the Unitarian Home Missionary Board, in 1889 it changed its name to Unitarian Home Missionary College and 1925 became the Unitarian College, Manchester.

[12] Leonard Smith, "The 1851 Religious Census and the Unitarian Home Missionary Board 1854", *TUHS* (2005), pp. 625-628. See also Geoffrey Head, "The Founders: John Relly Beard and William Gaskell" in Leonard Smith (ed.) *Unitarian to the Core: Unitarian College Manchester, 1854-2004* (2004), pp. 30-51.

[13] C. Gordon Bolam, "John Relly Beard and the New Function of Unitarianism in the 1850s", *TUHS* (1962), pp. 155-162.

[14] Alan Ruston, "John Relly Beard", DUUB.

[15] William Binns, "Unitarianism, its Mission and Missionaries" in *Unitarian Missionary Papers* (1861), p. 71.

[16] Dennis G. Wigmore-Beddoes, *Yesterday's Radicals: A Study of the Affinity between Unitarianism and Broad Church Anglicanism in the Nineteenth Century* (1971), p. 15.

17 Wigmore-Beddoes, *Yesterday's Radicals*, pp. 104-105.

18 David Young, *F. D. Maurice and Unitarianism* (1992), p. 96.

19 In the 1880s and 1890s attention was diverted from the co-operatives by the growth of Fabian collectivism, state socialism and the Independent Labour Party (ILP), although later "the cooperative ideal again became dominant — in the new form of Guild Socialism." Jones, *The Christian Socialist Revival*, p. 445.

20 "Andrew Mearns, with two colleagues, wrote *The Bitter Cry of Outcast London*, which the Congregational Union published in 1883 to advertise its missionary and philanthropic work in the slums." K. S. Inglis, "English Nonconformity and Social Reform, 1880-1900", *Past & Present* (1958), pp. 73-88.

21 The first settlement was started in Manchester in 1877 by Charles Rowley. Like Toynbee Hall it was non-denominational, had links with Victoria University of Manchester and was known as "University Settlement". Leonard Smith, *Religion and the Rise of Labour: Nonconformity and the Independent Labour Movement in Lancashire and the West Riding 1880-1914* (1993), p. 64.

22 K. S. Inglis, *Churches and the Working Classes in Victorian England* (1963), p. 166, gives 1893 as the foundation year, which is a mistake. In 1961 the Women's University Settlement changed its name to Blackfriars Settlement. See http://www.blackfriars-settlement.org.uk/history.

23 Katharine Bentley Beauman, *Women and the Settlement Movement* (1996), p. 222.

24 Gillian Darley, "Hill, Octavia (1838-1912)", ODNB. Octavia Hill was brought up in a Unitarian family with freedom on religious matters. Through her friendship with F. D. Maurice she became an undogmatic Anglican for whom religion was a personal matter.

25 Jose Harris, "Booth, Charles (1846-1916)", ODNB. Booth was President of the Royal Statistical Society 1892-94, Fellow of the Royal Society 1899 and Privy Councillor 1904. He was related by marriage to Beatrice Potter (Mrs Sidney Webb). His Unitarianism was later replaced with Comtist ideas.

26 Paul Robert Flatau, *Essays in the Development, Methodology and Policy Prescriptions of Neoclassical Distribution Theory* (2006), pp. 94-95 n. 12. Clara Collett was born into a Unitarian family; they attended South Place chapel where her father was musical director. She became one of the first women to obtain an M.A. degree (in political economy) at London University. After working with Charles Booth she went on to become Senior Investigator in the Labour Department, working with Lloyd George and Winston Churchill. Deborah McDonald, *Clara Collett 1860-1948: An Educated Working Woman* (2004), Introduction and pp. 2-3.

Notes

27 Browning Hall under the Wardenship of the Rev. F. H. Steed "rapidly became a trade-union and labor headquarters". Jones, *The Christian Socialist Revival*, p. 82.

28 Emily K. Abel, "Toynbee Hall, 1884-1914", *Social Services Review* (1979), pp. 606-832. There were 49 university settlements in Britain and over 400 in the United States by 1911.

29 Smith, *Religion and the Rise of Labour*, p. 65.

30 Timothy Sprigge, "Mrs Humphry Ward", DUUB. In 1889 Mrs Ward set out to promote modernism and obtained the "active interest of Canon Barnett, Warden of Toynbee Hall, Lord Carlisle, Dr Blake Odgers, Miss F. P. Cobbe, and Stopford Brooke, with the professors of Manchester College, and Philip Wicksteed." C. H. Herford, *Philip Henry Wicksteed: His Life and Work* (1931), p. 96.

31 Lester Burney, *Cross Street Chapel Manchester and its College* (1983), p. 73.

32 John Sutherland, *Mrs Humphry Ward: Eminent Victorian and Pre-eminent Edwardian* (1990), p. 218.

33 Sutherland, *Mrs Humphry Ward*, pp. 229-230. Wicksteed's misgivings were shared by his friend J. Estlin Carpenter, a member of settlement committee, who wrote to Mrs Ward that he did not understand the connection of the course of lectures with the settlement.

34 Mrs Humphry Ward gave the second lecture in a series initiated by the B&FUA on liberal Christianity and progressive thought. In her lecture, delivered at Essex Hall in 1894, she equated the "new Christian teaching" with Unitarianism, although she personally would only take the name Christian. She thought that the free development of the Christian spirit was due to Unitarianism and that Unitarian domestic missions had made real progress amongst the poor. Mrs Humphry Ward, *Unitarians and the Future* (1894).

35 A. J. A. Morris, "Edwards, John Passmore (1823-1911)", ODNB. Edwards gave £14,000 towards the settlement that bore his name. A humanitarian who had Chartist sympathies, he was active in the peace movement and political reform societies, and attracted by ideas of education for working men. He twice declined offers of a knighthood.

36 Herford, *Philip Henry Wicksteed*, p. 220.

37 Duncan Bythell, "Tillett, Benjamin (1860-1943)", ODNB. Tillett was a trade unionist who had come to national prominence with his leadership of the dock workers' strike. Tillett supported the Labour Church, speaking at it on many occasions. In 1898 he visited New Zealand and spoke at meetings of the Socialist Church.

38 John Trevor, *My Quest for God* (1897), p. 239.

39 *The Inquirer*, 25 April 1891, p. 275, quoted in Leonard Smith, *John Trevor and the Labour Church Movement* (1985), p. 21. Trevor thought "both these men prophesied the Labour Church". Trevor, *My Quest for God*, p. 239.

40 Trevor, *My Quest for God*, p. 241.

41 David Fowler Summers, *The Labour Church and Allied Movements of the Late 19th and Early 20th Centuries* (1958), p. 40.

42 For a detailed discussion of these points see Mark Bevir, "The Labour Church Movement, 1891-1902", *Journal of British Studies* (1999), pp. 217-245. Trevor also had mystical experiences which gave him feelings of peace and joy and unity with God's purpose. His experiences are described in the chapter on "Mysticism" in William James, *The Varieties of Religious Experience* (1902).

43 I. Sellers, "Unitarians and the Labour Church Movement", *TUHS* (1959), pp. 1-6.

44 As did his friend J. Estlin Carpenter, who is recorded as a donor to the first Labour Church founded in Manchester in October 1891. Summers, *The Labour Church and Allied Movements*, Appendix, p. 509.

45 *Labour Prophet*, No. 2, February 1892, quoted in Herford, *Philip Henry Wicksteed*, p. 223.

46 Philip H. Wicksteed, *What Does the Labour Church Stand For?* (c. 1895), p. 8.

47 Herbert Roth, "Atkinson, Harry Albert 1867-1956", DNZB. After working for the Labour Church between December 1891 and July 1893, Harry Atkinson left to study at Cambridge for a year. In September 1893 Rose Bell and Harry Atkinson were married by John Trevor. They then travelled to New Zealand and in 1896 formed the Christchurch Socialist Church based on the Manchester model. The church continued until 1905. Herbert Roth, "Labour Churches and New Zealand", *International Review of Social History* (1959), pp. 361-366.

48 Summers, *The Labour Church and Allied Movements*, Appendix, pp. 375-476 describes each Labour Church in Britain, Canada, the United States, and New Zealand. Although there was discussion of a Labour Church in Melbourne, Australia, it does not appear to have eventuated. However, a Labour Church was established in Perth, Western Australia, about 1897 by Montague David Miller (1839-1920). Eric Fry, "Miller, Montague David (1839-1920)", ADB.

49 H. A. Atkinson, letter to C. H. Herford, in Herford, *Philip Henry Wicksteed*, p. 227. "It should be a cause for some pride that a native New Zealander was among the founders" of the British Labour Party. Herbert Roth, "In Memoriam: Harry Albert Atkinson", *Here & Now* (1956), pp. 18-20.

Notes

⁵⁰ Summers, *The Labour Church and Allied Movements*, Appendix, pp. 425-426.

⁵¹ Jones, *The Christian Socialist Revival*, p. 397. Stopford Brooke "made the connection between a liberal theology and Socialism, and in later years was a member of the Fabian Society. Significantly, he published a sermon on the *Life and Work of Maurice*." Warren Sylvester Smith, *The London Heretics 1870-1914*, (1968), p. 314.

⁵² Smith, *Religion and the Rise of Labour*, p. 114. Hargrove's was the only paper set down for the afternoon of the second day of the conference and there was ample time for discussion afterwards. *Manchester General Reception Committee, Guide Book and Order of Proceedings to the National Conference* (1894).

⁵³ Smith, *Religion and the Rise of Labour*, p. 114.

⁵⁴ *Birmingham Daily Post*, 18 May 1894.

⁵⁵ *The Times*, 7 June 1895, p. 7.

⁵⁶ Jones, *The Christian Socialist Revival*, p. 396.

⁵⁷ Brooke Herford, letter to William Jellie, 18 March 1896, giving suggestions to Jellie who, with "one or two more of the younger London ministers", could identify themselves as "hosts" of the meeting with red ribbons in their buttonholes.

⁵⁸ James Martineau, letter to William Jellie, 20 May 1896, saying he will be out of London on the date of the meeting. The meeting in question was that of the London Unitarian Ministers, held on 27 May 1896.

⁵⁹ Jones, *The Christian Socialist Revival*, p. 402.

⁶⁰ Beatrice Webb, quotation from *Problems of Modern Industry*, recorded by William Jellie in his Work Book of Quotations. This appears under "Law, the mother of freedom". Under "Freedom" there is a cross reference to "Law".

⁶¹ These words were transposed and should be at the end of the sentence.

⁶² Jellie appears to have been quoting from Beatrice Webb, "Women and the Factory Acts", chapter IV in Sidney and Beatrice Webb, *Problems of Modern Industry*, (1898), p. 85. Nearly all of the chapters in this book are reprints of previously published articles. The one in question had been read at the Nottingham Conference of the National Union of Women Workers in October 1895 and the Fabian Society in January 1896. We cannot be sure whether Jellie is quoting from the book or an earlier article.

The same year the book was published, the Webbs toured America and Australia and stayed in New Zealand between 3 August and 2 September 1898. During their visit they took a particular interest in the Industrial Conciliation and Arbitration Act and local government. D.A. Hamer (ed.), *The Webbs in New Zealand 1898*

Notes

(1974), Introduction. Their main contact was a relative of Beatrice's, Richard Oliver (1830-1910), member of the House of Representatives for Dunedin 1878-1881, member of the Legislative Council 1881-1901. Obituary, *Evening Post*, 30 November 1910, p. 5.

63   Quoted in Mark Bevir, "The Long Nineteenth Century in Intellectual History", *Journal of Victorian Culture* (2001), pp. 313-335.

Chapter 4: Two English Ministries

1   Frank Castle, *Annals of the Auckland Unitarian Church* (1981), p. 6, incorrectly states that Jellie worked for "a six year period as assistant to Philip Wicksteed, minister of the Stanford [sic] Street Domestic Mission. "This confuses Wicksteed's ministry at Little Portland Street and his assistant John Trevor, with Jellie's sole ministry at Stamford Street and what is usually known as the Blackfriars Domestic Mission.

2   The chapel closed in 1962. When it was demolished to provide a school playground the portico was preserved. Graham Hague et. al., *The Unitarian Heritage: An Architectural Survey of Chapels and Churches in the Unitarian tradition in the British Isles* (1986), p. 67. The London Nautical School has occupied the area since 1965. See http://www.lns.org.uk/historical.htm.

3   Virginia Clark, "Stamford Street Unitarian Chapel 6 April 1868: A Unitarian First for Women's Suffrage", *TUHS* (2000), pp. 142-149.

4   Clark, "Stamford Street Unitarian Chapel," p. 143.

5   "Stamford Street," in *Survey of London: Volume 22, Bankside (The Parishes of St. Saviour and Christchurch Southwark)* (1950), pp. 122-124.

6   Charles Dickens [Jr], "Unitarian Places of Worship," in *Dickens's Dictionary of London, 1879*.

7   These advertisements have been found in the *Daily News*, 29 November 1890, 27 December 1890, 3 January 1891, and 22 October 1891.

8   "Stamford Street and the High Pavement Chapel," *High Pavement Chapel & Christ Church Chronicle*, January 1914. pp. 18-19. From Rev. George Eyre Evans' collection of press cuttings, HMC Library.

9   Frederick Summers, "The Origin and Progress of Our Domestic Missions", *The Christian Life*, 10 May 1913, pp.278-280.

10   Blackfriars Mission was amalgamated with the Stamford Street Chapel in 1880 when a number of organisations were brought together. See W. A. P. Facer, *William Jellie and the Development of the Auckland Unitarian Church*, p. 42. The

Notes

Mission was located at 33 New Cut and had a resident Warden, James Westwood Tosh. *Post Office London Directory, Part 6, London* (1895), pp. 2710, 2726.

11 Michael Slater, "Dickens, Charles John Huffam (1812-1870)", ODNB. Dickens was later to join the Unitarians in reaction to sectarian fighting over public education. Wesley Hromatko, "Charles Dickens", DUUB. Dickens associated with Unitarians for the remainder of his life. Although it is often claimed that he later adopted Broad Church Anglicanism, John P. Frazee, "Dickens and Unitarianism", *Dickens Studies Annual* (1989), pp. 119-143, has shown that he retained his Unitarian beliefs throughout his life.

12 V. D. Davis, *The Domestic Mission Society Record of a Hundred Years 1835-1935* (1935), p. 17.

13 *Post Office London Directory, Part 6, London* (1895), p. 2720. The Blackfriars Mission premises at New Cut closed at the end of William Jellie's ministry and located at the Stamford Street Chapel.

14 *Pall Mall Gazette*, 29 October 1892.

15 *The Times*, 23 November 1895, p. 9; 26 November 1895, p. 7; 28 November 1895, p. 7; 3 December 1895, p. 3.

16 *The Times*, 15 August 1896, p. 4.

17 *Daily News*, 11 March 1893.

18 *The Times*, 19 May 1894.

19 "Lord Carlisle at all events in the eighties of the last century, held Unitarian opinions. There used to be daily morning service in the chapel at Castle Howard with Dr Martineau's hymn book ... He was prominent in Unitarian conferences and gatherings." Charles Roberts, *The Radical Countess* (1962), pp.132-133.

20 [Kenneth Thomas], "The Rev. William Jellie 1865-1963", Auckland Unitarian Church *News & Views*, May 1963. The obituary was unsigned, but the June 1963 issue of *News & Views* identified Ken Thomas as the author.

Thomas incorrectly stated in Jellie's obituary that "In Scotland as a young man he was a friend of that great social reformer, the Countess of Carlyle." Through incorrect spelling, Thomas identified the wrong family, suggesting that Jellie was acquainted with the wife of the well-known writer Thomas Carlyle (1795-1881). Thomas Carlyle's wife, Jane Welsh Carlyle, died in 1866, and could not have met Jellie.

21 Edward M. Moore, "William Poel", *Shakespeare Quarterly* (1972), p. 24.

22 [Thomas], "The Rev. William Jellie 1865-1963".

23   *The Belfast News-Letter*, 11 August 1894.

24   W. Copeland Bowie, letter to H. McCready, 5 October 1899, confirming the appointment of Jellie to Auckland.

25   Brooke Herford, letter to William Jellie, 18 March 1896.

26   Chapel accounts show Jellie being paid £35 at the end of each quarter for ministerial services. The first payment was on 30 September 1896. Thus his annual salary was £140. His last payment for ministerial services was made on 12 November 1899. Suffolk Record Office FK4/1/3/2 Church Accounts 1891-1928.

27   *The Ipswich Journal*, 1 August 1896.

28   *The Ipswich Journal*, 1 July 1898.

29   *The Ipswich Journal*, 24 June 1898.

30   *The Ipswich Journal*, 24 February 1900.

31   Sydney Herbert Mellone, *Liberty and Religion: The First Century of the British & Foreign Unitarian Association* (1925), p.165. Brooke had been Anglican and for a time was Chaplain to the Queen.

32   *The Ipswich Journal*, 4 February 1898.

33   *East Anglian Daily Times*, 8 November 1899.

Chapter 5: In New Zealand: Auckland

1   John Bradshaw, *New Zealand As It Is* (1883), p. 309. This view may have been imperfect so far as the Crown Colony period was concerned, when the Governor could and did act capriciously in penalizing views on religion that he disliked. See Wayne Facer, "The Governor, Voltaire and the Nelson Magistrate," *The Open Society* (2007), pp. 15-17. Furthermore, it is arguable that, after the establishment of the Crown Colony on 21 May 1840, Unitarians in New Zealand may have been subject to the common law penalties for antitrinitarianism. "When New Zealand came under British sovereignty in 1840, it acquired, as a colony of settlement, the law of England — that is, the common law, together with those statutes applicable to the circumstances of the colony at the time." A. H. McLintock (ed.), *An Encyclopaedia of New Zealand* (1966), vol. 2, p. 291.

Unitarians remained subject to legal penalties until the passing of the Dissenters' Chapels Act on 19 July 1844, which, in order to allow Unitarians to hold property in their Chapels on the same basis as other dissenters, had to negate part of the Act of Toleration to remove the crime of denial of the Trinity. "Such denial nevertheless remained a criminal offence under the common law. As a consequence, the Unitarians lost control of Wolverhampton Chapel and Lady Hewley's Charities,

Notes

which were given over to orthodox Dissenters." Frank Schulman, *"Blasphemous and Wicked": The Unitarian Struggle for Equality 1813-1844* (1997), p. 1.

The Lady Hewley's Charities case was reported in the *New Zealander*, 12 July 1849, p. 3; the litigation went on for 18 years. Fifty years on the ramifications were still being felt in New Zealand: when the Dunedin Presbytery debated the issue of union with the northern church in 1897, one objection was that the proposed change to doctrine could mean that "Unitarianism might become the creed of the Presbyterian Church" with the resultant "risk to which they were exposing their property" because of such a departure from their constitution. *Otago Witness*, 13 May 1897, p. 11.

2   Erik Olssen, "Social Class in Nineteenth Century New Zealand," in David Pitt (ed.), *Social Class in New Zealand* (1977), pp. 25, 34.

3   Mr Newman, Member of the House of Representatives for Manawatu, introduced the Hereditary Titles Prevention Bill in 1911, which would have prevented any title or honour held by a New Zealand resident from being an incorporeal hereditament. The Bill lapsed. *New Zealand Parliamentary Debates*, Fourth Session, Seventeenth Parliament, July 22 to August 25, 1911, pp. 7, 681.

4   "Notes from New Zealand: The Passing of a Pioneer," *The Inquirer*, 25 May 1963, p. 6. This obituary of William Jellie is based on that written by Kenneth Thomas in the Auckland Unitarian Church *News & Views*, May 1963. Kenneth Thomas (1903-1978) was a lay leader of the Auckland Unitarian Church between 1939 and 1948 and knew Jellie well.

5   Sidney Webb mentioned Philip Wicksteed as one of the Christian ministers who "wrote approvingly on Socialism." Sidney Webb, *Socialism in England* (1890), p. 70.

6   The favourable perception of New Zealand's "socialist experiments" should not be underestimated. Even a generation later they were the focus of attention when John Mulgan (1911-1945) lectured a WEA class at Kidlington, near Oxford, on "Social Legislation in New Zealand." Mulgan wrote to Marguerita and Alan Mulgan, 26 February 1938: "They wanted to know about pensions, unemployment rates etc.— the most interesting things to them. Given those and they are much better here [in New Zealand] they want to know how they can get there."

7   Keith Sinclair, "Reeves, William Pember 1857-1932", NZDB. William Pember Reeves had intended to study law in England, but a breakdown in his health forced his return home to Christchurch. He qualified as a barrister and solicitor but soon gave it up for politics, having adopted the radical view of society expounded by the English Fabians. Initially appointed Minister of Education and Minister of Justice in the Ballance cabinet, in 1893 he was appointed Minister of Labour, the first in the British Empire.

Notes

8   Tim McIvor, "Ballance, John 1839-1893", DNZB; Timothy McIvor, *The Rainmaker: A Biography of John Ballance, Journalist and Politician 1839-1893* (1989), pp. 115-117. Born in County Antrim, Northern Ireland, John Ballance came to New Zealand with his first wife Fanny (née Taylor) in 1863. He gained prominence as a newspaper publisher in Wanganui before entering politics in 1875. He was Minister of Education and Colonial Treasurer in Sir George Grey's ministry, and Minister of Lands, Native Affairs and Defence in the Stout-Vogel ministry. During his Premiership he not only supported labour reforms but also introduced moves to enfranchise women, a cause promoted by his second wife Ellen. Ballance had the misfortune to be the first New Zealand premier to die in office. Like his friend Robert Stout, Ballance was a prominent freethinker. He published the *Freethought Review*, which became the successor throughout the Colony to Stout's *Echo*.

9   For income data see G. R. Hawke, *The Making of New Zealand: An Economic History* (1985), pp. 76-79. During this period "unemployment largely took the form of chronic structural underemployment that was widespread and was particularly marked in the rural economy and associated primary industries. It was also found in particular urban industries such as the building trade." John E. Martin, "Unemployment, Government and the Labour Market in New Zealand, 1860-1890", *New Zealand Journal of History* (1995), pp. 170-196.

10 *Sweating Commission: Report of the Royal Commission* (1890). The commission was set up following publicity given to the Rev. Rutherford Waddell's (1850-1932) sermon on the "sin of cheapness" concerning exploitation of Dunedin workers. Waddell had been attracted to Unitarianism when a theology student in Belfast: "The high character and literary quality of great Unitarian leaders made a strong appeal to him," but he felt they had "an inadequate conception of Christ." J. Collie (ed.) *Rutherford Waddell Memoir and Addresses* (1932), pp. 35-36; Ian Breward, "Waddell, Rutherford", DNZB.

11 William Pember Reeves, *The Long White Cloud Ao Tea Roa*, 4th ed., (1898), p. 317.

12 K. R. Howe, "Tregear, Edward Robert 1846-1931", DNZB. Edward Robert Tregear was a surveyor working in the public service, with broad humanitarian and socialist sympathies. He had become friendly with Ballance, Stout and Reeves and published in the *Freethought Review*. He was interested in Maori origins and worked on a Maori dictionary. As secretary of the Department of Labour he helped Reeves plan and draft legislation, and ensured that his Department faithfully administered it. Tregear achieved an international reputation for publicizing New Zealand's labour reforms. After Reeves went to Britain in 1896 Tregear was influential in getting Prime Minister Richard Seddon to introduce the Old Age Pension Bill just before the 1896 election. It was passed in 1898.

Notes

Tregear "was keen to employ a woman inspector of factories: Grace Neill held the position from 1893." K. R. Howe, *Singer in a Songless Land: A Life of Edward Tregear 1846-1931* (1991), p. 90. Elizabeth Grace Neill (1846-1926) a Scots-born trained nurse, transferred from the Department of Labour in 1895 to join Dr Duncan MacGregor as Deputy Director at the Department of Hospitals, Asylums and Charitable Institutions. She was influential in achieving a world first, the registration of nurses, in 1901. Grace Neill was a lifelong Unitarian attending the Wellington Unitarian Free Church. At her request Mr J. Rushden Salt, lay minister, conducted her funeral service. Margaret Tennant, "Neill, Elizabeth Grace 1846-1926", DNZB; *The Inquirer*, 22 January 1927, p. 60.

[13] A. H. McLintock and G. A. Wood, *The Upper House in Colonial New Zealand* (1987), pp. 120-121.

[14] W. B. Sutch, *Poverty and Progress in New Zealand*, rev. ed. (1961), pp. 123-124. It was not until 1914 with the passing of the Legislative Council Act that there was provision for an elected Upper House, a provision that was never used. Earlier, Reeves had supported Earl Grey's proposal to elect members to the Legislative Council from the Provincial Councils, which would have made abolition of the Provinces difficult. A. H. McLintock, *Crown Colony Government in New Zealand* (1958), pp. 357-358.

[15] J. Estlin Carpenter, letter to William Jellie, 23 December 1899.

[16] *Illustrated London News*, 18 March 1893. Pat Moloney, "State Socialism and William Pember Reeves: A Reassessment" in Pat Moloney and Kerry Taylor (eds.), *On the Left: Essays on Socialism in New Zealand* (2002), p. 50. Onslow also quoted from a Parliamentary speech by Sir Robert Stout saying that as New Zealand was not encumbered by privilege or prejudice it was free to undertake various social experiments. Peter J. Coleman, "The Spirit of New Zealand Liberalism in the Nineteenth Century", *Journal of Modern History* (1958), pp. 227-235. Stout had already been active in describing these reforms in some detail; see Robert Stout, "State Experiments in New Zealand", *Journal of the Royal Statistical Society* (1892), pp. 388-414.

[17] Ruth Fry, "Reeves, Magdalene Stuart 1865-1953", DNZB. Maud Reeves attended Canterbury University College, where she led a women's movement dedicated to women's suffrage. In 1890 she was president of the women's branch of the Canterbury Liberal Association. In England she joined the Fabian Society and was elected to the executive in 1907. She gained fame for an investigation she organised into the effect of poverty among mothers and children living in Lambeth. In 1917 she was director of women's services at the Ministry of Food.

Notes

[18] Keith Sinclair, *William Pember Reeves: New Zealand Fabian* (1965), pp. 248-249.

[19] William Pember Reeves, *The State and its Functions in New Zealand*, Fabian Tract No. 74 (1896). Another Fabian tract compared the systems in England, New Zealand and Australia, and concluded that despite the success in New Zealand "it is doubtful whether it is applicable to this country" (i.e. England). *State Arbitration and the Living Wage*, Fabian Tract No. 83, p. 13.

[20] Margaret McClure, *A Civilised Community: A History of Social Security in New Zealand 1898-1998* (1998), p. 23. The English popular press reported how "happy old people" went to New Zealand Post Offices on pension day. The pension was far from universal, only applying to the qualifying "deserving poor", and excluding people of Asian descent. The members of Parliament for Christchurch, G. W. Russell and W. W. Collins, supported universal coverage, which Richard Seddon had opposed. David Hamer, *The New Zealand Liberals: The Years of Power, 1891-1912* (1988), pp. 146-148.

[21] William Jellie, *Our Aims* and *The Principles and Doctrines of Unitarians* (1900), p. 3.

[22] Jellie, *Our Aims* and *The Principles and Doctrines of Unitarians*, p. 5.

[23] Jellie, *Our Aims* and *The Principles and Doctrines of Unitarians*, pp. 5-6.

[24] Jellie, *Our Aims* and *The Principles and Doctrines of Unitarians*, p. 8.

[25] Jellie, *Our Aims* and *the Principles and Doctrines of Unitarians*, pp. 8-9. Jellie argued that science, art and "all other branches of human endeavour" have won themselves a free position, which was a "prime necessity of human progress."

[26] Jellie, *Our Aims* and *The Principles and Doctrines of Unitarians*, p. 10.

[27] Jellie, *Our Aims* and *The Principles and Doctrines of Unitarians*, p. 11. Beliefs about Christ was a topic Jellie would return to. On 21 September 1902 he claimed that Christ was "the highest and noblest specimen of mankind" but denied that he was God, which drew a published response critiquing his heterodox opinions. Chas. Watt, *The Deity of Christ: A Review of a Lecture by the Rev. W. Jellie, B.A. (Unitarian Minister)* (c. 1902), p. 4.

[28] AUCMB, minutes of committee meeting, 4 April 1900. A more detailed account of the development of the church during Jellie's early years is found in Wayne Facer, *William Jellie and the Development of the Auckland Unitarian Church* (2009).

[29] Charles and Annie Newland (née Ockenden, 1868-1942) moved into 55 Ranfurly Road, Epsom, in April 1901. "There is even documentation of Newland House in Ranfurly Road serving as a gathering [place] for Unitarians." Graham

Notes

W.A. Bush (ed.), *The History of Epsom* (2006), p. 167. I am grateful to Barbara Holt for drawing this reference to my attention. An obituary for Charles Newland appeared in *The Inquirer*, 7 December 1946, p. 366.

30 AUCMB, minutes of a special meeting of the congregation 29 September 1901.

31 T. H. White file, University of Auckland School of Architecture Library.

32 Frank Castle claims in *Annals of the Auckland Unitarian Church* (1981), p. 7, that White's design was "based upon one he had constructed in Johannesburg, S.A." This claim is repeated in John Maindonald, *A Radical Religious Heritage*, rev. ed. (1993), p. 16. These claims are wrong. There is no evidence that Thomas White was ever in South Africa, and until the Johannesburg church started in 1911 there was only one Unitarian church, the Free Protestant congregation founded at Cape Town in 1867. Eric Heller-Wagner, *The Unitarians of South Africa: A Socio-Historical Study* (1995), pp. 127-166.

33 Hugh Clyde McCready was secretary and treasurer of the committee formed in 1898. He appears to have been a mainstay in the congregation, especially after the chairman Edward Russell Shawcross (1838-1899) and his wife Annie (1848-1927) went to farm at Cambridge, where Edward died in 1899. McCready came from Larne, County Antrim, in Northern Ireland. For many years he lived with his family in Whangarei where he was in business as a tailor. By 1896 they had moved to Auckland. When he was involved with the Auckland Unitarians he had a prosperous business as a master tailor at 398 Queen Street, Auckland. Unfortunately, though he had enthusiasm for the cause, he lacked tact. It appears he may have resigned from the committee because he was unable to work harmoniously with his colleagues. He retired in 1918. In 1932 he moved to Hamilton, where one of his sons lived, and died there a year later. There is a short obituary in *The New Zealand Herald and Daily Southern Cross*, 29 July 1933.

34 Macky Avenue in Devonport was named after Joseph Macky in 1926; see Auckland City Libraries, *North Shore Street Names*.

35 Due to the Depression, Macky, Logan, Caldwell Limited went into voluntary liquidation in 1933. By then Thomas Hugh Macky (1881-1965) was Managing Director following his father's death. Six separate companies were formed from sections of the old firm's businesses, including the Cambridge Clothing Company organised by Thomas Macky as Managing Director, which continues to this day.

36 The Symonds Street Cemetery tombstone records: "In loving memory of Isabella Campbell, the affectionate wife of J. C. Macky, who departed this life August 7th 1887 aged 38 years, also of our little Archie taken from us July 14th 1884 aged 13 months, to be with Jesus which is far better."

Notes

[37] It is incorrectly stated in Wayne Facer, *William Jellie and the Development of the Auckland Unitarian Church* (2009), p. 53, that all of Joseph's children were from the first marriage. This overlooked the children from his second marriage. The emotional bond between Mary and the children is clearly recorded in the Darlimurla Letters. See Neil Lloyd Macky, "The Macky Family in New Zealand" (1969), p. 19.

[38] Castle, *Annals of the Auckland Unitarian Church*, p. 12.

[39] Valerie Adams, Librarian, Presbyterian Historical Society of Ireland, Belfast, Northern Ireland, personal communication, 22 November 2010.

[40] Emmett A. Greenwalt, *The Point Loma Community in California 1897-1942: A Theosophical Experiment*, rev. ed. (1978), p. 33. Rev. Neill became Dean of the College of Divinity at Point Loma and a director of the Raja Yoga Academy, established by the Theosophists near San Diego, California, where he died on 22 June 1918. *Evening Post*, 2 August 1918, p. 6. The Rev. W. F. Kennedy, founder of the Dunedin Unitarian Church, wrote to Tom Macky on 21 August 1926, saying that the widow, Mrs Lillie Neill, was living in San Diego in difficult circumstances, that he had tried to help sort out her affairs, but "she would think a lot of even a five pound note to help her along." W. F. Kennedy, letter to Tom Macky, 21 August 1926.

[41] "The Latest Heresy Hunt", *The Observer*, 14 October 1893, p. 2.

[42] "Death to the Heretic", *The Observer*, 24 February 1894, p. 2. Following Rev. Neill's suspension there was a public meeting of support at which Joseph Macky gave an address which was later presented to Rev Neill signed by 1335 sympathizers, 700 from Thames and the rest Auckland city. *Hawke's Bay Herald*, 17 February 1894.

[43] Mary Macky, letters to Tom Macky, Easter Monday 1901; 1 September 1901; and 26 September 1901.

[44] For a more detailed account of these events see Facer, *William Jellie and the Development of the Auckland Unitarian Church*, pp. 53-63.

[45] Caroline Bingham, *History of Royal Holloway College 1886-1986* (1987), p. 89.

[46] Mary Macky, letter to Tom Macky, 14 December 1902. Joseph Macky held advanced views for a "captain of industry"; Neil Macky reports that "he was a strong believer in Unionism for workers in factories" and "he was a believer in taxation on unimproved values and a Liberal in his political views." Neil Macky, "The Macky Family in New Zealand" (1969), p. 20.

[47] "Strong's earnest and strenuous advocacy of unpopular economic and social views was a factor in the decline of the Australian Church." C. R. Badger, "Strong,

Notes

Charles (1844-1942)", ADB. In comparing the extent of each man's involvement in social action, Mary Macky overlooks the fact that William Jellie devoted considerable effort in this sphere while at Stamford Street, which she recalled in another letter to Tom: "Mr Jellie came over and had dinner with us and stayed a long time. He is very interesting and well read. He is doubly interesting to me now for he knows Stamford Street well, worked 6 years there in connection with the Unitarian Church ... He feels as you do about the children on the streets. He says he used to have a happy evening for them once a week and have 200 children regularly." Mary Macky, letter to Tom Macky, Easter Monday 1901.

48 Facer, *William Jellie and the Development of the Auckland Unitarian Church*, p. 59.

49 Joseph Macky, letter to Tom and Ella Macky, 24 May 1903.

50 AUCMB, minutes of committee meeting 5 August 1903. "That a letter of approval [of Mr Macky's proposal and specifications for the new organ] and thanks be sent to Mr Macky in connection forthwith. The Treasurer reported that the loan for the organ would be available from the same source as soon as the Church debt was extinguished."

51 Organ Historical Trust of Australia, *Indigenous and Exotic: Some Organs of the Upper North Island, New Zealand* (2006).

52 Auckland Unitarian Church, *Dedication of Organ and Opening Recital*, 2 April 1904. The organist at the opening recital was Mr T. E. Midgley, who played at the Anglican Church of All Saints. The next week it was Arthur Towsey from St Matthew's Church, and the week after that Mr W. T. Sharp, previously organist at the Napier Cathedral.

53 AUCMB, minutes of committee meeting 13 January 1904. "Mr C. J. Macky reported that he had entered into a bond with the Trustees in connection with the installation of the organ for £400 and further that the arrangements in progress were satisfactory." (In March 2015, £400 was equivalent to about £32,000 or $60,000). The report of the dedication in the *Auckland Star*, 4 April 1904, states that the organ was presented to the Unitarian Church by Joseph Macky. His son Jack Macky became seriously ill with typhoid in February 1903 and did not recover until May. Writing to Tom and Ella, Joseph Macky said: " I would like the organ, which is to be put in the church, to be regarded as a thanksgiving offering and a commemoration of Jack having been spared to us all." Joseph Macky, letter to Tom and Ella Macky, 24 May 1903.

54 Auckland Unitarian Church *Calendar*, May 1904.

55 Castle, *Annals of the Auckland Unitarian Church*, p. 18.

Notes

⁵⁶ Wayne Facer, "From Manchester to Auckland: Jessie Heywood and the Auckland Unitarian Church", *TUHS* (2014), pp. 253-258.

⁵⁷ Herbert Otto Roth, "Fowlds, Sir George", *Encyclopedia of New Zealand*. George Fowlds was in the left wing of the Liberal Party and was a disciple of Henry George, the single tax proponent. In 1906 he became Minister of Education and Minister of Public Health, but resigned in 1911 to promote his own radical views. The following year he joined the United Labour Party. Subsequently his main activities were in education, as a member of the Senate of the University of New Zealand and chairman of Auckland University College and Massey Agricultural College. He also had a strong interest in the Workers Educational Association.

⁵⁸ David Hamer, "Stout, Robert", DNZB. Robert Stout immigrated to New Zealand, arriving in Dunedin in 1864. He qualified as a teacher, surveyor, and lawyer. He was elected to the House of Representatives in 1875 and within a few years he held cabinet rank. From 1884 to 1887 he was premier. He was Chief Justice 1899-1926 and appointed to the Judicial Committee of the Privy Council in 1921. Both he and his wife Anna Logan Stout (1858-1931) favoured abolition of the liquor traffic. He was a vigorous proponent of secular education and had a strong interest in Herbert Spencer's philosophy. An active rationalist and Unitarian, he was President of the Wellington Unitarian Free Church at the time of his death. Wayne Facer, "Sir Robert Stout", DUUB.

⁵⁹ On 1 March 1901 there is an entry for Sir Robert Stout in Jellie's Diary, and on 7 March an entry that he made calls on both George Fowlds and Robert Stout.

⁶⁰ The Dunedin Freethought Association included theists, agnostics, Unitarians, pantheists and spiritualists, which Stout found acceptable because "we have recognised that the deeper questions of life can never be solved by all men alike; and we have united to discuss them freed from creeds and to teach our children their duties to themselves and their fellows." Jim Dakin, "New Zealand's Freethought Heritage Chapter 3: The rise and decline of Freethought in Dunedin, 1880-90", *New Zealand Rationalist & Humanist* (2001), pp. 8-12.

⁶¹ In 1908 George Fowlds donated the loom used by his father, Matthew Fowlds (1806-1907), to the Auckland War Memorial Museum. The loom is well over 200 years old. There is a painting in the Auckland Art Gallery of Matthew Fowlds weaving blankets on it in his 100th year. I am grateful to Finn McCahon-Jones, Associate Curator Arts & Design, Auckland War Memorial Museum, for this information.

⁶² D. A. Hamer, *The Law and the Prophet: A Political Biography of Sir Robert Stout (1844-1930)* (1960), pp. 341-366. Robert Stout's rationale for the social

Notes

legislation was: "The great organisation of the State is being used to give an equal chance to all." Sir Robert Stout and J. Logan Stout, *New Zealand* (1911), p. 177.

63   J. D. Salmond, *New Zealand Labour's Pioneering Days: The History of the Labour Movement in N.Z. from 1840 to 1894* (1950), p. 63. The first president appears to have been Rev. Waddell, although David Pinkerton (1836-1906), a trade union friend of Sir Robert's from the Dunedin Freethought Association, is also claimed for this position, which possibly reflects a timing difference. Pinkerton was certainly on the executive. See Erik Olssen, "Pinkerton, David", DNZB.

64   Facer, *William Jellie and the Development of the Auckland Unitarian Church*, p. 10. The friendship spanned 40 years and it is most likely that John Gammell introduced Stout to Unitarians in Wellington. See Wayne Facer, "John Gammell", DUUB.

65   From the beginning of his involvement with William Jellie, Sir Robert Stout also provided support to the Unitarian cause in Auckland. The Auckland Unitarian Church *Calendar* for December 1901 records his donation of one guinea toward the building fund. While in Wellington Joseph Macky met with Stout to discuss the proposed visit of Rev. Richard Acland Armstrong (1843-1905) and Stout agreed to take part in promoting and welcoming the visitor. AUCMB minutes of committee meeting 1 July 1903.

Rev. Armstrong was the brother-in-law of Philip Wicksteed, and in 1902-1903 was President of the B&FUA. For many years he had been minister at the Hope Street Unitarian Church in Liverpool. His health began failing in 1903, so his trip to New Zealand was put off. "In Memoriam Richard Acland Armstrong", *The Inquirer*, 14 January 1905, pp. 27-30.

66   Robert Stout's views on secular education are well known. William Jellie's position will be the subject of later discussion. Less well known are the views of George Fowlds, who "supports the colony's present system of free, secular, and compulsory education". *Cyclopedia of New Zealand* [Auckland Provincial District] Auckland City and Suburban Members of the House of Representatives. He became president of the Auckland branch of the National Schools Defence League when it was formed in 1913. Ian Breward, *Godless Schools?* (1967), p. 60.

67   William Jellie, *The Modern Genesis* (1909), p. 3. This booklet contains five sermons on this theme given over the preceding year.

68   J. Arthur Thomson, *The Bible of Nature* (1908). Sir John Thomson, as he became, was later Regius Professor of Natural History at Aberdeen University. He promoted Darwin's concept of evolution.

69   Jellie, *The Modern Genesis*, pp. 13, 14, 19.

70   Jellie, *The Modern Genesis*, p. 26.

71 Jellie, *The Modern Genesis*, pp. 30, 33. I doubt if William Jellie would have imagined that the ideas he was dismissing as untenable in 1908 would still have currency in the twenty-first century.

72 Jellie, *The Modern Genesis*, pp. 39, 43, 44.

73 Jellie, *The Modern Genesis*, p. 45.

74 Copies of William Jellie's sermons I have located are: "Our Aims" and "The Principles and Doctrines of Unitarians", 1900; "The Methods of Biblical Criticism", 3 July 1904; "The Modern Genesis" (five sermons), 1908; "Why There Are Not More Unitarians", 1908; "Responsibility of Parenthood", 1908; "Thanksgiving Service V. J. Day", 1945; and "The Power of Personality", n.d.

75 [Kenneth Thomas], "The Rev. William Jellie 1965-1963", Auckland Unitarian Church *News & Views*, May 1963. The June 1963 issue of *News & Views* identifies Thomas as the author.

76 Joseph Macky, letter to Tom Macky, 24 April 1902. The date is six years earlier, but it is the same theme which has been reworked in 1908 with the use of current reference material. Joseph Macky makes an important observation about working men attending the evening service.

77 "A Journal Containing a trustworthy though imperfect Account of the Rambles of the Auckland Unitarian Church Young People's Club and the Adventures which befell its members by the way. By a lady member." The cover of the notebook states: "C. M. Guy, Haslett Street, Eden Terrace." I am grateful to Dr Laurie Guy for lending me this family document.

Charlotte Mary (Lottie) Guy was born in Yorkshire in 1875. Her mother died in 1884. In 1886 she travelled to New Zealand with her father, younger sister and brother. When the family moved to Auckland in 1895 Lottie began attending the Auckland Adult School run by the Society of Friends. Her fiancé Harry Jackson died in an accident in 1899 and she never married. She joined the Auckland Unitarian Church and was active in the choir, sewing guild, tennis club and Sunday School and the young people's camps at Waiheke Island, where the children called her "Mother Guy". Margaret Howie and Jean Leyland, *A Guy Family History from Leeds to 'Lealands'* (2000), pp. 63-70.

78 "February 5th-14th 1910. Camp Pleasant Waiheke." The handwriting looks like that of Lottie Guy. I am grateful to Dr Laurie Guy for lending me this document.

79 Hilary Theodore Jellie (1909-1997) was the first of Ella and William's children. When the family lived at Southport, Lancashire, Hilary attended the Terra Nova School from 1917-1921. Upon their return to New Zealand he boarded at Waitaki Boys High School, where he was a contemporary of James Bertram and Ian Milner

Notes

and in 1927 won a University Scholarship. At Auckland University College he graduated B.A. in Pure Mathematics in 1933 and B.Com. in Accounting in 1935. In his final university year Hilary rowed in the Auckland University eights when it was the champion team winning the Hebberly Shield. The Auckland Rowing Club awards the Hilary Jellie Memorial Shield annually to the best crew.

When Hilary married Phyllis Moira Roe (1905-1989) on 27 March 1937 his father officiated. They had two daughters, Margot and Valerie. After joining Cambridge Clothing as company secretary in 1935 he became a Director in 1959 and remained on the Board until his death. He was Treasurer of the Organising Committee of the 1950 British Empire Games held in Auckland, for which he was awarded the Alwyn Moon Memorial Trophy by the Auckland Amateur Sports Association. For many years he was honorary auditor of the Auckland Unitarian Church.

80   A. A. Shawcross, letter to William Jellie, August 1907.

81   W. Copeland Bowie, letter to William Jellie, 20 November 1907.

82   W. Tudor Jones, letters to William Jellie, 12 and 14 November 1907.

83   W. Copeland Bowie, letter to William Jellie, 16 December 1908.

84   William Jellie, *Report to the British and Foreign Unitarian Association for the Colonial Conference, 1910*. This report was in response to a notice dated 11 February 1910, so the information contained would be for the first ten years, 1900 to 1909. *Eighty-fifth Annual Report of the B&FUA, 1910*, pp. 19-20, refers to Jellie's report, but not in much detail. It also quotes from a letter sent by Joseph Macky, then chairman of the Church committee, pointing to the need for a South Island church and another official visit. The following year the Rev. William and Mrs Wooding visited Australian churches and Auckland, Wellington and Timaru. *Eighty-sixth Annual Report of the B&FUA, 1911*, p. 25.

85   William Jellie had a great love of Shakespeare, leading the Church Shakespeare Society, using Shakespeare in sermons, joining the Auckland Shakespeare Society and acting in public performances. Wayne Facer, *William Jellie and the Development of the Auckland Unitarian Church*, pp. 61-62.

86   William Jellie, *Report to the British and Foreign Unitarian Association for the Colonial Conference, 1910*.

87   R. A. S., "Some Sermons Worth While", *The Triad*, 1 September 1909, pp. 30-31. For an appreciation of the place of *The Triad* and the life of its founder in New Zealand social history, see Joanna Woods, *Facing the Music: Charles Baeyertz and The Triad* (2008).

88   James Chapple, letter to William Jellie, 29 September 1909.

⁸⁹ Geoff Chapple, "Chapple, James Henry George", DNZB, updated 1 September 2010.

Chapter 6: In New Zealand: Wellington

¹ *The Star*, 6 August 1888, p. 4. The sermon was widely reported in the newspapers around the Colony. The title was a clear reference to "The Bitter Cry of Outcast London", published by the Congregational Union in 1883, which is mentioned in Chapter 3.

² G. H. Scholefield (ed.), *Dictionary of New Zealand Biography* (1940), vol.1, p. 234.

³ Rev. Samuel Edger married Louisa Harwood (d. 1880) in 1846 and they had two sons and four daughters. He moved to Auckland, where he established a non-denominational church and was an advocate of liberal causes and social reform. Rev. Edger was a strong supporter of "Polly Plum", Mary Ann Colclough (1836-1885), who championed women's rights. Peter J. Lineham, "Edger, Samuel", DNZB, updated 1 September 2010. Judy Malone, "Colclough, Mary Ann", DNZB, updated 1 September 2010.

⁴ According to the 1893 Electoral Roll, Charles Bradbury shared a house with William and Kate Evans at 69 Brougham Street, Mount Victoria, Wellington.

⁵ *Congregational Yearbook for 1916*, pp. 7-8. Extract supplied by Patricia Hurry, Librarian and Research Secretary, Congregational History Society, personal communication 28 October 2009. "Several young ministers in the neighbourhood ... like himself ... united they moved the district, preaching in mills and coal pits and advocating temperance and social reform."

⁶ James O'Bryen Dolt Richard Hoare attended Christ's College, Cambridge University, where he graduated B.A. in 1859 and M.A. in 1864. He entered the Church of England. In 1865 he married Frances Eleanor Henderson (d. 1911) and later that year they arrived in New Zealand. He was appointed vicar at St John's Church, Christchurch. In 1871 the family returned to England and he was appointed vicar of Weston in Hampshire. For a year in 1880 he was secretary of the Church of England Temperance Society, after which he did not work for the next two years, living off investment income.

Returning to New Zealand in 1883, he accepted a number of Anglican appointments until 1894, when he left to establish Our Father's Church. For two years before leaving he gave addresses about Our Father's Church movement, which had been established in London by the Unitarian minister John Page Hopps (1834-1911). Hopps was something of a radical in Unitarian circles, an advocate of secular

Notes

education; he once chaired a public meeting in Leicester for Charles Bradlaugh, the prominent secularist. The idea behind Our Father's Church was that men and women of all races, bound by no creed and controlled by no organisation, should join together in religious worship. Our Father's Church met in the morning at 151 Gloucester Street and in the evening at the Art Gallery in Durban Street. By 1902 it had grown to 300 members. The church had two branches: the Metaphysical Club for those interested in mental science and the School of Brotherhood for those interested in studying sociology.

In 1909 O'Bryen Hoare joined the New Zealand Rationalist Association, then centred in Christchurch under the leadership of W. W. Collins. By 1911 he was elected vice-president and occupied the public platform whenever Collins was absent from Christchurch. Jim Dakin, "New Zealand's Freethought Heritage, Chapter 6: Freethought in Canterbury with W. W. Collins", *The Open Society* (2002), pp. 8-14. "Memorial Notice: The Rev. John Page Hopps", *The Inquirer*, 15 April 1911, pp. 235-237. "Mr James O'Bryen Dolt Richard Hoare", *Cyclopedia of New Zealand* (1903).

Hugh Mostyn Trevor (1882-1927), the son of Labour Church founder John Trevor, settled in New Zealand in 1906 and in 1910 married Rev. O'Bryen Hoare's daughter Helen Hoare (1878-1954). He owned a cheese factory in Ohakune. Hugh Trevor followed Harry Atkinson into the Canterbury Fabian Society, becoming a member in 1909; the membership roll records him as "Cheese Factory Owner Ohakune."

7   *The Star*, 18 April 1891, p. 1.

8   *The Star*, 21 January 1891, p. 4; 27 July 1891, p. 3.

9   *The Star*, 21 October 1892, p. 4; 10 June 1892, p. 2.

10   *The Star*, 6 March 1893, p. 3. Presentations were made by Bradbury's admirers, "outside as well as within the pale of the church", recognizing the public esteem in which he was held. A congregational farewell of about 200 people gave him a purse of sovereigns and collection of books. *The Star*, 21 March 1893, p. 3; 29 April 1893, p. 2.

11   *The Star*, 10 November 1893, p. 1. There is very little election press coverage of Rev. Bradbury, supporting the view he returned late in the year to take part. With six clergymen standing in this election, one commenter contended there was now a Clerical Party based on female suffrage, prohibition and the Bible in schools. *The Star*, 25 November 1893, p. 7.

12   Christopher William Richmond was the eldest son of Christopher (1785-1832) and Maria "Lely" Richmond (née Wilson, 1791-1872). Both parents were Unitarian; his father was elected third president of the B&FUA in 1828. When

Notes

William, as the family called him, was sent to the Unitarian school Hove House, he formed a lifelong friendship with the headmaster Richard Holt Hutton, later editor of the *Spectator*. He followed his father into law in 1847. In 1852 he married Emily Elizabeth Atkinson (1829-1906) and they had five daughters and two sons. While in England William Richmond became interested in Christian Socialism, reading and listening to F. D. Maurice. Two brothers, James Crowe and Henry Robert Richmond, had joined a relative, John Hursthouse, in New Plymouth, and William and Emily followed in 1853. When their sister Jane Maria (1824-1914) married Arthur Samuel Atkinson (1833-1902) in 1854, the connection between the two families was cemented.

Elected to represent New Plymouth in Parliament in 1855, William Richmond joined the ministry of Edward Stafford (1819-1901) and became colonial treasurer, colonial secretary and minister of native affairs. In 1860, during Stafford's absence for six months in England, William Richmond was acting Premier. However, politics had never been entirely to his liking. He resigned his seat and in 1862 accepted an appointment to the Supreme Court based in Dunedin. When Edward Stafford offered him the Premiership if he returned to politics in 1865 he declined. In 1873 he moved to Wellington where as senior Puisne Judge he continued to serve on the Supreme Court and the Court of Appeal until his death. His Unitarianism was influenced by Dr Martineau and he gave addresses on his religious and philosophical interests to the Nelson Institute and the New Zealand Institute. Austin Graham Bagnall, "Richmond, Christopher William", *Encyclopedia of New Zealand*, updated 23 April 2009. Keith Sinclair, "Richmond, Christopher William", DNZB, updated 1 September 2010. Edmund Bohan, "Stafford, Edward William", DNZB. Obituary, Mr Justice Richmond, *Evening Post*, 5 August 1895, p. 2.

[13] C. W. Richmond, letter to Alice Blake, 30 August 1893. Alice Richmond was the sixth child of William and Emily Richmond. In 1892 she married Mr E. J. Blake, a solicitor and Unitarian, in Somerset where she then lived.

[14] W. A. Evans, "Aims of the Forward Movement", *The Citizen* (1895), pp. 1-3.

[15] See Appendix 2: Forward Movement Literary Society Lectures. Judge Richmond was due to deliver a lecture on his favourite poet Robert Browning to the Forward Movement Literary Society the night he died on 3 August 1895.

[16] *Evening Post*, 18 March 1895. Unfortunately Rev. Bradbury's role in the Forward Movement, including his co-Presidency, is too often completely overlooked. See for example Margaret J. McArthur, *Collectivist Tracts and Altruistic Sermons: A Study of "Socialism" in Late Nineteenth Century New Zealand*, (1981), pp. 87-89, which talks about Rev. Evans as the sole founder without mention of Rev. Bradbury.

Notes

[17] Mrs Annie Hislop was Mayoress of Wellington 1905-1909. When she died, "the funeral service was impressively conducted by the Rev. Dr Tudor Jones of the Unitarian Church." *New Zealand Free Lance*, 11 September 1909, p. 15.

[18] After studying at Bedford College in London, Dolla Richmond went to the Slade School of Fine Art for two years. When she returned to New Zealand she was appointed art mistress at the Nelson College for Girls in 1883, when Kate Edger became principal. Janet Paul, "Richmond, Dorothy Kate", DNZB, updated 1 September 2010.

[19] Most of the Richmond-Atkinson supporters of the Forward Movement are identified in Frances Porter, *Born to New Zealand* (1995), p. 329.

[20] Ernest Beaglehole was appointed to the management committee of the Forward Movement at the first meeting on 27 August 1893 and became Secretary; the committee included Arthur Richmond Atkinson, his wife Lily and Maurice Richmond. (The two founders would also have been on the committee; and the Treasurer was T. Pringle. *Evening Post*, 18 March 1895.) Tim Beaglehole, *A Life of J. C. Beaglehole, New Zealand Scholar* (2006), p. 33. The Beaglehole family was to have an extensive involvement with the Wellington Unitarian Free Church (pp. 50-52).

[21] Brigid Pike, "Tasker, Marianne Allen", DNZB, updated 1 September 2010.

[22] *Evening Post*, 9 March 1896. The Workers Union passed a resolution opposing an independent labour party as they saw no reason to desert the Liberal Party "who have done so much for labour". *Hawera and Normanby Star*, 30 April 1898, p. 2.

[23] *Southland Times*, 11 February 1896, p. 2.

[24] *Evening Post* 17 June 1896, p. 5. The Clarion Club lectures were given over four weeks. The Clarion Clubs were derived from Robert Blatchford's *Clarion* newspaper. As we have seen, Blatchford supported the Labour Church and the Independent Labour Party in Britain. The newspaper's financial backer, William Ranstead (1859-1944), later immigrated to New Zealand with the intention of establishing a Clarion Colony, having persuaded about 190 men and women to come out to form a co-operative settlement. Eventually the settlement plan was abandoned. Herbert Otto Roth, "Socialist (N.Z.) Party", *Encyclopedia of New Zealand*, updated 22 April 2009.

[25] H. Roth, "The New Zealand Socialist Party", *Political Science* (1957), pp. 51-60.

[26] G. H. Scholefield (ed.), *Dictionary of New Zealand Biography* (1940), vol. 1, p. 234. William Evans was an advocate of a university, and when Victoria University College was established in 1897 he was a member of council, 1898-1921, and chairman, 1902-1903. He also served on the Wellington City Council.

Notes

27 Charles Bradbury remained at Prahran until 1905. He then had Congregational parishes at Leederville in Western Australia and Milton in Brisbane. He was president of the Congregational Union in Australia and principal of the Congregational College. He died on 30 April 1914, survived by his third wife and four sons. *Brisbane Courier*, 1 May 1914, p. 8.

28 "The move provided [Rev. Evans] greater financial security, since the role with the Forward Movement had not been salaried. Despite earlier reservations about such a ministry, he exercised considerable influence there and within the wider church. This influence, and the growth of his parish, suggests that a constituency for progressive social Christianity existed." Geoffrey Michael Troughton, *Jesus in New Zealand 1900-1940* (2007), p. 136.

29 *Evening Post*, 9 December 1893, p. 2, and 11 December 1892, p. 2, gave a summary of Atkinson's Sunday night address, saying that the object of the Labour Church was to "unite the workers in a common bond of brotherhood, with the view of realising higher objects for the well-being of the community as a whole." Both Rev. Evans and Rev. Bradbury were present, the latter having just returned from Christchurch, where he was involved in the General Election. James E. Taylor, *"To me, Socialism is not a set of dogmas but a living principle": Harry Atkinson and the Christchurch Socialist Church, 1890-1905* (2010).

30 Joseph Macky, letter to Tom Macky, 27 October 1902.

31 Joseph Macky, letter to Tom Macky, Darlimurla Sunday night [2 November 1902].

32 Christine Berry, *The New Zealand Student Christian Movement, 1896-1996: A Centennial History* (1998), pp. 9-10. Rev. Evans addressed SCM students in Wellington in 1906.

33 William Jellie visited Wellington in April 1910 following Dr Tudor Jones' departure; this was an opportune time for the committee to discuss an appointment with him. *Evening Post*, 15 April 1910, p. 8. He arrived to take up his position on 7 September 1910. *Evening Post*, 8 September 1910, p. 9.

34 William C. Stephens, letter to William Jellie, 14 February 1908. The church site was in Ingestre Street, later renamed Vivian Street, and was occupied by a "Chinese Laundryman" paying 30/- a week rent, which paid the interest on the loan and rates.

35 Margaret Richmond was educated at Newnham College, Cambridge University. She married Walter Fell, M.A., M.D., MRCS, LRCP (1855-1932), who attended Rugby School and University College, Oxford. They had two daughters who attended Victoria University College, Wellington, and Margaret Fell often

Notes

acted as chaperone at College dances. Fred de la Mare wrote her obituary, entitled "A Great Lady", in the 1933 edition of *The Spike: or, Victoria College Review*.

36 James Bennie was born in Ayrshire, Scotland and came to New Zealand as a child with his family when his father took up a position as engineer at the Brunner coal mine on the West Coast. He went to Melbourne and trained as an architect under Thomas Searell at the Working Men's College. Upon returning to New Zealand he practiced at Greymouth and then Christchurch before settling in Wellington in 1903. He did most of his work in the Wellington area and developed interests in designing cinemas and churches, undertaking work for Methodist, Anglican and Presbyterian clients as well as Unitarian. He was a follower of the British Israelites. Although he retired in 1935, the owners of the Paramount cinema asked him to carry out repairs and alterations following the 1942 Wellington earthquake. Tony Froude, *James Bennie, Wellington Architect 1873-1945* (2005).

37 An article by Dr Tudor Jones in *The Inquirer*, 11 April 1908, confirms the price of the land and says that £1500 more will be needed for the building. Reporting on the opening of the church, *The Inquirer*, 12 June 1909, says that £2450 had been collected, which would leave a shortfall of £337. But another report in *The Inquirer*, 16 April 1910, has Dr Tudor Jones saying that £3500 had been raised. Given that there was still a substantial deficit, how much did the building cost? At the annual meeting in 1910 it was reported there was a bank overdraft of £141 and a debt on the property of £1500. (*Evening Post*, 18 October 1910, p. 4) Did the building really cost nearly twice the original estimate? The Balance Sheet as at 30 September 1923 gave the cost of the building at £2807-7-0 with a mortgage of £1200. Wellington Unitarian Free Church *Calendar*, December 1923. The Auckland church six years earlier had leased the land and the building cost less than one third that of Wellington.

38 *Evening Post*, 9 October 1908, p.3.

39 Wellington Unitarian Free Church *Calendar*, March, April, and May 1911.

40 Margaret Campbell Jellie was born on 12 November 1911 and was two years old when the family left Wellington for England. After returning to New Zealand the family moved to Timaru when William Jellie accepted the call to the Unitarian Church there. Margaret attended Craighead Diocesan Girls School and when the family returned to Auckland in 1925 she continued her secondary education at St Cuthbert's College. She went on to Auckland University College and graduated B.A. in 1932 and M.A. in English with honours in 1934. Concurrently she attended Auckland Teachers College for a year. She taught at Hamilton High School between 1934 and 1939. From there she joined the staff of Marlborough

College where she remained until 1945, followed by Whangarei High School and New Plymouth Girls High School. In 1952 she was appointed Head of the English Department at Matamata College where she remained until her retirement in 1969. At Matamata College she spent a lot of time working in the Memorial Library. She was very involved in local community affairs, served two terms as president of the Matamata Arts Society and worked for charities. She was a member of the Bronte Society and in 2004 donated her collection of Bronte Society *Transactions* to the University of Auckland. Margaret was a member of the Auckland Unitarian Church throughout her adult life. She sang in the church choir and became church librarian, taking over from Jessie Heywood. Wayne Facer, "Margaret Campbell Jellie", Auckland Unitarian Church *News & Views*, Supplement December/January, (2006), pp. 5-6.

41   William Jellie had called for "twelve men and women, good and true, of sound judgment, experienced in business if possible; zealous in the cause, faithful in attendance." Wellington Unitarian Free Church *Calendar*, October 1911. The committee for 1912-13 comprised: Chairman, Mary E. Richmond; Secretary, David Beaglehole; Treasurer, William Stephens; Committee, Jessie Oakley-Browne, Professor Hugh Mackenzie, Messrs John Gammell, James Geddis, W. R. Gibson, James McDowell, D. Pollock, F. Sampson and W. J. Thompson. Wellington Unitarian Free Church *Calendar*, December 1912. In February 1913 the *Calendar* reported that Mr W. R. Gibson had been elected Treasurer.

42   Frances Porter, "Richmond, Mary Elizabeth," *DNZB*, updated 1 September 2010. For details of Mary Richmond's educational activities and the Unitarian network that supported her views see Kerry Bethel, "To Bring into Play: Miss Mary Richmond's Utilization of Kindred Networks in the Diffusion of Kindergarten Ideals into Practice", *History of Education* (2006), pp. 225-244.

43   John Gammell, former Unitarian minister and retired educationalist, was the first President, 1906-1908. He was followed by Hugh Mackenzie (1861-1940), Professor of English at Victoria University College, and then Sir Robert Stout, who was President until his death in 1930. James McRoberts Geddis (1856-1935), publisher of the *New Zealand Free Lance*, became President in 1930, and finally Edmund Charles Isaac (1855-1949), former Congregational minister and Inspector of Technical Education, who was President 1933-1945.

44   Wellington Unitarian Free Church Committee 1912/13 and Church Roll. Assuming the roll is a complete document, which it appears to be, this was a very slender number on which to erect such a financial structure.

45   Wellington Unitarian Free Church *Calendar*, August 1912.

Notes

[46] Gammell gave three lectures. Attendance averaged about 100 and £14 was raised.

[47] *Evening Post*, 28 February 1912, p. 2.

[48] James Chapple resigned from the Presbyterian Church on 13 September 1910. He was employed for just over two years as librarian in the Timaru Public Library, but with the opening of the Timaru Unitarian Hall devoted more time to the cause. As a pacifist he left for America in July 1915 along with his wife Florence and 13 children, where they stayed at Oakland, California. Returning to New Zealand in 1917 he started a Unitarian Church in Christchurch, but in March 1918 was convicted of sedition and sentenced to 11 months imprisonment. Upon release he returned to the Christchurch Unitarian church where he remained until 1925. Eventually he retired in Auckland and joined William Jellie in sharing the Auckland pulpit during the Second World War. But his support for Soviet Union neutrality before the German invasion was very unpopular and he ceased his involvement in the church. Geoff Chapple, "Chapple, James Henry George," DNZB, updated 1 September 2010.

In 1930 James Chapple was unsuccessfully nominated for the Nobel Peace Prize by William Lee Martin (1870-1950), MP for Raglan. In the first Labour Government Lee Martin was Minister of Agriculture and later became a member of the Legislative Council. Dr Olav Njølstad, Research Director, Nobel Institute, confirmed that the nomination of James Chapple was made by William Lee Martin. Personal communication 12 March 2003.

[49] Joseph McCabe arrived in New Zealand In June 1910 on a tour sponsored by the Rationalist Press Association of London. On 6 June 1910 he addressed the Auckland Unitarian Church on "The Religion of Women" to a capacity audience. After a number of other very popular public addresses he went to Wellington, where the city council had decided to refuse him use of the town hall, until a deputation of civic leaders including Professor Hugh Mackenzie and John Gammell persuaded them to rescind the ban. At a meeting chaired by Sir Robert Stout, Joseph McCabe spoke to a crowded town hall on "Secular Education" which resulted in the formation of a National League for the Defence of Secular Education. His other public meetings were packed out and people were turned away. At the Unitarian Free Church he spoke to another full audience on "The Evolution of the Social Position of Women". From there he went to Timaru where on 12 July he spoke on "The Present Conflict between Science and Theology" with Rev. James Chapple in the chair. Bill Cooke, *A Rebel To His Last Breath: Joseph McCabe and Rationalism* (2001), pp. 45, 83, 303.

[50] Wellington Unitarian Free Church *Calendar*, August 1911.

[51] William Fleming Kennedy was born in Ireland and came to New Zealand as a child, about 1870. At the age of 43 he decided to train as a Unitarian minister. He

went to Manchester College, Oxford on his own initiative and applied for admission as a Special Student in 1907. The Regulations under which he was admitted required two satisfactory testimonials from "competent and disinterested persons" as to his character and attainments. One was supplied by Dr Tudor Jones. Did William Jellie provide another, or was he accepted with only one? In his letter of application dated 20 June 1907, he said that his father "belonged to an old Dublin Unitarian family, known to the Rev. Dr Drummond." This would have been the Strand Street Meeting House in Dublin where Dr William Hamilton Drummond (1778-1865) was minister between 1815 and 1859. William Fleming Kennedy, letter to A. H. Worthington, 20 June 1907.

W. F. Kennedy was admitted to Manchester College without fees and after a minimum of one year's satisfactory study was awarded a Manchester College Certificate. Jeannie Forsyth Ewing (1863-1936) from Dunedin probably married William Kennedy while he was minister at the (Unitarian) Free Christian Church, Barnard Castle, 1910-1911.

Besides founding the Dunedin Unitarian Church he took a strong interest in the National Peace and Anti-Militarist League, being elected President on 6 November 1913. National Peace and Anti-Militarism League, Dunedin Branch, minutes of meeting, 6 November 1913.

52 Wellington Unitarian Free Church *Calendar*, June 1912. Mr and Mrs George Wells had bought the Unitarian Hall site for £750 and underwritten a further £450 toward the building. Wellington Unitarian Free Church *Calendar*, September 1911.

53 William Jellie, *Report by William Jellie on the Unitarian Church newly started in Dunedin by the Rev. Mr Kennedy, September 1912*.

54 Although William Jellie did not give the first name or initial it is possible that he was referring to Arthur Sidey, as the eldest Sidey brother, John, died in 1895. The Sidey family was Presbyterian.

55 That support was forthcoming: James Chapple, being closest, made many visits; and William Jellie made quite a number of trips as well. Richard Hall came from Auckland on a number of occasions and as a fellow pacifist attended a meeting of the National Peace and Anti-Militarism League with Rev. Kennedy on 10 June 1913, where he spoke about the work of the Peace and Freedom League in Auckland. National Peace and Anti Militarism League, Dunedin Branch, minutes of special meeting, 10 June 1913. "An array of groups came together to form the National Peace Council, which within a few months had perhaps thirty thousand men and women on its roll throughout the country. Other groups also fought conscription. Among them were the National Peace and Anti-Militarist League, the Freedom League and the Passive Resisters Union. The socialist movement, growing rapidly

Notes

among workers and some of the middle class, threw its weight against the law." Stevan Eldred-Grigg, *The Great Wrong War: New Zealand Society in WW1* (2010), p. 18.

56   William Evans had been an early defender of the existing secular education system, speaking in its favour at a public meeting in 1896 where he was identified as representing the Forward Movement. *Marlborough Express*, 23 May 1896, p. 2.

57   Geoffrey Michael Troughton, *Jesus in New Zealand 1900-1940* (2007), p. 210.

58   *Evening Post*, 15 December 1910, p. 3.

59   *Evening Post*, 24 March 1911, p. 2.

60   *Evening Post*, 10 May 1913, p. 3.

61   *Evening Post*, 30 May 1911, p. 8.

62   Wellington Unitarian Free Church *Calendar*, April 1913. The committee wrote to Rev. W. Copeland Bowie, secretary of the B&FUA, asking if he could find a young unmarried minister who would accept a greatly reduced salary. William Jellie continued on in his position until August 1913.

63   *New Zealand Truth*, 6 September 1913, p. 4.

Chapter 7: Return to England

1   Amongst their excursions Ella and Thomas Macky took a cruise to the Norwegian fiords on board the steam yacht *Argonaut* which departed from Hull on 13 June 1903. Passenger List for *Argonaut*.

2   *Unitarian Monthly*, January 1914, p. 31.

3   *The Times*, 4 August 1913, p. 8.

4   *The Christian Life*, 28 March 1914.

5   Eric Glasgow, "Memorials of a Library", *Library Review* (2001), pp. 461-465.

6   Eric Glasgow, "Memorials of a Library". James Noble's daughter Helen Noble (1877-1967) married the poet Edward Thomas (1878-1917), who was killed in the First World War at Arras. He was encouraged by his father-in-law to write. His first poems were written in 1914 and collections of his verse were published posthumously.

7   I have been generously assisted by the Rev. Daphne Roberts, Chair of the Southport Unitarian Church Committee and her husband, Rev. John Roberts, who provided a select synopsis of the Minute Book of the Council and the Soldiers Entertainment Committee during the term of William Jellie's ministry. They also looked through the local press for news items. John Maindonald kindly provided

Notes

his copy of a report by Mr J. G. A. Wallace, honorary secretary of the Southport Unitarian Church, "The Rev. William Jellie, B.A. and Southport Unitarian Church" dated 7 February 1990. Together these comprise the main sources of William Jellie's church activities.

8   *Southport Visitor*, 17 December 1914.

9   Jack Macky joined the Royal Navy Division formed at the direction of Winston Churchill from surplus reserves of the Royal Navy not required at sea. He was commissioned as Lieutenant in June 1915 and after training at the Crystal Palace and Blandford went to the eastern Mediterranean early in 1916. He then saw service in France and was wounded twice, severely on the Somme, and was invalided back to England at the end of 1916. He rejoined the Drake Battalion in July 1917 which saw heavy fighting for the next six months including the Battle of Passchendaele. He then transferred to Palestine where he was attached to the Motor Machinegun Corps with the rank of Captain. While on duty there he was awarded the Military Cross for gallantry and devotion to duty at Baku on 14 September 1918. During the defence of the town he manoeuvred his car against the enemy's right flank at a critical moment holding up their advance so that reinforcements could arrive. *Evening Post*, 18 October 1918, p. 8 and 18 December 1919, p. 7.

10   Joseph Macky, letter Tom Macky, 8 April 1915.

11   Tom Macky, letter to Ella Jellie, 4 April 1915.

12   Joseph Macky, letter to Tom Macky, 22 April 1915.

13   Joseph Macky, letter to Tom Macky, Saturday morning [1 May 1915].

14   There had been extensive press coverage of the sinking of the *Lusitania*, including lists of those feared dead and, later, lists of those who had perished. (Of those on board, 1198 died and 761 were rescued. On the *Titanic* 1517 lost their lives and 706 were rescued.) There was considerable mention of Mary and Joseph Macky in these reports and also coverage when it was known that Jack Macky and Sam Hannah were safe. It was reported that the lady to whom Mrs Macky had given her seat in the lifeboat had advertised to meet Jack Macky and that Mary Macky, when offered the seat, reportedly said: "I am getting old, and would rather stay with my husband. You are younger, and have life before you." *Evening Post*, 24 August 1915, p. 9. Presumably Joseph and Mary Macky had told this lady during the voyage that they had a son in London.

15   William Jellie, letter to Ella Jellie, "G.E.R. Tuesday. 4.30" [June 1915]. This eyewitness account does not agree with the press report of Mary Macky being offered the one seat left but declining it for a younger woman. William Jellie and Jack Macky travelled to London to meet Miss Neatby of Wimpole Street, the

Notes

friend of Miss Manly who confirmed all the important details. Because of his delay in getting home, William decided to write to Ella straight away with news from the first meeting. He also sent an account to Tom Macky in a letter dated 7 June 1915.

16   William Williams came from Cardiff and was educated at University College, South Wales, 1895-1900, where he graduated with a B.A. and then went school teaching. He decided to enter the ministry and studied at Manchester College, Oxford, 1904-1907. He had ministries at Wimbledon, an affluent London suburb, and at Evesham in the county of Worcestershire, where the Unitarian chapel dated from 1737. He went to the Auckland Unitarian Church in 1914. He took great care in preparing his sermons, which reflected his deep appreciation of English literature. The duration of his ministry was marked by the First World War. After he returned to England he had a settled ministry at Stourbridge in 1920 and then moved to his last ministry at Bournemouth in 1929. *The Inquirer*, 24 January 1942, p. 28. Unlike his predecessor Richard Hall, who was strongly pacifist, William Williams held patriotic views supporting the war.

17   *Evening Post*, 20 May 1915, p. 8. *The Inquirer*, 14 August 1915, p. 403.

18   Margaret Jellie, letter to Barbara Holt, 8 November 1991.

19   Before the war Thomas Macky had been in business as a land agent. He was unmarried when he joined the New Zealand Rifle Brigade and became a sergeant in the 3rd Battalion. He gained promotion to second lieutenant upon passing his examinations while in camp in England and transferred to the Otago Infantry Regiment. An old boy of Auckland Grammar School, his name is recorded on the School War Memorial. *Evening Post*, 23 October 1917, p.7. Auckland War Memorial Museum Cenotaph Database.

20   Neil Macky attended Auckland University College and graduated LL.B. in 1912. A second lieutenant in the New Zealand Rifle Brigade, he went to France in 1916 and took part in the battle of the Somme. He was awarded the Military Cross and Mentioned in Despatches. After recovering from his wounds in England he returned to France in 1917 and was promoted to captain. Upon return to New Zealand in 1919 he resumed legal practice and merged his firm with Russell, Campbell and McVeagh. He continued serving in the Territorial Army as did many of his law partners, becoming a lieutenant colonel commanding an Auckland Regiment in 1931. A reorganisation of the Territorial Force under the first Labour government reduced numbers and duties of senior officers. Neil Macky and three other colonels, following an unsatisfactory response from the minister of defence, Frederick Jones, publicly challenged the government over its policies. They were posted to the retired list as a result. All four had connections to the National Party opposition and some saw their actions as bringing party politics into the Army.

With the outbreak of Second World War the colonels' "revolt" was largely forgotten and Neil Macky was re-appointed to active service. During the retreat from Greece in 1941 he led a battalion that successfully held up a German panzer division for 36 hours and then, alongside two Australian battalions, held back the Germans for three days allowing the ANZAC troops to retreat. He was invalided home in 1941. After the war he continued to practice law and to follow his interest in yachting. He was commodore of the Royal New Zealand Yacht Squadron, which has a memorial trophy named after him. W. David McIntyre, "Macky, Neil Lloyd," *DNZB*, updated 1 September 2010.

For an account of the colonels' revolt, see L. H. Barber, "The New Zealand Colonels' 'Revolt', 1938", *New Zealand Law Journal* (1977), pp. 496-502. What would William Jellie have made of Neil Macky's class-based comment: "To kow-tow to a boot-maker as a Minister of Defence was too much for me"? See also Erik Olssen and Shawn Ryan, "Jones, Frederick", *DNZB*, updated 1 September 2010.

[21] Frank Macky was educated at Prince Albert College, Auckland, and Box Hill School, Melbourne. He studied medicine at Melbourne University and graduated in 1914, taking up a post at Auckland hospital later that year. He returned to Australia in 1915 and joined the Australian Medical Corps. Promoted to the rank of captain, he went to Cairo and while there contracted typhoid and was repatriated home. Medically unfit for overseas service, he was posted to Bulford Camp hospital in 1917. In 1918, with the rank of major, he was posted to the General Hospital at Havre, where he was stationed until the end of the war. Neil Macky, "The Macky Family in New Zealand" (1969). Margo Osborne kindly provided me with a copy of a postcard Frank Macky sent from Bulford Camp to his sister-in-law Josephine, Tom Macky's wife.

[22] Hilary wrote to his mother from Carrickfergus and although the letters (kindly supplied by Margo Osborne) are undated, he sends his love "to Margaret and baby" a reference to Mary Jellie, born 17 April 1918. As Hilary asks "how is baby getting on" it seems that their trip was close to the date of Mary's birth. (The Rev. John Jellie died on 25 November 1918.)

[23] Margaret Jellie, letter to Barbara Holt, 8 November 1991. Margaret wrote that it was wrong to describe her father as being of Irish extraction, as he was "Irish through and through." He took an interest in Irish culture and supported the preservation of its national heritage, becoming a member of the Royal Society of Antiquaries of Ireland, Dublin, while working in London. His proposer was John Smyth Crone, another old boy of the Royal Belfast Academical Institution, who is best remembered for his *Concise Dictionary of Irish Biography*. Pursuing this interest, William Jellie was a subscriber to the *Ulster Journal of Archaeology* while working at Ipswich.

Notes

24 Francis E. Mineka, *The Dissidence of Dissent* (1944), pp. 136-137, 152, 153.

25 Philip Noble Tindale, "Roman Catholics and Unitarians: An Account of Reciprocal Help and Comfort, Part 1", *TUHS* (1993), pp. 177-186.

26 Philip Noble Tindale, "Roman Catholics and Unitarians: An Account of Reciprocal Help and Comfort, Part 2", *TUHS* (1994), pp. 271-282.

27 H. McLachlan, *The Unitarian Movement in the Religious Life of England* (1934), p. 295.

28 Leonard Smith, *Unitarian to the Core*, pp. 71-72, says that it was a minority of Unitarians who broke with the Liberals over Home Rule for Ireland. Joseph Chamberlain, the Birmingham Unitarian MP, crossed the floor of the House in 1886 in opposition to the Home Rule Bill, which led to the formation of the Liberal Unionist Party. "From then on Unitarian allegiance to the Liberal Party could not be assumed." Ruth Rowntree, *"Religious Devils" of Hampstead* (2004), p. 180. On the other hand, some Unitarians strongly supported Irish home rule from the start. One such was C. P. Scott, influential editor of the *Manchester Guardian*; he deplored the suppression of the Easter uprising in Dublin in 1916 and the military action at the end of the war. Trevor Wilson, "Scott, Charles Prestwich (1846-1932)", ODNB.

29 R. P. Davis, "Sir Robert Stout and the Irish Question", *Historical Studies, Australia and New Zealand* (1966), pp. 417-434.

30 Winston Churchill, letter to Clementine Churchill, 31 July 1914.

31 William Jellie, letter to Robert Harris, 30 November 1920. Jellie's letter of resignation gave the customary three months' notice. The secretary of the Church Council, Dr Robert Harris, replied on 7 December 1920 that the Church Council "in accepting the resignation owing to ill health of the Rev. William Jellie deeply regrets its necessity, and trust that the rest he anticipates may completely restore him." Both letters were published in the Southport Unitarian Church *Calendar*, January, February & March, 1921. (Jellie, producing his last issue of the *Calendar*, combined three months.) This is the only *Calendar* I have been able to find.

32 Alan O'Day, *Irish Home Rule 1867-1921* (1998), p. 300. "In January 1921 the Labour party declared: 'things are being done in the name of Britain which must make our name stink in the nostrils of the whole world.'"

33 Jellie was not the first Unitarian minister to find his views on the Irish question out of step with his congregation. When the Melbourne Unitarian Church rejected Rev. George Walters's proposal to debate the Irish question he resigned. Dorothy Scott, *The Halfway House to Infidelity: A History of the Melbourne Unitarian Church, 1853-1973* (1980), p. 71. Rev. Walters was from an Anglo-Irish family.

[34] John Jellie began school when the family had moved into their new house at 14 Warren Avenue, Mt Roskill. From the local primary school he then attended Auckland Grammar School between 1934 and 1937, obtaining university matriculation and playing rugby, cricket and winning the tennis championship. Later he played interclub tennis competitions. When growing up he went to Auckland Unitarian Church services with his family, but later pursued his sporting interests rather than church.

At the outbreak of war he applied to join the Fleet Air Arm of the Royal Navy. He sailed to England as a civilian and went to Portsmouth Harbour, HMS *St Vincent*, training as a seaman, then to Elmdon near Birmingham and Kingston, Ontario, Canada where he trained on Harvard planes. He returned to Royal Naval Air Station Yeovilton in Somerset as a sub lieutenant and joined 800 squadron flying Hurricanes. In 1943 he was based on HMS *Emperor* flying American Hellcats; a year later he was involved in the attacks on the battleship *Tirpitz* in Norway. He took part in the naval cover provided for the D-Day landings in Normandy. He was awarded the Distinguished Service Cross for his skill and leadership in dive bombing and was promoted to the rank of lieutenant. He was involved in a series of air strikes in the Aegean and during these operations was Mentioned in Despatches. He returned home in 1946 and returned to his former job at the Guardian Trust.

In 1948 he married Nancy Greville and they had a family of six children. Meanwhile John changed his occupation, going into the clothing industry, where he became company manager to a number of manufacturers, including one that had been started by his maternal grandfather. After his retirement in 1982 he donated the collection of William Jellie's WEA lecture notes, which he had carefully preserved since his father's death, to the University of Auckland. Wayne Facer, "In Memoriam: John Hugh Jellie 1920-2010", Auckland Unitarian Church *News & Views*, October 2011, attachment, pp. 1-8.

[35] William Jellie, letter to members of the Southport Unitarian Church congregation, 23 July 1921.

Chapter 8: In New Zealand: Timaru

[1] Mary Isabella Jellie (1918-2008) was educated at St Cuthbert's College, Epsom Girls Grammar School and the Auckland Business College. She sang in the Auckland Unitarian Church choir, sometimes as soloist during radio broadcasts. She also sang in the Lyric Harmonists' choir, which gave town hall concerts and radio broadcasts. In 1942 she performed a broadcast solo recital. After the war she travelled to Australia, working in Melbourne and Adelaide. When she returned she met Joop Kok, a Dutchman repatriated to New Zealand after the war from Dutch

Notes

East Indies. They married in 1966 and continued living in Auckland. Wayne Facer, "In Memoriam: Mary Isabella Kok (née Jellie)", Auckland Unitarian Church *News & Views*, June 2009, pp. 4-7.

2   Radio broadcasting was only starting: by the end of 1922 there were seven stations in the main centres, none of which were broadcasting for more than a few hours a week. Patrick Day, *The Broadcasting Years: A History of Broadcasting in New Zealand* (1994), p. 48.

3   Albert Thornhill, letter to William Jellie, 19 February 1922. Born in Stalybridge, a Cheshire town that became one of the first textile centres in the industrial revolution, Albert Thornhill came from a working class background: his father was a boot maker and Albert started work when he was eleven. After studying University Extension courses and gaining a scholarship to the Oxford summer school, he joined Fitzwilliam Hall at Cambridge University, established by the Non-Collegiate Students Board for underprivileged students. From Cambridge, where he completed a B.A. in 1902 and received an M.A. in 1906, he studied at Manchester College, Oxford 1902-1905, attaining first class honours in Old and New Testament studies. He had ministries at Carlisle, 1905-1907; Failsworth, Manchester, 1907-1908; and Derby, 1908-1911. Following a ten-year ministry at Brookfield Church, Gorton, Manchester, Rev. Thornhill arrived at Auckland in April 1920 with his wife Daisy and three children. His time at Auckland was successful; he was instrumental in arranging radio broadcasts of the church services, undertook missionary work well beyond Auckland and was active in the Unitarian Association of New Zealand. In 1929 he left Auckland for Sydney. He resigned from his Sydney ministry in January 1932. The following year Daisy divorced him for adultery with Alice Harris, former secretary of the Sydney Unitarian Church. Meanwhile Albert Thornhill returned to England and, failing to get another church appointment, studied dietetics. He then returned to Sydney and set up practice as a dietician. Rev. William Bottomley married Albert and Alice at the Melbourne Unitarian Church four years before Albert died in 1938.

4   Educated at Trinity College, Oxford where he took a B.A., Wyndham Heathcote was ordained in the Church of England in 1889. He was a chaplain to the Argyle and Sutherland Highlanders during the South African war, after which he came to Australia and was vicar at Bundaberg, Queensland, 1903-1910. He became Unitarian and was minister at the Melbourne Unitarian Church, 1912-1918. From there he went to the Adelaide Unitarian Church until December 1920. While planning a trip to San Francisco in 1921, he offered to visit Wellington and provided temporary supply for three months. Wellington at that stage was waiting for its settled minister, Rev. James Shaw Brown (1862-1948), to arrive

from England. When his sailing was delayed Wyndham Heathcote was engaged for a further three months. He visited Timaru in September 1921 before sailing on the SS *Tahiti* in October 1921.

The Rev. James Shaw Brown arrived in August 1921 to a joint welcome and farewell to Heathcote at which the farewell dominated proceedings. He found it impossible to work constructively with the Wellington Church committee, some of whom wanted to recall Wyndham Heathcote and divert James Shaw Brown to Timaru. Shaw Brown resigned in April 1922 and during May visited Christchurch, Timaru and Dunedin. He married Ina Lee, a member of the congregation, in June 1922, and then left for England.

Meantime Wyndham Heathcote, who had provided temporary supply to the Ottawa Unitarian Church since December 1921, left in May 1922 (a month earlier than agreed) and arrived in Wellington the same month Shaw Brown left; he remained until 1923. Some saw him as an enthusiast who indulged in Spiritualism and Theosophy, opposed prohibition and was anti-Catholic, to the detriment of the Unitarian cause. Others saw him as an eloquent and cultured speaker who attracted audiences. Unable to get work at any North American church, despite trying, he accepted the Sydney pulpit when the Rev. George Walters (1852-1926) died, but resigned in 1928. He was reappointed in 1932 following the departure of Albert Thornhill and remained at the Sydney Unitarian Church until 1945, retiring as Minister Emeritus aged 83. Geoffrey Ronald Usher, *Four Decades of Leadership* (1989), pp. 9-13, 41-48; Tim Beaglehole, *A Life of J. C. Beaglehole, New Zealand Scholar* (2006), p. 51.

5   A. M. Paterson, letter to William Trimble, 18 June 1915, discussing his prospects of providing lay leadership.

6   Unitarian Association of New Zealand, minutes of the executive council, 15 September 1916. The B&FUA were notified by cable that McDonnell had resigned for financial reasons. At the meeting of 2 March 1917 the council decided to pay £7-7-0 to McDonnell for "his work for Liberal Religion in New Zealand." Timaru representatives attended each conference of the Unitarian Association of New Zealand before William Jellie's appointment, indicating that the church organisation continued to function.

7   The Rev. J. K. Archer (1865-1949) of Christchurch spoke under the auspices of the Timaru Labour Party on "Rights of Property and Rights of the People", claiming that the Labour Party "stood in the best interests of the people as a whole." *New Zealand Truth*, 16 July 1921, p. 6. Rev. Archer was prominent in the Canterbury WEA, teaching economic history. He was a Christian socialist and a notable Baptist, from 1916 to 1918 president of the Baptist Union. Sir Robert

Notes

Stout, Chancellor of the University of New Zealand, accused him of being a "revolutionary communist", comments which he later successfully sued a newspaper for publishing. He went on to become Mayor of Christchurch, 1925-1931, and was appointed to the Legislative Council in 1937. Roy Shuker, *Educating the Workers? A History of the Workers' Educational Association in New Zealand* (1984), pp. 56-59; Barry Gustafson, "Archer, John Kendrick", DNZB, updated 1 September 2010.

8   That same year Michael James Liston, Catholic Bishop of Auckland, was charged with sedition for claiming that the Anglo-Irish Treaty was not a final settlement and that Ireland had suffered under foreign occupation which resulted in murder. Though he supported the Bishop's freedom of speech, William Jellie was Anglo-Irish and did not go so far as to adopt the republican cause. Bishop Liston was acquitted of the charges. Nicholas Reid, *James Michael Liston: A Life* (2006), pp. 110-126.

9   *The Inquirer*, 21 April 1923, p. 254. Rosalind Lee wrote in *The Inquirer*, 24 May 1924, pp. 336-337, that a generous grant from the B&FUA for missionary work in New Zealand made it possible to station William Jellie in Timaru "last year." Albert Thornhill had suggested in a letter to William Jellie, 19 October 1922, that he should consider visiting Timaru: "I think it might be possible to scrape funds together for a year's trial." On 23 February 1923 he wrote confirming funds of £300, split equally between a private donor, the congregation and the B&FUA.

10   The Unitarian Hall building still exists at 65 Church Street, Timaru. It was used by the Unitarian Progressive Society at least until the 1930s, when the YWCA met there. In November 1935 it was sold to the Open Brethren who renamed the building Church Street Chapel. Alistair J. Pike, *An Unfinished Story: A History of Church Street Chapel 1935-1985*, p. 3. The Bible of the Rev. James Chapple remains in the Church Street Chapel.

11   Notices of Unitarian services in the *Timaru Herald*, 7 April 1923, p. 14; 14 April 1923, p. 4; 28 April 1923, p. 2; and 28 July 1923, p. 12. I am indebted to Alistair Pike for providing a schedule of Unitarian Church and WEA notices from the *Timaru Herald* during William Jellie's term.

12   New Zealand was the final country on Hickson's world tour. He arrived in Auckland in October 1923. After World War I there was a marked decline in church attendance due to the disenchantment with religion following the war, although some attributed it to "liberal theology and rationalism." Despite the increased awareness of psychosomatic illness, Hickson's ministry was supported by the Anglican Church not only to help the sick but also to restore "the Church to some of its former vigour". A. Fay Farley, "A Spiritual Healing Mission Remem-

bered: James Moore Hickson's Christian Healing Mission at Palmerston North, New Zealand, 1923", *Journal of Religious History* (2010), pp. 1-19.

[13] John Ellis was educated at Grenville College and the School of Mines in Ballarat, Victoria, Australia. He entered the Methodist Church in 1885 and the next year came to Christchurch, where he assisted the Rev. J. Orchard. He was ordained in 1890 and married Ada Lydia Orchard (1865-1926) in 1891. He resigned from the ministry in 1909 and worked as an Instructor in Agriculture and Dairy Science for the Department of Education. He was a Fellow of the Royal Horticultural Society. (During his Unitarian ministry he was elected to the Council of the New Zealand Institute of Horticulture.) In 1920 he and his wife were in charge of a Methodist orphanage. He took his first service at the Wellington Unitarian Church on 16 September 1923, although his formal appointment was later.

In November 1923 the annual conference of the Unitarian Association of New Zealand set up an Advisory Board to examine the credentials of ministers applying for admission to the Unitarian ministry in New Zealand. *The Inquirer*, 23 February 1924, p. 133. John Ellis was the first and possibly only applicant examined by the Board, which approved his application and welcomed him into the ministry, notifying the B&FUA of its decision. He finished his Wellington ministry in December 1924, once again due to financial reasons. Wellington Unitarian Free Church *Calendar*, April 1924, January 1925. He and Ada returned to Christchurch. After her death there in 1926, John went to Australia. I am grateful for information supplied by Jo Smith, Archivist, Methodist Church of New Zealand Archives, personal communication, 8 June 2011.

[14] The report of the annual meeting of the South Canterbury WEA for March 1924 does not record a president being present or elected, so it is possible the position was vacant. *Timaru Herald*, 25 March 1924, p. 4.

[15] *Timaru Herald*, 25 March 1924, p. 4.

[16] William Jellie's first report in his role as WEA President is in the *Timaru Herald*, 22 May 1924, p. 5. The report of his last Council meeting is in the *Timaru Herald*, 28 April 1925.

[17] *Timaru Herald*, 22 May 1924, p. 5.

[18] *Timaru Herald*, 21 August 1924, p. 6.

[19] Frank Holmes, "Belshaw, Horace", DNZB, updated 1 September 2010. Grant Fleming, "Condliffe, John Bell", DNZB, updated 1 September 2010.

[20] Albert Mansbridge (1876-1952), coming from the cooperative movement, founded the WEA after realising that the university extension movement, begun

Notes

by Cambridge University in 1873, was failing to attract working class students. He proposed a joint committee of university and WEA representatives, with the WEA having a controlling voice in the selection of tutors. Classes were to be conducted on a tutorial model, which was called the "Oxford formula". The resulting report, *Oxford and Working-Class Education* (1908), was considered quite revolutionary for its time. Summer schools were introduced in 1910. Once adopted, the association spread throughout Britain and overseas. In 1913 Mansbridge with his wife Frances visited all the Australian states. Bernard Jennings, "Mansbridge, Albert (1876-1952)", ODNB. The Mansbridges only managed to spend a few days in New Zealand at Auckland. Jean E. Sharfe, *The Canterbury Workers' Educational Association: The Origins and Development, 1915 to 1947. A Working Class Organisation?* (1990), pp. 21, 61.

[21] Ian Carter, "Shelley, James", DNZB, updated 1 September 2010. Ian Carter's biography, *Gadfly: The Life and Times of James Shelley* (1993), tells much about Shelley's life but fails to mention that for nine years he was vice-president of the New Zealand Rationalist Association. With the advent of the first Labour government, Shelley was appointed to the new position of Director of Broadcasting and had a great influence over New Zealand's cultural life. He was knighted and returned to live the remainder of his life in England.

[22] *Timaru Herald*, 27 October 1924, p. 9.

[23] David O. W. Hall, *New Zealand Adult Education* (1970), p. 54.

[24] Michael Bassett, "Airey, Willis Thomas Goodwin", DNZB, updated 1 September 2010.

[25] *Timaru Herald*, 6 February 1925, p. 7.

[26] Vic Elliott, "Miller, Harold Gladstone", DNZB, updated 1 September 2010.

[27] George Manning was born in Wales and emigrated to New Zealand in 1910. He had a nonconformist background but for a while conducted rationalist funerals in Christchurch. He went on to part-time university study, gaining a diploma in social science in 1927 and an M.A. in economics in 1930. He was WEA national president, 1942-1948, and became mayor of Christchurch, 1958-1968. Jean Sharfe, "Manning, George", DNZB, updated 1 September 2010.

[28] *Timaru Herald*, 6 February 1925, p. 7.

[29] Formerly a Methodist minister, Clyde Carr became a Congregational minister, but resigned over the opposition that arose when he preached the social gospel. He was a friend of James Chapple, supporting his Unitarian church in Christchurch. He joined the Labour Party and in 1928 was elected to the Timaru seat, which he held for 33 years. Colin Brown, "Carr, Clyde Leonard", DNZB, updated 1

Notes

September 2010. His involvement with Unitarianism continued over many years and he is recorded as a Unitarian minister under the Marriage Act in *The New Zealand Gazette*, 26 January 1928, p. 217.

[30] The Rev. Albert Thornhill wrote in *The Inquirer*, 25 July 1925, p. 471: "Timaru found itself unable to maintain a minister and Mr Jellie, after doing valuable service there, has brought his family to Auckland where he and they are entering joyfully into the work of the church he did so much to build up in its infant days. Timaru's loss is Auckland's gain." If Albert Thornhill had realised what the Timaru failure portended for liberal religion he may have been less sanguine.

[31] James Chapple left the Christchurch Unitarian Church by the end of 1925 and moved to Tauranga. Services were continued by Clyde Carr and his friend Norman Murray Bell (1887-1962). Both were teachers in the church's Socialist Sunday school that Chapple established (in 1932 the name was changed to the Socialist Guild of Youth). The Socialist Sunday schools became the model of "The Young Comrades" children's league organised by the West Coast socialists at Blackball. Len Richardson, *Coal, Class & Community* (1995), p. 210.

When Clyde Carr's radio duties (followed by politics) took his time in 1927 Norman Bell became leader and the church was renamed the Free Religious Movement. Norman Bell was a Labour Party member and lifelong peace activist. A brilliant academic, he was educated at Christ's College and Canterbury University College, completing an M.A. with honours in Classics and Chemistry in 1909, and was awarded the first scholarship to Trinity College, Cambridge, completing a B.A. in Classics in 1912. He graduated with a B.D. from London University in 1915. He studied education at St Andrews University in Scotland. At the time he was conscripted into the Army in 1917 he was teaching at Canterbury University College. His refusal of an order to accept his kit resulted in a court martial sentencing him to two years imprisonment with hard labour. Subsequent loss of civil rights barred him from standing as a Labour candidate in the 1919 election or teaching at a public institution; he survived as a private tutor to university students. Archives New Zealand Defence Force Records, WW1 64795-Army, Norman Murray Bell. David Grant, *Out in the Cold* (1986), pp. 41-43. Bell's address to the Unitarian Church, *Education for Freedom* (1921) is extant, as is his *Maori Myths and Rites in the Light of Human Ontogeny* (1928).

In 1926 William Jellie became secretary of the Unitarian Association of New Zealand. He corresponded with Clyde Carr and James Chapple, who wrote telling him the Free Religious Movement was doing well; Chapple also forwarded reports he received from Norman Bell. Clyde Carr thought the attendances "exceptionally good" and wanted to ensure the Christchurch movement was "linked up", presumably with the Unitarian Association. He described them as "extreme radicals" and wondered how they would appeal to William Jellie. None of Jellie's replies has survived. Clyde Carr, letters to William Jellie, 13 December 1928, 16 April 1929 and 9 December 1929; James Chapple, letters to William Jellie, 13 December 1928 and 20 December 1929. The Free Religious Movement was active in the 1930s, with press coverage in the *Evening Post*, 23 April 1934, p. 14, but how long it continued is unknown.

32 For the effects on the Methodist and Presbyterian Churches see Peter J. Lineham, *New Zealanders and the Methodist Evangel* (1983), pp. 44-47.

33 H. R. Jackson, *Churches and People in Australia and New Zealand 1860-1930* (1987), pp. 115-117; see also pp. 125 and 136: "However the statistics are analysed they indicate a substantial decline. Assuming that Sunday school children were not included, then the level of adult attendances was 43 percent lower in 1926 than it had been in 1891." The decline in Protestant children attending Sunday schools was similar; whereas it was thought attendance of Sunday school age was about 90 percent at the turn of the century, by 1926 it was about 55 percent. Ian Breward, *Godless Schools?* (1967), p. 78.

Chapter 9: The Poor Person's University

1 Raymond V. Holt, *The Unitarian Contribution to Social Progress in England* (1952), pp. 267-270.

2 Mechanics Institutes were established in Wellington, Nelson and Auckland in 1842, Dunedin in 1851 and Hutt Valley in 1854. "By the 1880's most towns, and indeed townships, had their mechanics' institute or athenaeum, as many of these institutions came to be called. Many of them acquired their own buildings and all maintained a reading room and library." Mutual improvement societies were important, if often overlooked, contributors to adult education and some of their supporters "were pioneers of the Workers' Educational Association". James C. Dakin, "The prevalence of mutual improvement in adult education in New Zealand 1870-1915", *International Journal of Lifelong Education* (1991), pp. 243-254.

3 John R. Read, "Healthy Intercourse: The Beginning of the London Working Men's College", *Browning Institute Studies* (1988), pp. 77-90.

4 The intention was "to design a cheap and direct system of university extension by which young scholars ventured forth to spread knowledge and to prove that privilege had its social conscience". This classic example of top-down thinking faltered when a later generation of scholars, including R. H. Tawney, G. D. H. Cole and William Temple, built strong links with the working class and labour movement, and the subsequent emergence of the WEA. Lawrence Goldman,

Notes

"Education as Politics: University Adult Education in England since 1870", *Oxford Review of Education* (1999), pp. 89-101.

5   Adult Schools started in Auckland in 1891, and spread into the suburbs; at one time there were four, followed by schools in Wellington, Christchurch and Dunedin. Their activity had peaked by 1915. Margaret West and Ruth Fawell, *The Story of New Zealand Quakerism 1842-1972* (1973), pp. 92-95. The schools were non-sectarian, aimed at the "working man and artisan class, whom it is nobody's concern to look after, and who are utterly neglected. It is these the school desires to reach and give a helping hand to, and we want them to come along just as they are, and never mind their clothes or personal appearance, as they will be heartily welcome." *Evening Post*, 3 April 1908, p. 3.

6   Lottie Guy's attendance at the Auckland Adult School is mentioned in Chapter 5. Her brother George Herbert Guy (1880-1969) enrolled at the Adult School in 1895 and her brother John Beecher Guy (1872-1938) in 1896. Their father John Guy (1845-1929) became vice-president and by 1898 was chairman of the school. Margaret Howie and Jean Leyland, *A Guy Family History* (2000), pp. 34-35, 52, 82.

7   *The Colonist*, 24 December 1914, p. 4.

8   "The Workers' Educational Association occupied the other half of the old Grammar School building in Symonds Street where Elam [School of Fine Arts] was now situated. An adult outreach educational wing of the Auckland University College, the WEA was a poor person's university." Nicola Green, *By the Waters of Babylon: The Art of A. Lois White* (1993), p. 29. Auckland University College provided rooms for the WEA in the Old Grammar School in 1925 until it was burned down in 1949. After the fire the WEA was housed in the Auckland Unitarian Church until 1976.

9   Ruth Watts, *Gender, Power and the Unitarians in England 1760-1860* (1998), p. 184, citing MSS Biggs *Scrapbooks*, I, John Hollings' speech at the Boston Mechanics Institute, 1852.

10   William Jellie's son John could not recall his father discussing politics at home and there is no record of him discussing it in a party political sense. Wayne Facer, "In Memoriam: John Hugh Jellie 1920-2010", Auckland Unitarian Church *News & Views*, October 2011, attachment, pp. 1-8.

11   "The suggested course is one of twenty four lectures at the rate of £60 per course, and I should be glad to have an opportunity of talking matters over with you..." L. A. Mander letter to William Jellie, 19 February 1926.

Linden Alfred Mander (1897-1967) was educated at Prince Alfred College, Adelaide after being awarded a public exhibition, and at Adelaide University. He was honorary secretary of the South Australia League of Nations Union in

Notes

1920. *The Advertiser*, 29 October 1920, p. 10. In April 1922 he was appointed Tutor-Organiser of the Auckland WEA. This was changed a year later to Director of Tutorial Classes, a position he held until his resignation in 1927. He returned to speak at the League of Nations Union, visiting Adelaide in 1926 and 1927, where he was identified as the Director of the Auckland WEA. *The Advertiser*, 20 January 1926, p. 12; 25 January 1927, p. 2. He took up a chair in political science at Washington University, Seattle in 1927; his specialty was the United Nations and international organisations. He received a distinguished service award from the United Nations International Children's Emergency Fund (UNICEF). Hugh A. Bone, "Linden A. Mander: 1897-1967", *Western Political Quarterly* (1967), p. 513.

[12] John A. Colquhoun, *History of the Auckland Workers' Educational Association until the passing of the Adult Education Act, 1947* (1976), p. 9.

[13] Quoted in Roy Shuker, *Educating the Workers? A History of the Workers' Educational Association in New Zealand* (1984), p. 76.

[14] Ellen Elizabeth Ferner (née Aley) was a portrait painter and photographer, awarded a gold medal for portraiture at the Auckland Exhibition in 1914. She spent a lifetime working in the interests of children: organising support for the passage of the Child Welfare Act in 1925 and working in the Children's Court, first as an associate member, then appointed a Justice of the Peace in 1926. She organised the Community Sunshine School for sick and convalescing children and a residential camp for undernourished children at Waiheke Island. She served on the Boards of Seddon Memorial Technical College and Elam School of Art and was instrumental in establishing the Rocklands Hall residence for women teacher's college students. Bronwyn Dalley, "Ferner, Ellen Elizabeth", DNZB. She was a member of the Auckland Unitarian Church from 1900. Her funeral was conducted by the Revs. William Constable and William Jellie. A memorial tablet was unveiled in the Auckland Unitarian Church by Sir George Fowlds. *The Inquirer*, 3 January 1931, p. 9; *Evening Post*, 25 February 1931, p. 13.

[15] When the Rev. George Walters (1856-1926) died, Wyndham Heathcote provided temporary supply at the Sydney Unitarian Church until February 1928. He was replaced in January 1929 by Albert Thornhill, who "it seems more than likely ... had heard of the vacancy through Rev. William Jellie, his retired predecessor in Auckland to whom the Sydney Church had made overtures." Geoffrey Ronald Usher, *Four Decades of Leadership Ministers of the Sydney Unitarian Church 1927-1968* (1989), p.14.

[16] Anthony Taylor, "Shakespeare and Radicalism: The Uses and Abuses of Shakespeare in Nineteenth-Century Popular Politics", *Historical Journal* (2002), pp. 357-379.

[17] In addition to delivering his lecture courses on Dante, William Jellie prepared an extensive Dante Dictionary in an A-Z style, which is still in manuscript form.

[18] Alison Milbank, *Dante and the Victorians* (1998), pp. 16-17.

[19] "It is not until we come to Dante that we find a layman writing with full knowledge of the ecclesiastical philosophy of his time. Until the fourteenth century, ecclesiastics have a virtual monopoly of philosophy, and philosophy, accordingly, is written from the standpoint of the Church." Bertrand Russell, *A History of Western Philosophy* (1945), p. 302.

[20] William Jellie, Scrap & Newscutting Book.

[21] J. B. Bury concurrently held chairs in modern history and Greek at Trinity College, Dublin and went on to become Regius Professor of Modern History at Cambridge in 1902. He produced a seven-volume edition of Edward Gibbon's *Decline and Fall of the Roman Empire* as well as many books on classical Greece. His rationalist views on history can be seen in his *History of Freedom of Thought* (1913) and *History of the Idea of Progress* (1920). Michael Whitby, "Bury, John Bagnell (1861-1927)", ODNB.

[22] Bury, *History of Freedom of Thought*, p. 34.

[23] Bury, *History of Freedom of Thought*, p. 240.

[24] Jellie's "Philosophy of Modern Pacifism" is undated and does not appear on any schedule of lectures, although it may have been part of a series and not separately identified. It is likely to have been given in 1939 as the threat of war approached.

[25] Cyril Edwin Mitchinson Joad was educated at Balliol College, Oxford. While working for the civil service he joined the Fabian Society and wrote book reviews for the *Daily Herald* and *New Statesman*. He wrote from an agnostic viewpoint and his publications included popular works, *Common Sense Ethics* and *Common Sense Theology*. In 1930 he became head of philosophy at Birkbeck College, University of London. Later he was promoted to reader and received a D.Litt. Since the First World War he had been a pacifist and was active in the National Peace Council, but later abandoned his pacifism and agnosticism. Jason Tomes, "Joad, Cyril Edwin Mitchinson (1891-1953)", ODNB.

[26] The plight of the Republican government in Spain was well known at this time. The Labour government elected in November 1935 supported collective security, which justified intervention against the fascists in the Spanish civil war that broke out in July 1936; the Labour party *Standard* covered the war in detail and supported the Republic. New Zealand had volunteers serving in the International Brigade. Dr D. G. MacMillan, Minister of Health, became president of the Spanish Medical Aid Committee. New Zealand was critical of British foreign

Notes

policy over this matter, something that had never happened before. The Catholic Church stood out in its support for Franco and the fascists. John Shennan, "The Labour Party: A principled stand", in Mark Derby (ed.), *Kiwi Compañeros: New Zealand and the Spanish Civil War* (2009), pp. 185-203.

27 William Jellie used the topic of "Utopias Through the Ages" as the theme for a series of sermons at the Timaru Unitarian Church in 1923.

28 For a review of this literature see Dominic Alessio, "Promoting Paradise: Utopianism and National Identity in New Zealand, 1870-1930", *New Zealand Journal of History* (2008), pp. 22-41; and Lyman Tower Sargent, "Utopianism and the Creation of New Zealand National Identity", *Utopian Studies* (2001), pp. 1-18.

29 Herbert Roth, "Bellamy Societies of Indonesia, South Africa and New Zealand", in Sylvia E. Bowman et. al., *Edward Bellamy Abroad* (1962), p. 232.

30 Walter Edward Murphy, "Bellamy Society", in A. H. McLintock (ed.), *Encyclopaedia of New Zealand* (1966), vol. 2, pp. 793-794.

31 Roth, "Bellamy Societies of Indonesia, South Africa and New Zealand", p. 246.

32 Murphy, "Bellamy Society", pp. 793-794.

33 Robert Pemberton, *The Happy Colony* (1854). Each illustration in the book proclaimed it was a design "To be established in New Zealand by the workmen of Great Britain." On his class reading guide Jellie marked this book "out of print", so students would have to be satisfied with his notes or try the public library for a copy.

34 Pemberton lived in London and Paris and was present during the French Revolution of 1848. Education was his abiding interest. He founded an infant school based on his own theory, blended from Owenism and Transcendentalism, a form of socialism using reasoning as the basis of all knowledge. This concern for education is seen in the town design Pemberton produced for New Zealand: Queen Victoria Town has been described as "little more than a university campus incorporating accommodation for agricultural and industrial workers" with a model farm at the centre. The design is a series of circles: the first, of 50 acres, contains the four colleges of the natural university, swimming baths, riding school, botanic and horticultural gardens; the second contains manufactories and public workshops; and the outer circles have parks, public buildings and dwelling houses. Robert Pemberton's son Charles ffrench Pemberton (1835-1905), a Sorbonne-educated civil engineer, emigrated to New Zealand in 1859, perhaps with plans for his father's colony in mind. See John Rockey, "From Vision to Reality: Victorian Ideal Cities and Model Towns in the Genesis of Ebenezer Howard's Garden City",

Notes

The Town Planning Review (1983), pp. 83-105; and "An Australasian Utopist", *New Zealand Journal of History* (1981), pp. 157-178.

35 Gregory Claeys, "Owen, Robert (1771-1858)", ODNB. J. F. C. Harrison, *Robert Owen and the Owenities in Britain and America* (1969), p. 252 and n.3.

36 The Clover Street Unitarian Chapel was known as "The Co-op Chapel" because a significant number of its members were founders in the Rochdale Pioneers. Based on Robert Owen's principles of co-operation rather than competition, the co-ops had a set of rules: capital provided by members carried a fixed rate of interest; only pure food was supplied; a full weight or measure was to be given; all purchases were to be cash and not credit; dividends were to be divided among members in proportion to their purchases; management was based on democratic principles with one vote per member; and part of the profits was to go to education. R. S. Roper and Alan Ruston, "The Rochdale Pioneers — 150th Anniversary", *TUHS* (1994), pp. 283-286; and Nikola Balnave and Greg Patmore, "'Practical Utopians': Rochdale Consumer Co-operatives in Australia and New Zealand", *Labour History* (2008), pp. 97-110.

37 John A. Colquhoun, *History of the Auckland Workers' Educational Association until the passing of the Adult Education Act, 1947* (1976), p. 40.

38 *New Zealand Highway*, April 9, 1927, pp. 7-9.

39 *New Zealand Highway*, March 10, 1928, pp. 10-11.

40 N. M. Richmond, "Workers Education in New Zealand", *International Labour Review*, April 1938, pp. 440-462.

41 Upon his return to New Zealand in 1923, Norman Richmond was a housemaster at Christ's College and studied education at Canterbury University College with Professor James Shelley. In 1925 he moved to Auckland University College as assistant to WEA director Linden Mander. Christopher Horton, "Richmond, Norman Macdonald 1897-1971", DNZB, updated 22 June 2007. Information about his father, Maurice Norman, is found in J. C. Beaglehole, *Victoria University College: An Essay towards a History* (1949), pp. 50-51, 60-61, 100, 103-104.

42 Tim Beaglehole, *A Life of J. C. Beaglehole, New Zealand Scholar* (2006), p. 160.

43 Margaret Howie and Jean Leyland, *A Guy Family History from Leeds to 'Lealands'* (2000), pp. 18-21. It was Ruskin's intention that the community land "would be managed, if not owned, by 'Companions' of the Guild". W. H. G. Armytage, *Heavens Below: Utopian Experiments in England 1560-1960* (1961), p. 291.

44 Laurie Guy, *Shaping Godzone: Public Issues and Church Voices in New Zealand 1840-2000* (2011), p. 515, n.41.

Notes

45   Howie and Leyland, *A Guy Family History from Leeds to 'Lealands'*, p. 37.

46   *New Zealand Highway*, October 10, 1928, p. 9.

47   Colquhoun, *History of the Workers' Educational Association*, p. 46.

48   J. L. J. Wilson, "Thirty-Eight Years in Adult Education", paper presented at the National Conference on Adult Education held at Warburton, Victoria, Australia, 1963, p. 13. There was also an opportunity for William Jellie and William Constable to deliver radio talks. Constable took part in the 1YA radio broadcast of WEA talks in 1933, discussing "The Plays of Ibsen". This was followed in 1934 by Jellie talking on "The French Revolution in English Literature". The radio talks had begun in 1928 but were stopped in 1935, probably because the WEA allowed free discussion of controversial material. David O. W. Hall, *New Zealand Adult Education* (1970), p. 66.

49   Rachel Barrowman, *A Popular Vision: The Arts and the Left in New Zealand 1930-1950* (1991), pp. 177-180. The same author has written *Mason: The Life of R. A. K. Mason* (2003), a definitive account of Ron Mason's life. Both Ron Mason and Arthur Sewell gave WEA courses and were active in the Rationalist Association; Mason was secretary in 1936 and Sewell was vice-president, 1934-1943.

50   John Gordon, *All the World's a Stage* (1981), pp. 31-32.

51   The Constables were inducted into the Auckland Unitarian Church on 13 July 1929, by the Reverends Jellie, Chapple and Hall. Sir George Fowlds gave "A Dominion Welcome" speech in the evening.

William Constable graduated from the University of Edinburgh with a M.A. in 1912 and then went to the Congregational Yorkshire United Independent College at Bradford. Wilna also attended the University of Edinburgh and the United Independent College. They married in Bradford in 1915. Wilna became Unitarian in 1921 and was minister at the Unitarian Church in Warwick, 1921-1929; during that period William was an adult education lecturer. Wilna Constable was notable as the first ordained woman minister in New Zealand. Upon leaving New Zealand in 1934 the Constables served at the Unitarian Church of Vancouver, 1934-1937. From there they went to the Free Protestant (Unitarian) Church in Cape Town, 1938-1941. In Cape Town they were adversely affected by financial strain attributed to the obligations entered into by the church with the previous minister, Rev. Ramsden Balmforth (1861-1941), who had the use of the manse free for life and a retiring allowance from the Church of £150 a year (in addition to his pension from Britain.) Partly because of this issue, the Constables decided to seek an appointment in the United States. (See the correspondence in the Inactive Ministers Files, 1825-1999, Andover-Harvard Theological Library, Harvard

Divinity School, bMS 1446, Box 36.) Between 1941 and 1953 they were joint ministers at the First Unitarian Church of Orlando, Florida. In Florida William had the opportunity to return to teaching with his appointment to an associate professorship in the English Department at Rollins College, a Congregational-established university college.

52 [WEA] Annual Tutor's Reports 1926-1939.

53 WEA Reports 1937.

Chapter 10: The Epilogue

1 By 1933 nearly 80,000 people were registered unemployed in New Zealand.

2 "We have a special interest in the hardships of our own people and desire to keep in touch with them." Auckland Unitarian Church *Calendar*, July 1934. The Registrar of the unemployed was Mr Whittaker of 4 Dickens Street, Ponsonby.

3 Auckland Unitarian Church *Calendar*, May 1935.

4 Cyprus Mitchell took ministerial charge of the Wellington Unitarian Free Church in March 1934. He exchanged pulpits with William Jellie in April 1935 and within a year had moved to Auckland. His induction into the Auckland Unitarian Church on 1 March 1936 was broadcast from Radio 1YX.

Born in Coomooroo, Clare, South Australia, Mitchell was the eldest child and only boy in a family of four children. Life was not easy for the family after his parents divorced in 1898. As a young man he spent time in Western Australia hunting kangaroos and working in the Kalgoorlie goldfields and the copper field at Phillips River. In 1905 he began studying as a mature student and the same year went to America to study for the ministry. In 1911 he graduated B.A. from Eureka College, Illinois, which had been established by abolitionist members of the Christian Church (Disciples of Christ). He was ordained by the Disciples on 18 June 1911. He attended the Bible College of Missouri in 1912-1913. From there he went to Union Theological Seminary, 1913-1914, and the University of Missouri, where he completed an M.A. in 1914 with a thesis on "Pragmatism in John Henry Cardinal Newman". *Alumni Catalogue of the Union Theological Seminary 1836-1936* (1937), p. 307.

After graduation Mitchell spent a year preaching in Bendigo, Victoria, Australia, before returning to America. While at the University of Chicago, where he studied for two quarters, he was recruited into the YMCA for service in Russia and entered that country via Japan in 1917, becoming one of the 442 YMCA officials in Russia during the period 1917-1921. He was in charge of the association's work with the Russian army in Kazan on the Volga River during the civil war and in November 1918 was in Moscow a year after the Bolshevists came to power. After 15 months

Notes

in Russia he went to London where he filed his report with YMCA headquarters there. *Missouri Alumnus*, November 1915, p. 44; November 1917, p. 57. His YMCA service record is in the Kautz Family YMCA Archives, University of Minnesota Libraries.

Returning to America in October 1919, Mitchell became pastor to the Sikeston Christian Church in Missouri. Subsequently he entered Yale University and graduated B.D. in 1923. He was enrolled for a B.Litt. at Oxford in 1923, where he proposed continuing his study of John Henry Cardinal Newman, but did not complete the degree. (I am grateful to Michelle Conway, Archives Assistant, Oxford University Archives, for supplying this information.) Between 1924 and 1926 he was Chaplain at the Veterans Hospital, New Haven, Connecticut. Returning to Melbourne, he became director of religious education at the YMCA. He left the YMCA in February 1927 to join Dr Strong as associate minister at the Australian Church, a position he filled as "an able and helpful colleague" until April 1928. C. R. Badger, *The Reverend Charles Strong and the Australian Church* (1971), p. 152.

In 1928 Cyprus Mitchell was married in that church to Lillian McCashney; the same year they moved to America, where Cyprus became pastor to the Congregational-led Federated Church of Pullman, Washington State. Returning to Yale, he completed a Ph.D. in 1931 with a dissertation on "Cardinal Newman's Theory of Religious Knowledge". He separated from Lillian, who remained in America, becoming a naturalised citizen in 1936; later they divorced. Cyprus returned to Australia in 1933, where he provided temporary supply to the Melbourne Unitarian Church before coming to Wellington. His Auckland ministry was successful, particularly with radio broadcasts and his missionary work outside Auckland. He introduced *The Torch* in place of the Church's *Calendar* each month.

It is not known whether Mitchell resumed church work when he returned to Australia in his sixtieth year. However, he maintained his friendship with Miles Franklin (1879-1954), the eminent feminist littérateur who wrote *My Brilliant Career*. By 1951 Mitchell was in a convalescent hospital suffering from Parkinson's disease and rheumatoid arthritis. Miles wrote from Carlton, New South Wales, that she "was sorry I could not make a second visit to you ... but I am so glad I saw you once again" and said she had since heard he had been moved to another hospital near Melbourne. Like Mitchell she had spent many years in America and went on to lament that "All my old American associates are passing..." Jill Roe, "Franklin, Stella Maria Sarah Miles (1879-1954)", ADB. Miles Franklin, letter to Rev. Dr Cyprus Mitchell, 23 March 1952.

5   In 1940 Joseph Coyne married Eileen May Smee (1911-1992), an active member of the People's Theatre who worked for Progressive Books and was involved with family planning. Rachel Barrowman, *A Popular Vision: The Arts and the Left in New Zealand 1930-1950* (1991), pp. 111-129.

⁶ The script of the play is in the R. A. K. Mason Papers. It was Mason's only play to deal with a New Zealand issue. After its performance at the Auckland Unitarian Church, the play appeared at Labour Party branches and Fabian clubrooms. Barrowman, *A Popular Vision*, p. 239.

⁷ Unitarian Church leaflet, October 1939, copy in the R.A.K. Mason Papers.

⁸ Frank Walters, "Rationalism: What It Is and What It Is Not" in Robert B. Drummond (ed.), *Free Thought and Christian Faith* (1890), pp. 3-4.

⁹ Walters, "Rationalism: What It Is and What It Is Not", p. 6.

¹⁰ Extracts from a sermon by Rev. W. Jellie published in *The Truth Seeker*, 6 September 1930, p. 1. An earlier report on Sir Robert Stout's death, in *The Truth Seeker*, 2 August 1930, pp. 1-2, reported William Jellie as saying that Sir Robert did not take upon himself the name of Christian or of any form of religion but had been loyal to the great law of love to man. A fuller account of his sermon was published in the later edition at Jellie's request.

¹¹ The first meeting was on 16 October 1930 organised by the State Education Defence League; the second was on 12 July 1931. Four days later, on 16 July 1931, William Jellie chaired a meeting of the State Education Defence League. Bill Cooke, *Heathen in Godzone* (1998), pp. 42-43, 49 n. 62; Bill Cooke, "Rationalist Association Chronology 11 January 1923 to 9 June 1994".

¹² *The Truth Seeker*, September 1931, p. 3. A delegation which met the Prime Minister and Minister of Education on 6 August 1931 included fellow Unitarian Hugh Ronald Atkinson (1863-1956), whose statement opposing the Bill was reproduced in the same issue of *The Truth Seeker*, pp. 3-4. Ronald Atkinson, as he was known, was the elder brother of Harry Albert Atkinson, founder of the Socialist Church in Christchurch, who joined Ronald and his wife Mary (née Gledstanes, 1886-1964) at Katikati in the Bay of Plenty after the death of his wife Rose in 1955. Harry Atkinson died at his brother's home and is buried along with Ronald and Mary in the Katikati cemetery.

¹³ Peter Fraser had grown up in a working class family in Scotland. He continued his education by reading many socialist writers and, in New Zealand, by studying with the WEA. His exposure to religion had turned him to rationalism, although he was never a member of the Rationalist Association: "His distaste for organised religion in middle life stemmed from the narrowness of mind he observed in many strict adherents to the Bible, and their refusal to apply the gospel to burning social issues of the day." His wife Janet was not religious and her son from a previous marriage attended the socialist Sunday school. When she died she "was given a state funeral service at St John's Presbyterian Church, for which an elegant order of service was prepared by J. C. Beaglehole". After his wife's death Fraser occasionally

Notes

attended evening church services. Michael Bassett and Michael King, *Tomorrow Comes the Song: A Life of Peter Fraser* (2000), pp. 20, 77, 283, 350.

[14] *The Truth Seeker*, December 1937, p. 1. The loophole involved officially closing the school for a period of time during which religious instruction was given to pupils unless their parents did not want them to attend. This was often referred to as the Nelson system, having originated in that province.

[15] The January 1938 issue of *The Truth Seeker* published an abstract of William Jellie's address to the Minister of Education, pp. 1-2.

[16] According to Frank Castle, *Annals of the Auckland Unitarian Church*, p. 30, James Chapple attended meetings of the Movement Against War and Fascism. Established in the four main cities in 1933, the Movement did not survive past 1938; the mixture of Christian pacifism and "militant left-wing antimilitarism were poles apart". This organisation had been declared incompatible with Labour Party membership in 1935 because it was communist led. David Grant, *Out in the Cold* (1986), pp. 27-30. I am grateful to Dr Kerry Taylor for drawing my attention to this reference.

[17] Frank Castle, *Annals of the Auckland Unitarian Church*, p. 30. James Chapple had also maintained a close relationship with the Rationalist Association. Having offered his services to the Association, he became the second most frequent speaker at their Free Forums between 1935 and 1941. The Forums were held at the Strand Cinema, Queen Street, Auckland City, on Sunday evenings, with a lecture delivered before a film was shown. Bill Cooke, *Heathen in Godzone* (1998), p. 64; Bill Cooke, "The Rationalist Association's Free Forums, 1935-1941: An Examination" (2008). See Appendix 4 for James Chapple's lecture topics.

[18] Rex Mason became Minister of Education in 1940 when Peter Fraser was appointed Prime Minister. Jonathan Hunt, "Mason, Henry Greathead Rex", DNZB.

[19] Ministerial Conference on Education, Christchurch, October 1944.

[20] Ministerial Conference on Education, Christchurch, October 1944, pp. 56-57. William Jellie is identified as the author of this submission by Joan Walsh, President of the New Zealand Society of Unitarians, who quotes from the submission and says "The Liberal Religious position in New Zealand is set out in a paper prepared in 1944 by the late Rev. W. Jellie." *Motive* (1963), p. 23.

[21] See the editorial "A Win for Secular Education", *The Truth Seeker*, December 1944-January 1945, p. 7.

[22] "Unitarianism in New Zealand", *The Christian Life*, 10 May 1913, pp. 290-291.

23 "Unitarians in Early New Zealand", *Motive*, Winter 1958, pp. 5-6.
24 "Unitarians in Early New Zealand", *Motive*, Winter 1958, pp. 5-6.
25 William Jellie, letter to Lincoln Gribble, 1 July 1952.
26 Born in 1930, Lincoln Ashton Gribble was dedicated as an infant at the Auckland Unitarian Church by the Rev. Wilna Constable. The family association began when his grandfather William Gribble (1858-1939) was the first church organist. Lincoln's father Horace Victor Gribble (1893-1955) and several aunts were members during William Jellie's ministries; his mother Avis Ida Maude (née Simpson) was Anglican. Lincoln joined the church as a university student in 1948, when the Rev. Ellis Henry Morris was minister. In his first year at MCO he won the Mansfield Evans Prize in Philosophy for his essay on "The Relation between Religion and Science". Upon completing his studies he intended going to St. Lawrence University in New York to study religious education before returning home. However he met Dolores Micallef at the London hostel of the International Voluntary Service for Peace; he was applying for an American visa, she was intending to return to Malta. They married in 1956.

In 1957 Lincoln Gribble was inducted into a joint pastorate of the Memorial Church, Wallasey and Matthew Henry's Chapel, Chester, the charge being given to him by the Rev. Ellis Morris. By now Gribble had met the Rev. Will Hayes (1890-1959), or "Brother John" as he was known, at his Church of the Great Companions, Chatham. Will Hayes taught a Universalist religious view which Gribble readily adopted. When he returned to New Zealand with his family at Christmas 1960, the Auckland Unitarian Church had filled Rev. Morris' vacancy with Maurice James Wilsie (1908-1977) as lay charge, a position he held until 1963. Gribble became a secondary school teacher; while at Warkworth District School, 1961-1964, he was also associate editor of *Motive*, the periodical published by the New Zealand Society of Unitarians. At Motueka High, 1964-66, he was head of French. In Fiji, 1967-1970, he taught at Queen Victoria School and the University of the South Pacific. He returned as head of English to Dannevirke High School and went to Te Aute College in 1981 as House Master. His teaching career continued until 1990. Throughout this time he provided occasional supply to the Auckland Unitarian Church, participated as a key speaker at Unitarian conferences and led services when various celebrations occurred in the life of the church.

27 William Jellie donated his considerable collection of Dante and other Italian literature, part of a library of some 8,000 books, to the University of Auckland. In expressing gratitude on behalf of the University Council, the Chancellor said that the Deed of Gift provided for Jellie to retain the collection during his lifetime and for family members to select other books from his library after his death.

Notes

W. Cocker, letter to William Jellie, 26 June 1961. When the residue of his library was sold after his death it was found to contain a collection of prints based on the *Liber Veritatis* (Book of Truth) by Claude Lorrain in three volumes, published in London in 1819. These were bought by Keith Townley. *New Zealand Herald*, 1 February 1964. Most are now in the Auckland City Art Gallery and four in the writer's possession.

[28] William Jellie, letter to Lincoln Gribble, 13 December 1961. The day before he had written to Gribble telling him he was unable to attend the Christmas service Gribble was to conduct at the Auckland Unitarian Church. William Jellie, letter to Lincoln Gribble, 12 December 1961.

[29] Frederick Hale, "Interpreting South African Cultural Clashes through Darwinian Eyes: Ramsden Balmforth in Cape Town (1902-1911)", *South African Journal of Cultural History* (2011), pp. 26-45. According to F. Kenworthy, "The Unitarian Tradition in Liberal Christianity", *TUHS* (1944), pp. 58-67, Unitarianism "is still the most radical and thoroughgoing element in modern Liberal Christianity; it is the left-wing".

Bibliography

Abbreviations

The following abbreviations are used in the Bibliography:

ACLSC	Auckland City Library Special Collection
ADB	Australian Dictionary of Biography
ATL	Alexander Turnbull Library
AUCMB	Auckland Unitarian Church Minute Book
AWMMIL	Auckland War Memorial Museum and Institute Library
B&FUA	British & Foreign Unitarian Association
DNZB	Dictionary of New Zealand Biography
DUUB	Dictionary of Unitarian and Universalist Biography
HL	Hocken Library, University of Otago
HMC	Harris Manchester College
ODNB	Oxford Dictionary of National Biography
TUHS	Transactions of the Unitarian Historical Society
UASC	University of Auckland Special Collections
WEA	Workers Educational Association

Bibliography

Primary Sources

Manuscripts, Archives, and Other Unpublished Sources

Auckland Unitarian Church. *Calendar*, 1901-1935. Copies held by author.

———. Church Minute Book 1900-1909. MS 91/72, Series A1. AWMMIL.

———. *News & Views*, 1963-2011. Copies held by author.

Cooke, Bill. "Rationalist Association Chronology, 11 January 1923 to 9 June 1994". Unpublished manuscript, n.d. I am grateful to Dr Cooke for providing a copy of this document.

Cyprus Richard Mitchell file. Kautz Family YMCA Archives, University of Minnesota Libraries.

Darlimura Letters: Letters of Macky family of Darlimurla, Devonport, 1875-1915, 1993. ACLSC, Macky Family NZMS 935, Box "Additional". I am grateful to Barbara Holt for telling me about this collection of letters compiled by Helen Kominik (née Macky).

de la Mare, Fred. "A Great Lady" [obituary of Margaret Richmond Fell]. *The Spike: or, Victoria College Review*, 1933. ATL ref. no. 77-173-24/4.

Fabian Society Minute Book. ATL, ref. no. 94-106-07/05.

[Guy, Charlotte M.] "February 5th–14th 1910. Camp Pleasant Waiheke". Guy Family collection.

———. "A Journal Containing a trustworthy though imperfect Account of the Rambles of the Auckland Unitarian Church Young People's Club and the Adventures which befell its members by the way. By a lady member", n.d. Guy Family collection.

Howie, Margaret and Jean Leyland. *A Guy Family History from Leeds to 'Lealands'*. Auckland: The Guy Family Committee, 2000.

Jellie, William. Dante Dictionary in an A-Z style manuscript, n.d. UASC, MSS A-70, Box 3 uncatalogued.

———. Diary. AWMMIL, MS 91/71, Series D 7.

———. Journal. Held by the Jellie family.

———. Lectures. UASC, MSS A-70 and 91/4.

———. Notes on "Social Problems In the Light of Economic Theory". Two notebooks containing notes of lectures on sociology given by P. H. Wicksteed

Bibliography

at Manchester New College. One of the notebooks is signed by William Jellie. HMC, MSS. Wicksteed 2e.

———. "The Philosophy of Modern Pacifism", n.d. UASC, MSS A-70, Box 2, Item 36.

———. Draft of *Report on the Unitarian Church newly started in Dunedin by the Rev. Mr. Kennedy, September 1912*. Copy held by author.

———. *Report to the British and Foreign Unitarian Association for the Colonial Conference 1910*. Copy held by author.

———. Scrap & Newscutting Book. UASC, MSS A-70, Box 2, Item 36.

———. Work Book of Quotations with A-Z dividers, n.d. This is Jellie's first notebook, judging from the clarity of writing which is very similar to his student handwriting, whereas later writing is much more difficult to read. The book is the only one with A-Z dividers and only contains quotations; later work books contain collections of notes, quotes and drafts for sermons and lectures without alphabetical arrangement. This foolscap book has vellum covering, disintegrating especially on the spine and still bears the label of "Richard Flint & Co. Stationers, Account-Book Makers, Printers, &c. 49, Fleet Street, London." No other work book is in this style. The book is in the possession of the Jellie family.

Macky, Neil Lloyd. "The Macky Family in New Zealand". Unpublished manuscript, 1969. Macky.net/history.html

Mason, R. A. K. Papers, HL, MS-0990/028.

National Peace and Anti Militarism League, Dunedin Branch. Minutes of meetings. HL, MS 1016/3.

Passenger List for *Argonaut*. Macky Family Papers, ACLSC, NZMS 935, Box 4/F1.

T. H. White file. University of Auckland School of Architecture Library, File W588t.

Unitarian Association of New Zealand. Minutes. AWMMIL, 91/72 Series A2.1.

Workers Educational Association (WEA). Annual Tutor's Reports, 1926-1939. UASC MSS & Archives E-23, item 299a.

———. Auckland University District City Classes Programme, 1928, 1929, 1930, 1934, 1935. Copies held by author.

———. Auckland University District Tutorial Classes, 1931, 1932, 1933. Copies held by author.

Bibliography

Wellington Unitarian Free Church. *Calendar*, 1911-1925. Copies held by author.

———. Committee 1912/13 and Church Roll. AWMMIL, 91/72, Series F7.

Wilna and William Constable file. Inactive Ministers Files, 1825-1999, bMS 1446, Box 36. Andover-Harvard Theological Library, Harvard Divinity School.

Letters

Atkinson, H. A. Letter to C. H. Herford. In C. H. Herford, *Philip Henry Wicksteed: His Life and Work*. London & Toronto: J. M. Dent & Sons, 1931.

Bowie, W. Copeland. Letter to H. McCready, 5 October 1899. AWMMIL, MS 91/72, Series E3.

———. Letters to William Jellie, 20 November 1907, 6 December 1908. AWMMIL, MS 91/72 Series C, F4.

Carpenter, J. Estlin. Letter to William Jellie, 23 December 1899. HMC, folio 52-74, MS Misc 2.

Carr, Clyde. Letters to William Jellie, 13 December 1928, 16 April 1929 and 9 December 1929. AWMMIL, MS 91/72 Series C, F 6.

Chapple, James. Letter to William Jellie, 29 September 1909. AWMMIL, MS 91/72 Series C, F4.

———. Letters to William Jellie, 13 December 1928 and 20 December 1929. AWMMIL, MS 91/72 Series C, F6.

Churchill, Winston. Letter to Clementine Churchill, 31 July 1914. In Mary Soames (ed.), *Speaking for Themselves: The Personal Letters of Winston and Clementine Churchill*. London: Doubleday, 1998.

Cocker, W. Letter to William Jellie, 26 June 1961. Copy held by author.

Franklin, Miles. Letter to Rev. Dr Cyprus Mitchell, 23 March 1952. Rivett Family Correspondence, National Library of Australia, MS 6219.

Harris, Robert. Letter to William Jellie, 7 December 1920. Southport Unitarian Church *Calendar*, January-March 1921.

Herford, Brooke. Letter to William Jellie, 18 March 1896. HMC, MS Misc 2, folios 49-51.

Jellie, Arthur B. Letter to his extended family in New Zealand including a Jellie family tree, 20 August 1982. Copy held by author.

Jellie, John. Letter to Rev. H. Enfield Dowson, 8 April 1884. Copy supplied by the Librarian, HMC. (Not found in Dennis Porter, *A Catalogue of Manuscripts in Harris Manchester College Oxford*. Oxford: Harris Manchester College, 1998.)

Bibliography

Jellie, Margaret. Letter to Barbara Holt, 8 November 1991. Letter held by author.

Jellie, William. Letter to James Martineau, 5 April 1884, enclosing letters from James C. Street and others, n.d.; W.A. Adamson, 9 April 1884; and John McDowell, n.d. Copies supplied by the Librarian, HMC. (Not found in Dennis Porter, *A Catalogue of Manuscripts in Harris Manchester College Oxford*. Oxford: Harris Manchester College, 1998.)

———. Letter to Ella Jellie, "G.E.R. Tuesday. 4.30" [June 1915]. Copy held by Jellie family.

———. Letter to Tom Macky, 7 June 1915. *Darlimurla Letters*, vol. 2.

———. Letter to Robert Harris, 30 November 1920. Southport Unitarian Church *Calendar*, January-March 1921.

———. Letter to members of the Southport Unitarian Church congregation, 23 July 1921. Copy held by author.

———. Letter to Mary Richmond, 18 January 1943. ATL ref. no. 77-173-12/3.

———. Letters to Lincoln Gribble, 1 July 1952, 12 and 13 December 1961. Letters held by author.

Jones, W. Tudor. Letters to William Jellie, 12 and 14 November 1907. AWMMIL, MS 91/72 Series C, F 4.

Kennedy, William Fleming. Letter to A. H. Worthington, 20 June 1907. HMC Library.

———. Letter to Tom Macky, 21 August 1926. ACLSC, Macky Family NZMS 935, Box 4/F3.

Macky, Joseph. Letter to Tom and Ella Macky, 24 May 1903. *Darlimurla Letters*, vol. 1.

———. Letters to Tom Macky, 24 April 1902, 27 October 1902, Sunday night [2 November 1902], 8 April 1915, 22 April 1915, Saturday morning [1 May 1915]. *Darlimurla Letters*, vol. 2.

Macky, Mary. Letters to Tom Macky, Easter Monday 1901, 1 September 1901, 26 September 1901, 14 December 1902. *Darlimurla Letters*, vol. 1.

Macky, Tom. Letter to Ella Jellie, 4 April 1915. *Darlimurla Letters*, vol. 2.

Mander, L. A. Letter to William Jellie, 19 February 1926. Copy held by author.

Martineau, James. Letter to Rev. H. Enfield Dowson, 12 May 1884. Copy supplied by the Librarian, HMC.

———. Letter to William Jellie, 20 May 1896. HMC, MSS. Misc. 2, folio 52.

Bibliography

Mulgan, John. Letter to Marguerita and Alan Mulgan, 26 February 1938. In Peter Whiteford (ed.), *A Good Mail: Letters of John Mulgan*. Wellington: Victoria University Press, 2011, pp. 132-134.

Paterson, A.M. Letter to William Trimble, 18 June 1915. DPL, Archives 157, William Trimble Collection.

Richmond, C. W. Letter to Alice Blake, 30 August 1893. In Guy H. Scholefield (ed.), *The Richmond-Atkinson Papers*, vol. 2. Wellington: Government Printer, 1960, pp. 589-590.

Shawcross, A. A. Letter to William Jellie, August 1907. AWMMIL, MS 91/72 Series C, F4.

Stephens, William C. Letter to William Jellie, 14 February 1908. AWMMIL, MS 91/72 Series C, F4.

Thornhill, Albert. Letters to William Jellie, 19 February 1922, 19 October 1922. AWMMIL, MS 91/72 Series C, F6.

Wicksteed, P. H. Letter to William Jellie, 31 May 1924. HMC, MSS Misc. 2.

Newspapers and Periodicals

Australia

Note: many Australian daily newspapers were accessed online via Trove.

The Advertiser

Brisbane Courier

Britain

Note: many British daily newspapers were accessed online via Gale.

Birmingham Daily Post

The Christian Life

Daily News

East Anglian Daily Times

Illustrated London News

The Inquirer

The Ispwich Journal

Pall Mall Gazette

Southport Visitor

The Times

Unitarian Monthly

Bibliography

Ireland
Belfast News-Letter
The Disciple (Belfast)

New Zealand
Note: many New Zealand daily newspapers were accessed online via Papers Past.
Auckland Star
The Citizen
The Colonist
Evening Post
Hawera & Normanby Star
Hawke's Bay Herald
Marlborough Express
Motive (published by New Zealand Society of Unitarians, 1958-1969)
New Zealand Free Lance
New Zealand Herald and Daily Southern Cross
New Zealand Highway
New Zealand Truth
New Zealander
The Observer
Otago Witness
Southland Times
The Star
Timaru Herald
The Triad
The Truth Seeker

Books, Pamphlets and Reports

Anon. *State Arbitration and the Living Wage.* Fabian Tract No. 83, n.d.

[Auckland Provincial District] Auckland City and Suburban Members of the House of Representatives. *Cyclopedia of New Zealand.* http://nzetc.victoria. ac.nz/tm/scholarly/tei-Cyc02Cycl-t1-body1-d1-d9.html.

Bell, Norman. *Education for Freedom.* Greymouth: Grey River Argus, 1921.

Bibliography

Bellamy, Edward. *Looking Backward: 2000-1887* [1888]. https://archive.org/details/lookingbackward01bellgoog

Bradshaw, John. *New Zealand As It Is*. London: Sampson Low, Marston, Searle & Rivington, 1883.

British & Foreign Unitarian Association. *Essex Hall Year Book for 1904*.

———. *Eighty-fifth Annual Report of the B&FUA, 19 May 1910*.

———. *Eighty-sixth Annual Report of the B&FUA, 8 June 1911*.

Bury, J. B. *History of Freedom of Thought*. New York: Henry Holt & Co., 1913.

———. *History of the Idea of Progress* [1920]. New York: Dover Publications, 1955.

Carpenter, J. Estlin and P. H. Wicksteed. *Studies in Theology*. London, J. M. Dent, 1903.

Coleridge, John Duke (Lord Chief Justice of England). *The Law of Blasphemous Libel: The Summing Up in the Case of Regina v. Foote & Others*. London: Stevens & Sons, 1883. https://archive.org/details/lawblasphemousl00colegoog

Collie, J., ed. *Rutherford Waddell Memoir and Addresses*. Dunedin: A.H. Reed, 1932.

Congregational Yearbook for 1916. London: The Congregational Union of England and Wales.

Foote, G. W. *Prisoner for Blasphemy*. London: Progressive Publishing, 1886.

James, William. *The Varieties of Religious Experience* [1902]. London: Collins, 1968.

Jellie, William. *The Modern Genesis*. Auckland: Brett Printing and Publishing, 1909.

———. *Our Aims* and *The Principles and Doctrines of Unitarians*. Auckland, 1900.

Manchester General Reception Committee. *Guide Book and Order of Proceedings to the National Conference*. Manchester, 1894.

Manchester New College. *Report of Manchester New College, In Connection with The University of London, and University College, London; University Hall, Gordon Square*. 1885-1889 (99th Annual Meeting-103rd Annual Meeting). Library, HMC.

———. *Report of Manchester New College, 90, High Street, Oxford*. 1890-1891 (104th Annual Meeting-105th Annual Meeting). Library, HMC.

Bibliography

Ministerial Conference on Education, Christchurch, October 1944. Reports and Memoranda. Wellington: Government Printer, 1944.

Pemberton, Robert. *The Happy Colony*. London: Saunders and Otley, 1854.

Post Office London Directory for 1895, Comprising, Amongst Other Information, Official, Street, Commercial, Trades, Law, Court, Parliamentary, Postal, City & Clerical, Conveyance & Banking Directories. London: Kelly, 1895.

Reeves, William Pember. *The Long White Cloud Ao Tea Roa*, 4th ed. [1898]. London: George Allen & Unwin, 1950.

———. *The State and its Functions in New Zealand*. Fabian Tract No. 74. London: Fabian Society, 1896.

Ryle, Edward. Annual Reports of the Manchester Domestic Missionary Society, 1833-1908. Publication no. R97126, Microform Academic Publishers, 1979.

Stout, Robert and J. Logan Stout. *New Zealand*. Cambridge: University Press, 1911.

Sweating Commission: Report of the Royal Commission Appointed to Inquire into Certain Relations Between the Employers of Certain Kinds of Labour and the Person Employed. Appendix to the Journal of the House of Representatives, H.5, 1890.

Thomson, J. Arthur. *The Bible of Nature*. New York: Charles Scribner's, 1908.

Trevor, John. *My Quest for God*. London: Labour Prophet, 1897.

University of Auckland Library. *Dante and His Times: The Jellie Collection. Biographical Bulletin No. 1*. Auckland: University of Auckland, 1964.

Ward, Mrs Humphry [Mary Augusta Arnold]. *Unitarians and the Future*. London: Philip Green, 1894.

Watt, Chas. *The Deity of Christ: A Review of a Lecture by the Rev. W. Jellie, B.A. (Unitarian Minister)*. Auckland: Wilson and Horton, n.d. (c. 1902).

Webb, Sidney and Beatrice. *Problems of Modern Industry*. London: Longman Green, 1898.

Webb, Sidney. *Socialism in England*. London: S. Sonnenschein & Co, 1890. https://archive.org/details/socialisminengl00webbgoog

Wicksteed, Charles. *The Land for the People: How to Obtain It, How to Manage It*. London: William Reeves, 1885.

———. *Our Mother Earth: A Short Statement of the Case for Land Nationalisation*. London: Swan Sonnenschein, 1892.

Wicksteed, Philip H. *What Does the Labour Church Stand For?* London: Labour Prophet, n.d. (c. 1895).

Bibliography

Articles

Anon. "Evolution and the Existence of Satan". *The Christian Reformer*, April 1886, pp. 223-235.

Binns, William. "Unitarianism, its Mission and Missionaries". In *Unitarian Missionary Papers*. London: Edward Whitfield, 1861.

Bonar, James. "The Austrian Economists and their View of Value". *Quarterly Journal of Economics* 3:1 (1888), pp. 1-31.

Carpenter, Philip Herbert. "Evolution and the Existence of Satan II". *The Christian Reformer*, May 1886, pp. 269-276.

Dickens, Charles [Jr]. "Unitarian Places of Worship". In *Dickens's Dictionary of London, 1879*. http://www.victorianlondon.org/dickens/dickens-u.htm

Evans, W.A. "Aims of the Forward Movement". *The Citizen* 1:1 (1895), pp. 1-3.

R. A. S. "Some Sermons Worth While". *The Triad*, 1 September 1909, pp. 30-31.

Stout, Robert. "State Experiments in New Zealand". *Journal of the Royal Statistical Society* 55:3 (1892), pp. 388-414. http://www.jstor.org/stable/2979464.

Summers, Frederick. "The Origin and Progress of Our Domestic Missions". *The Christian Life*, 10 May 1913, pp. 278-280.

Walters, Frank. "Rationalism: What It Is and What It Is Not". In Robert B. Drummond (ed.), *Free Thought and Christian Faith*. London: B&FUA, 1890.

Wicksteed, P. H. "The Place of Sociology in the Circle of Theological Studies". In J. Estlin Carpenter and P. H. Wicksteed, *Studies in Theology*. London: J. M. Dent, 1903.

Secondary Sources

Books and Pamphlets

Armytage, W. H. G. *Heavens Below: Utopian Experiments in England 1560-1960*. London: Routledge and Kegan Paul, 1961.

Badger, C. R. *The Reverend Charles Strong and the Australian Church*. Melbourne: Abacada Press, 1971.

Barrett, Gladys. *Blackfriars Settlement: A Short History 1887-1987*. London: Blackfriars Settlement, 1985. [The publication date of 1985 is correct, although the title covers the period to 1987.]

Bibliography

Barrowman, Rachel. *A Popular Vision: The Arts and the Left in New Zealand 1930-1950*. Wellington: Victoria University Press, 1991.

———. *Mason: The Life of R. A. K. Mason*. Wellington: Victoria University Press, 2003.

Bassett, Michael and Michael King. *Tomorrow Comes the Song: A Life of Peter Fraser*. Auckland: Penguin Books, 2000.

Beaglehole, J. C. *Victoria University College: An Essay towards a History*. Wellington: New Zealand University Press, 1949.

Beaglehole, Tim. *A Life of J. C. Beaglehole, New Zealand Scholar*. Wellington: Victoria University Press, 2006.

Beauman, Katharine Bentley. *Women and the Settlement Movement*. London: Radcliffe Press, 1996.

Bebbington, D. W. *The Nonconformist Conscience: Chapel and Politics, 1870-1914*. London: George Allen & Unwin, 1982.

Berry, Christine. *The New Zealand Student Christian Movement, 1896-1996: A Centennial History*. Christchurch: Student Christian Movement of Aotearoa, 1998.

Bingham, Caroline. *The History of Royal Holloway College 1886-1986*. London: Constable, 1987.

Breward, Ian. *Godless Schools?* Christchurch: Presbyterian Bookroom, 1967.

Burney, Lester. *Cross Street Chapel Manchester and its College*. Manchester: Peter C. Woolley, 1983.

Bush, Graham W. A., ed. *The History of Epsom*. Auckland: Epsom and Eden District History Society, 2006.

Carter, Ian. *Gadfly: The Life and Times of James Shelley*. Auckland: Auckland University Press, 1993.

Carter, Matt. *T. H. Green and the Development of Ethical Socialism*. Exeter: Imprint Academic, 2003.

Castle, Frank. *Annals of the Auckland Unitarian Church*. Auckland: Auckland Unitarian Church, 1981.

Condliffe, J. B. *The Beginnings of the W. E. A.* Wellington: National Council of Adult Education, 1968.

Cooke, Bill. *Heathen in Godzone*. Auckland: New Zealand Association of Rationalist & Humanists, 1998.

Bibliography

———. *A Rebel To His Last Breath: Joseph McCabe and Rationalism*. New York: Prometheus Books, 2001.

Davie, Donald. *Essays in Dissent: Church, Chapel, and the Unitarian Conspiracy*. Manchester: Carcanet Press, 1995.

Davis, V. D. *A History of Manchester College from its Foundation in Manchester to its Establishment in Oxford*. London: George Allen & Unwin, 1932.

———. *The London Domestic Missionary Society: Record of a Hundred Years 1835-1935*. London: Lindsey Press, 1935.

Day, Patrick. *The Broadcasting Years: A History of Broadcasting in New Zealand*. Auckland: Auckland University Press, 1994.

Desmond, Adrian and James Moore. *Darwin*. London: Michael Joseph, 1991.

Eldred-Grigg, Stevan. *The Great Wrong War: New Zealand Society in WW1*. Auckland: Random House, 2010.

Froude, Tony. *James Bennie, Wellington Architect 1873-1945*. Paraparaumu: T. Froude, 2005.

Gordon, John. *All the World's a Stage*. Wellington: Mallinson Rendel, 1981.

Grant, David. *Out in the Cold*. Auckland: Reed Methuen, 1986.

Grassian, Victor. *Moral Reasoning: Ethical Theory and Some Contemporary Moral Problems*. Englewood Cliffs, NJ: Prentice Hall, 1981.

Green, Nicola. *By the Waters of Babylon: The Art of A. Lois White*. Auckland: Auckland City Art Gallery/David Bateman, 1993.

Greenwalt, Emmett A. *The Point Loma Community in California 1897-1942: A Theosophical Experiment*, rev. ed. Berkeley: University of California Press, 1979.

Guy, Laurie. *Shaping Godzone: Public Issues and Church Voices in New Zealand 1840-2000*. Wellington: Victoria University Press, 2011.

Hague, Graham et. al. *The Unitarian Heritage: An Architectural Survey of Chapels and Churches in the Unitarian tradition in the British Isles*. Unitarian Heritage, 1986.

Hall, David O. W. *New Zealand Adult Education*. London: Michael Joseph, 1970.

Hamer, David. *The New Zealand Liberals: The Years of Power, 1891-1912*. Auckland: Auckland University Press, 1988.

———, ed. *The Webbs in New Zealand 1898*. Wellington: Price Milburn, 1974.

Harrison, J. F. C. *Robert Owen and the Owenities in Britain and America*. London: Routledge and Kegan Paul, 1969.

Bibliography

Hawke, G. R. *The Making of New Zealand: An Economic History*. Cambridge: Cambridge University Press, 1985.

Herford, C. H. *Philip Henry Wicksteed: His Life and Work*. London & Toronto: J. M. Dent & Sons, 1931.

Holt, Raymond V. *The Unitarian Contribution to Social Progress in England*, 2nd rev. ed. London: Lindsey Press, 1952.

Howe, K. R. *Singer in a Songless Land: A Life of Edward Tregear 1846-1931*. Auckland: Auckland University Press, 1991.

Inglis, K. S. *Churches and the Working Classes in Victorian England*. London: Routledge & Kegan Paul, 1963.

Jackson, H. R. *Churches and People in Australia and New Zealand 1860-1930*. Wellington: Allen & Unwin, 1987.

Jamieson, John. *The History of the Royal Belfast Academical Institution 1810-1960*. Belfast: William Mullan and Son Limited, 1959.

Jones, Peter d'A. *The Christian Socialist Revival 1877-1914*. Princeton: Princeton University Press, 1968.

Lineham, Peter J. *New Zealanders and the Methodist Evangel*. Wesley Historical Society, 1983.

Maindonald, John. *A Radical Religious Heritage: Auckland Unitarian Church and its wider connections*, rev. ed. Auckland: Auckland Unitarian Church, 1993.

Marsh, Joss. *Word Crimes: Blasphemy, Culture, and Literature in Nineteenth-Century England*. Chicago and London: University of Chicago Press, 1998.

McClure, Margaret. *A Civilised Community: A History of Social Security in New Zealand 1898-1998*. Auckland: Auckland University Press, 1998.

McDonald, Deborah. *Clara Collett 1860-1948: An Educated Working Woman*. London: Woburn Press, 2004.

McIvor, Timothy. *The Rainmaker: A Biography of John Ballance, Journalist and Politician 1839-1893*. Auckland: Heinemann Reed, 1989.

McLachlan, H. *The Unitarian Movement in the Religious Life of England*. London: George Allen & Unwin, 1934.

McLintock, A. H. *Crown Colony Government in New Zealand*. Wellington: Government Printer, 1958.

———, ed. *An Encyclopaedia of New Zealand*. Wellington: Government Printer, 1966.

Bibliography

McLintock, A. H. and G. A. Wood. *The Upper House in Colonial New Zealand*. Wellington: Government Printer, 1987.

McMillan, William. *A History of the Moneyreagh Congregation*. Newtownards: Chronicle, 1969.

Mellone, Sydney Herbert. *Liberty and Religion: The First Century of the British & Foreign Unitarian Association*. London: Lindsey Press, 1925.

Milbank, Alison. *Dante and the Victorians*. Manchester: Manchester University Press, 1998.

Mineka, Francis E. *The Dissidence of Dissent*. Chapel Hill: University of North Carolina Press, 1944.

O'Day, Alan. *Irish Home Rule 1867-1921*. Manchester: Manchester University Press, 1998.

Pike, Alistair J. *An Unfinished Story: A History of Church Street Chapel 1935-1985*. Privately printed booklet, n.d.

Porter, Frances. *Born to New Zealand*. Wellington: Bridget Williams Books, 1995.

Reid, Nicholas. *James Michael Liston: A Life*. Wellington: Victoria University Press, 2006.

Richardson, Len. *Coal, Class & Community*. Auckland: Auckland University Press, 1995.

Roberts, Charles. *The Radical Countess*. Carlisle: Steel Brothers (Carlisle) Limited, 1962.

Rothenstein, William. *Men And Memories: Recollections of William Rothenstein 1872-1900*. London: Faber & Faber, 1931

Rowe, Mortimer. *The Story of Essex Hall*. London: Lindsey Press, 1959.

Rowntree, Ruth. *"Religious Devils" of Hampstead*. Oxford: Harris Manchester College, 2004.

Royle, Edward. *Radicals, Secularists and Republicans*. Manchester: Manchester University Press, 1980.

———. *Victorian Infidels*. Manchester: Manchester University Press, 1974.

Russell, Bertrand. *A History of Western Philosophy*. New York: Simon and Schuster, 1945.

Salmond, J. D. *New Zealand Labour's Pioneering Days: The History of the Labour Movement in N.Z. from 1840 to 1894*. Auckland: Forward Press, 1950.

Schulman, Frank. *"Blasphemous and Wicked": The Unitarian Struggle for Equality 1813-1844*. Oxford: Harris Manchester College, 1997.

Scott, Dorothy. *The Halfway House to Infidelity: A History of the Melbourne Unitarian Church, 1853-1973*. Melbourne: Unitarian Fellowship of Australia/ Melbourne Unitarian Peace Memorial Church, 1980.

Shuker, Roy. *Educating the Workers? A History of the Workers' Educational Association in New Zealand*. Palmerston North: Dunmore Press, 1984.

Sinclair, Keith. *A History of the University of Auckland 1883-1983*. Auckland: Auckland University Press, 1983.

———. *William Pember Reeves: New Zealand Fabian*. Oxford: Clarendon Press, 1965.

Smith, Barbara, ed. *Truth, Liberty, Religion: Essays Celebrating Two Hundred Years of Manchester College*. Oxford: Manchester College, 1986.

Smith, Leonard. *Religion and the Rise of Labour: Nonconformity and the Independent Labour Movement in Lancashire and the West Riding 1880-1914*. Keele: Keele University Press, 1993.

———, ed. *Unitarian to the Core: Unitarian College Manchester 1854-2004*. Manchester: Unitarian College, 2004.

Smith, Warren Sylvester. *The London Heretics 1870-1914*. London: Constable, 1967.

Sutch, W. B. *Poverty and Progress in New Zealand*, rev. ed. Wellington: A. H. & A. W. Reed, 1961.

———. *Poverty and Progress in New Zealand: A Re-Assessment*. Wellington: A. H. & A. W. Reed, 1969.

Sutherland, John. *Mrs Humphry Ward: Eminent Victorian and Pre-eminent Edwardian*. Oxford: Clarendon Press, 1990.

Thompson, Noel. *Political Economy and the Labour Party: The Economics of Democratic Socialism, 1884-2005*, 2nd ed. Oxford: Routledge, 2006.

Tribe, David. *100 Years of Freethought*. London: Elek Books, 1967.

Twells, Alison. *The Civilising Mission and the English Middle Class, 1792-1850*. Basingstoke: Palgrave Macmillan, 2009.

Watts, Ruth. *Gender, Power and the Unitarians in England 1760-1860*. London and New York: Longman, 1998.

West, Margaret and Ruth Fawell. *The Story of New Zealand Quakerism 1842-1972*. New Zealand Yearly Meeting of the Religious Society of Friends, 1973.

Wigmore-Beddoes, Dennis G. *Yesterday's Radicals: A Study of the Affinity between Unitarianism and Broad Church Anglicanism in the Nineteenth Century*. Cambridge: James Clarke, 1971.

Bibliography

Woods, Joanna. *Facing the Music: Charles Baeyertz and The Triad*. Dunedin: Otago University Press, 2008.

Young, David. *F. D. Maurice and Unitarianism*. Oxford: Clarendon Press, 1992.

Articles

Anon. "The Rev. William Jellie 1865-1963". Auckland Unitarian Church *News & Views*, May 1963.

Anon., assisted by William Jellie. "Unitarians in Early New Zealand". *Motive*, Winter 1958, pp. 5-6.

Abel, Emily K. "Toynbee Hall 1884-1914". *Social Services Review* 53:4 (1979), pp. 606-832.

Addison, Sam. "Archibald Henry Sayce 1845-1933, Professor of Assyriology, Oxford". Biographical introduction to Sayce's Gifford Lectures on "The Religions of Ancient Egypt and Babylonia" (1900-1902). http://www.giffordlectures.org/lecturers/archibald-henry-sayce

Alessio, Dominic, "Promoting Paradise: Utopianism and National Identity in New Zealand, 1870-1930", *New Zealand Journal of History* 42:1 (2008), pp. 22-41.

Bebbington, D. W. "Unitarian Members of Parliament in the Nineteenth Century: A Catalogue". *TUHS* 24:3 (2009), pp. 153-175 and Supplement.

Balnave, Nikola and Greg Patmore. "'Practical Utopians': Rochdale Consumer Co-operatives in Australia and New Zealand". *Labour History* 95 (2008), pp. 97-110. http://www.jstor.org/stable/27516311

Barber, L. H. "The New Zealand Colonels' 'Revolt', 1938". *New Zealand Law Journal* 22 (1977), pp. 496-502.

Bethel, Kerry. "To Bring into Play: Miss Mary Richmond's Utilization of Kindred Networks in the Diffusion of Kindergarten Ideals into Practice". *History of Education* 35:2 (2006), pp. 225-244.

Bevir, Mark. "The Labour Church Movement, 1891-1902". *Journal of British Studies* 38:2 (1999), pp. 217-245. http://www.jstor.org/stable/175956

———. "The Long Nineteenth Century in Intellectual History". *Journal of Victorian Culture* 6 (2001), pp. 313-335.

———. "Welfarism, Socialism and Religion: On T. H. Green and Others". *The Review of Politics* 55:4 (1993), pp. 639-661. http://www.jstor.org/stable/1407610

Bolam, C. Gordon. "John Relly Beard and the New Function of Unitarianism in the 1850s". *TUHS* 12:4 (1962), pp. 155-162.

Bibliography

Bone, Hugh A. "Linden A. Mander: 1897-1967". *Western Political Quarterly* 20:2 (1967), p. 513. http://www.jstor.org/stable/44546

Burrell, Audrey. "Dr Thomas Percival, MD: Eighteenth Century Pioneer in Medical and Social Reform". *TUHS* 23:4 (2006), pp. 649-662.

Clark, Virginia. "Stamford Street Unitarian Chapel 6 April 1868: A Unitarian First for Women's Suffrage". *TUHS* 22:2 (2000), pp. 142-149.

Coleman, Peter J. "The Spirit of New Zealand Liberalism in the Nineteenth Century". *Journal of Modern History* 30:3 (1958), pp. 237-235. http://www.jstor.org/stable/1872837

Cooke, Bill. "The Rationalist Association's Free Forums, 1935-1941: An Examination". Paper presented to the Religious History Association of Aotearoa/New Zealand Conference, University of Auckland, 28-29 November 2008.

Dakin, Jim [James C.]. "New Zealand's Freethought Heritage, Chapter 3: The rise and decline of Freethought in Dunedin, 1880-90". *New Zealand Rationalist & Humanist* 74:2 (2001), pp. 8-12.

———. "New Zealand's Freethought Heritage, Chapter 6: Freethought in Canterbury with W. W. Collins". *The Open Society* 75:1 (2002), pp. 8-14.

———. "The prevalence of mutual improvement in adult education in New Zealand 1870-1915". *International Journal of Lifelong Education* 10:3 (1991), pp. 243-254.

Davis, R. P. "Sir Robert Stout and the Irish Question". *Historical Studies, Australia and New Zealand* 12:47 (1966), pp. 417-434.

Eisen, Sydney. "Herbert Spencer and the Spectre of Comte". *Journal of British Studies* 7:1 (1967), pp. 48-67.

Elton, E. A. "A Victorian City Mission: The Unitarian Contribution to Social Progress in Holbeck and New Whortley, 1844-78". *Publications of the Thoresby Society* 19:4 (1977), pp. 316-332.

Facer, Wayne. "From Manchester to Auckland: Jessie Heywood and the Auckland Unitarian Church". *TUHS* 25:4 (2014), pp. 253-258.

———. "The Governor, Voltaire and the Nelson Magistrate". *The Open Society* 80:3 (2007), pp. 15-17.

———. "In Memoriam: John Hugh Jellie 1920-2010". Auckland Unitarian Church *News & Views*, October 2011, attachment, pp. 1-8.

———. "In Memoriam: Mary Isabella Kok (née Jellie)". Auckland Unitarian Church *News & Views*, June 2009, pp. 4-7.

Bibliography

———. "Margaret Campbell Jellie". Auckland Unitarian Church *News & Views*, Supplement, December/January 2006, pp. 5-6.

Farley, A. Fay. "A Spiritual Healing Mission Remembered: James Moore Hickson's Christian Healing Mission at Palmerston North, New Zealand, 1923". *Journal of Religious History* 34:1 (2010), pp. 1-19.

Flatau, Paul. "Jevons's One Great Disciple: Wicksteed and the Jevonian Revolution of the Second Generation". *History of Economics Review* 40 (2004), pp. 69-107.

Frazee, John P. "Dickens and Unitarianism". *Dickens Studies Annual* 18 (1989), pp. 119-143.

Frykstedt, Monica Correa. "*Mary Barton* and the Reports of the Ministry to the Poor: A New Source". *Studia Neophilologica* 52:2 (1980), pp. 333-336.

Glasgow, Eric. "Memorials of a Library". *Library Review* 50:9 (2001), pp. 461-465.

Goldman, Lawrence. "Education as Politics: University Adult Education in England since 1870". *Oxford Review of Education* 25:1 & 2 (1999), pp. 89-101. http://www.jstor.org/stable/1050702

Hale, Frederick. "Interpreting South African Cultural Clashes Through Darwinian Eyes: Ramsden Balmforth in Cape Town (1902-1911)". *South African Journal of Cultural History* 25:1 (2011), pp. 26-45.

Head, Geoffrey. "The Founders: John Relly Beard and William Gaskell". In Leonard Smith (ed.), *Unitarian to the Core: Unitarian College Manchester, 1854-2004*. Manchester: Unitarian College, 2004.

Inglis, K. S. "English Nonconformity and Social Reform, 1880-1900". *Past & Present* 13 (1958), pp. 73-88.

Kenworthy, F. "The Unitarian Tradition in Liberal Christianity". *TUHS* 8:2 (1944), pp. 58-67.

Kirzner, Israel M. "Philip Wicksteed: The 'Austrian' Economist". Ludwig von Mises Institute (2007). https://web.archive.org/web/20070623213702/http://www.mises.org/content/wicksteedbio.asp

Leighton, Denys P. "T. H. Green and the Dissidence of Dissent: On Religion and National Character in Nineteenth-Century England". *Parliamentary History* 27 (2008), pp. 43-56.

Long, Arthur J. "The Life and Work of J. Estlin Carpenter". In Barbara Smith (ed.), *Truth, Liberty, Religion: Essays Celebrating Two Hundred Years of Manchester College*. Oxford: Manchester College, 1986.

Bibliography

Martin, John E. "Unemployment, Government and the Labour Market in New Zealand, 1860-1890". *New Zealand Journal of History* 29:2 (1995), pp. 170-196.

Moloney, Pat. "State Socialism and William Pember Reeves: A Reassessment". In Pat Moloney and Kerry Taylor (eds.), *On the Left: Essays on Socialism in New Zealand*. Dunedin: University of Otago Press, 2002.

Moore, Edward M. "William Poel", *Shakespeare Quarterly* 23:1 (1972). http://www.jstor.org/stable/2868650.

Murphy, Walter Edward. "Bellamy Society". In A. H. McLintock (ed.), *Encyclopaedia of New Zealand*, vol. 2. Wellington: Government Printer, 1966.

Olssen, Erik. "Social Class in Nineteenth Century New Zealand". In David Pitt (ed.), *Social Class in New Zealand*. Auckland: Longman Paul, 1977.

Organ Historical Trust of Australia. "Indigenous and Exotic: Some Organs of the Upper North Island, New Zealand". 29th Annual Conference, 30 September-5 October 2006.

Packer, Brian A. "The Founding of the Liverpool Domestic Mission and its Development under the Ministry of John Johns". *TUHS* 18:2 (1984), pp. 39-53.

Pickstone, John V. "Ferriar's Fever to Kay's Cholera: Disease and Social Structure in Cottonopolis". *History of Science* 22 (1984), pp. 401-419.

Plowman, David H. and Genevieve Calkin. "The Origins of Compulsory Arbitration in Western Australia". *Journal of Industrial Relations* 46:1 (2004), pp. 53-83.

Raymond, Jean and John V. Pickstone, "The Natural Sciences and the Learning of English Unitarians: An exploration of the roles of Manchester College". In Barbara Smith (ed.), *Truth, Liberty, Religion: Essays Celebrating Two Hundred Years of Manchester College*. Oxford: Manchester College, 1986.

Read, John R. "Healthy Intercourse: The Beginning of the London Working Men's College". *Browning Institute Studies* 16 (1988), pp. 77-90. http://www.jstor.org/stable/25057829

Richmond, N. M. "Workers Education in New Zealand". *International Labour Review*, April 1938, pp. 440-462.

Rockey, John. "An Australasian Utopist". *New Zealand Journal of History* 15:2 (1981), pp. 157-178.

———. "From Vision to Reality: Victorian Ideal Cities and Model Towns in the Genesis of Ebenezer Howard's Garden City". *The Town Planning Review* 54:1 (1983), pp. 83-105. http://www.jstor.org/stable/40111935

Roper, R. S. and Alan Ruston. "The Rochdale Pioneers: 150th Anniversary". *TUHS* 20:4 (1994), pp. 283-286.

Bibliography

Roth, Herbert. "Bellamy Societies of Indonesia, South Africa and New Zealand". In Sylvia E. Bowman et. al., *Edward Bellamy Abroad*. New York: Twayne, 1962.

———. "In Memoriam: Harry Albert Atkinson". *Here & Now*, June 1956, pp. 18-20.

———. "Labour Churches and New Zealand". *International Review of Social History* 4:3 (1959), pp. 361-366.

———. "The New Zealand Socialist Party". *Political Science* 9:9 (1957), pp. 51-60.

Ruston, Alan. "London's East End Domestic Mission — Spicer Street, Buxton Street and Mansford Street". *TUHS* 21:2 (1996), pp. 117-135.

———. "Obituaries of Unitarian Ministers 1800-1849: Index and Synopsis". *TUHS* Supplement (April 2007).

———. "Obituaries of Unitarian Ministers 1850-1899: Index and Synopsis". *TUHS* Supplement (April 2006).

———. "Obituaries of Unitarian Ministers 1900-1999: Index and Synopsis". *TUHS* 22:2 (2000).

———. "Obituaries of Unitarian Ministers 1900-1999: Corrections and additions to the Index issued with the April 2000 Issue and extended to the end of 2004". *TUHS* Supplement (April 2005).

Sargent, Lyman Tower. "Utopianism and the Creation of New Zealand National Identity". *Utopian Studies* 12:1 (2001), pp. 1-18.

Schuff, H. W. "Education for the Neglected: Ragged Schools in Nineteenth-Century England". *History of Education Quarterly* 12:2 (1972), pp.162-183. http://www.jstor.org/stable/366975

Sellers, I. "Unitarians and the Labour Church Movement". *TUHS* 12:1 (1959), pp. 1-6.

Shennan, John. "The Labour Party: A principled stand". In Mark Derby (ed.), *Kiwi Compañeros: New Zealand and the Spanish Civil War*. Christchurch: Canterbury University Press, 2009.

Simmons, Jack. "A Victorian Social Worker: Joseph Dare and the Leicester Domestic Mission". *Leicestershire Archaeological and Historical Society Transactions* 46 (1970-71), pp. 65-80.

Smith, Leonard. "The 1851 Religious Census and the Unitarian Home Missionary Board 1854". *TUHS* 23:3 (2005), pp. 625-628.

"Stamford Street," in *Survey of London: Volume 22, Bankside (The Parishes of St. Saviour and Christchurch Southwark)*, ed. Howard Roberts and Walter H

Bibliography

Godfrey (London: London County Council, 1950), 122-124. British History Online. http://www.british-history.ac.uk/survey-london/vol22/pp122-124.

Steed, John. "Unitarianism, Political Economy and the Antimonies of Liberal Culture in Manchester 1830-50". *Social History* 7:1 (1982), pp. 1-25.

Steedman, Ian. "Rationality, Economic Man and Altruism in Philip H. Wicksteed's *Commonsense of Political Economy*". In Barbara Smith (ed.), *Truth, Liberty, Religion: Essays Celebrating Two Hundred Years of Manchester College*. Oxford: Manchester College, 1986.

Steers, David. "The Origins and Development of the Domestic Mission Movement, Especially in Liverpool and Manchester". *TUHS* 21:2 (1996), pp. 79-103.

Tarrant, William George and Joseph Worthington. "University Hall, London". *TUHS* 4:1 (1927-30), pp. 1-15.

Taylor, Anthony. "Shakespeare and Radicalism: The Uses and Abuses of Shakespeare in Nineteenth-Century Popular Politics". *Historical Journal* 45:2 (2002), pp. 357-379. http://www.jstor.org/stable/3133649

Tindale, Philip Noble. "Roman Catholics and Unitarians: An Account of Reciprocal Help and Comfort". Part 1: *TUHS* 20:3 (1993), pp. 177-186. Part 2: *TUHS* 20:4 (1994), pp. 271-282.

Vincent, Andrew. "Becoming Green". *Victorian Studies* 48:3 (2006), pp. 487-504.

Wagner, Alexandra. "Rescued from Obscurity: The impact of Henry George's ideas on Christian Socialist movement in England". Robert Schalkenbach Foundation, August 2005. http://schalkenbach.org/scholars-forum/RSF-Alex-Wagner.pdf

Webb, R. K. "The Unitarian Background". In Barbara Smith (ed.), *Truth, Liberty, Religion: Essays Celebrating Two Hundred Years of Manchester College*. Oxford: Manchester College, 1986.

―――. "Views of Unitarianism from Halley's Comet". *TUHS* 18:4 (1986), pp. 180-195.

Willis, Kirk. "The Introduction and Critical Reception of Marxist Thought in Britain, 1850-1900". *The Historical Journal* 20:2 (1977), pp. 417-459.

Wilson, H. G. "One Hundred Years of Religious and Social Work in Birmingham". *TUHS* 8:3 (1945), pp. 113-121.

Wilson, J. L. J. "Thirty-Eight Years in Adult Education". Paper presented at the National Conference on Adult Education held at Warburton, Victoria, Australia, 1963.

Wuthnow, Robert. "Altruism and Sociological Theory". *Social Service Review* 67:3 (1993), pp. 344-357. http://www.jstor.org/stable/30012503

Bibliography

Wykes, David L. "'Training Ministers suited to the wants of the less educated Classes': The Establishment of the Unitarian Home Missionary Board". *TUHS* 23:3 (2005), pp. 615-624.

Theses and Research Dissertations

Colquhoun, John A. *History of the Auckland Workers' Educational Association until the passing of the Adult Education Act, 1947.* M.Phil. Thesis in Education, University of Auckland, 1976.

Facer, Wayne Arthur Pickard. *William Jellie and the Development of the Auckland Unitarian Church.* P. G. Dip. Arts Research Exercise, Massey University, Albany, 2009.

———. *William Jellie Unitarian, Scholar and Educator.* M.Phil. thesis in History, Massey University, Albany, 2012.

Flatau, Paul Robert. *Essays in the Development, Methodology and Policy Prescriptions of Neoclassical Distribution Theory.* Ph.D. Thesis in Economics, Murdoch University, 2006.

Grosso, Diane Lee. *Hugh Price Hughes: Late Victorian Nonconformity and the Kingdom of God.* M.A. Thesis in History, Florida Atlantic University, 2004.

Hamer, D. A. *The Law and the Prophet: A Political Biography of Sir Robert Stout (1844-1930).* M.A. Thesis, University of Auckland, 1960.

Heller-Wagner, Eric. *The Unitarians of South Africa: A Socio-Historical Study.* Ph.D. Dissertation, University of Stellenbosch, 1995.

McArthur, Margaret J. *Collectivist Tracts and Altruistic Sermons: A Study of "Socialism" in Late Nineteenth Century New Zealand.* M.A. Thesis in Political Science, University of Canterbury, 1981.

Newman, R. K. *Liberalism and the Left Wing 1908-1911: A Study in Middle-Class Radicalism in New Zealand.* M.A. Thesis, University of Auckland, 1965.

Sharfe, Jean E. *The Canterbury Workers' Educational Association: The Origins and Development, 1915 to 1947. A Working Class Organisation?* M.A. Thesis in History, University of Canterbury, 1990.

Smith, Leonard. *John Trevor and the Labour Church Movement.* M.A. Thesis in History, Huddersfield Polytechnic, 1985.

Summers, David Fowler. *The Labour Church and Allied Movements of the Late 19th and Early 20th Centuries.* Ph.D. Thesis in History, University of Edinburgh, 1958.

Bibliography

Taylor, James E. *"To me, Socialism is not a set of dogmas but a living principle": Harry Atkinson and the Christchurch Socialist Church, 1890-1905*. M.A. Thesis in History, Victoria University of Wellington, 2010.

Troughton, Geoffrey Michael. *Jesus in New Zealand 1900-1940*. Ph.D. Thesis in History, Massey University, Albany, 2007.

Usher, Geoffrey Ronald. *Four Decades of Leadership: Ministers of the Sydney Unitarian Church 1927-1968*. M.A. Thesis in Religious Studies, Sydney University, 1989.

Biographical Dictionaries and Other Reference Works

Unless otherwise specified, all references to dictionaries of national biography (ADB, DNZB, ODNB) are to the online editions.

Anon. "Mr. James O'Bryen Dolt Richard Hoare". *Cyclopedia of New Zealand* [Canterbury Provincial District]. Christchurch: Cyclopedia Company, 1903. http://nzetc.victoria.ac.nz//tm/scholarly/tei-Cyc03Cycl-t1-body1-d3-d21-d107.html

Badger, C. R. "Strong, Charles (1844-1942)". ADB.

Bagnall, Austin Graham. "Richmond, Christopher William". *Encyclopedia of New Zealand*, updated 23 April 2009.

Bassett, Michael. "Airey, Willis Thomas Goodwin". DNZB, updated 1 September 2010.

Black, Collison R. D. "Jevons, William Stanley (1835-1882)". ODNB.

Bohan, Edmund. "Stafford, Edward William". DNZB.

Bonney, T. G. "Carpenter, Philip Herbert (1852-1891)", rev. V. M. Quirke. ODNB.

Breward, Ian. "Waddell, Rutherford". DNZB.

Brown, Colin. "Carr, Clyde Leonard". DNZB.

Bythell, Duncan. "Tillett, Benjamin (1860-1943)". ODNB.

Carter, Ian. "Shelley, James". DNZB, updated 1 September 2010.

Chapple, Geoff. "Chapple, James Henry George". DNZB, updated 1 September 2010.

Claeys, Gregory. "Owen, Robert (1771-1858)". ODNB.

Cleary, Maryell and Peter Hughes. "Harriet Martineau". DUUB. http://uudb.org/articles/harrietmartineau.html

Dalley, Bronwyn. "Ferner, Ellen Elizabeth". DNZB, updated 1 September 2010.

Bibliography

Darley, Gillian. "Hill, Octavia (1838-1912)". ODNB.

Davis, John. "Webb, (Martha) Beatrice (1858-1943)". ODNB.

Elliott, Vic. "Miller, Harold Gladstone". DNZB, updated 1 September 2010.

Elston, M.A. "Blackwell, Elizabeth (1821-1910)". ODNB.

Facer, Wayne. "John Gammell". DUUB. http://uudb.org/articles/johngammell.html

———. "Sir Robert Stout". DUUB. http://uudb.org/articles/robertstout.html

Fleming, Grant. "Condliffe, John Bell". DNZB, updated 1 September 2010.

Fry, Eric. "Miller, Montague David (1839-1920)". ADB.

Fry, Ruth. "Reeves, Magdalene Stuart 1865-1953". DNZB.

Galbreath, Ross. "Onslow, William Hillier 1853-1911". DNZB.

Goodhart, A.L. "Kenny, Courtney Stanhope (1847-1930)", rev. Richard A. Cosgrove. ODNB.

Gustafson, Barry. "Archer, John Kendrick". DNZB, updated 1 September 2010.

Hamer, David. "Stout, Robert". DNZB.

Harris, Jose. "Booth, Charles (1846-1916)". ODNB.

———. "Spencer, Herbert (1820-1903)". ODNB.

Holmes, Frank. "Belshaw, Horace". DNZB, updated 1 September 2010.

Horton, Christopher. "Richmond, Norman Macdonald 1897-1971". DNZB, updated 22 June 2007.

Howe, K.R. "Tregear, Edward Robert 1846-1931". DNZB.

Hromatko, Wesley, "Charles Dickens". DUUB. http://uudb.org/articles/charles-dickens.html

Hunt, Jonathan. "Mason, Henry Greathead Rex". DNZB.

Jennings, Bernard. "Mansbridge, Albert (1876-1952)". ODNB.

Kadish, Alan. "Toynbee, Arnold (1852-1883)". ODNB.

Lee, Matthew. "Neale, Edward Vansittart (1810-1892)". ODNB.

Lineham, Peter J. "Edger, Samuel". DNZB, updated 1 September 2010.

Long, A.J. "Carpenter, (Joseph) Estlin (1844-1927)". ODNB.

Malone, Judy, "Colclough, Mary Ann". DNZB, updated 1 September 2010.

McIntyre, W. David. "Macky, Neil Lloyd". DNZB, updated 1 September 2010.

McIvor, Tim. "Ballance, John 1839-1893". DNZB.

Bibliography

Mitchell, Charlotte. "Hughes, Thomas (1822-1896)". ODNB.

Morris, A. J. A. "Edwards, John Passmore (1823-1911)". ODNB.

Norman, E.R. "Ludlow, John Malcolm Forbes (1821-1911)", rev. H. C. G. Matthews. ODNB.

Olssen, Erik. "Pinkerton, David". DNZB.

Olssen, Erik and Shawn Ryan. "Jones, Frederick". DNZB, updated 1 September 2010.

Paul, Janet. "Richmond, Dorothy Kate". DNZB, updated 1 September 2010.

Pike, Brigid. "Tasker, Marianne Allen". DNZB, updated 1 September 2010.

Porter, Frances. "Richmond, Mary Elizabeth". DNZB, updated 1 September 2010.

Reardon, Bernard M. G. "Maurice, (John) Frederick Denison (1805-1872)". ODNB.

Roe, Jill. "Franklin, Stella Maria Sarah Miles (1879-1954)", ADB.

Roth, Herbert [Otto]. "Atkinson, Harry Albert 1867-1956". DNZB.

———. "Fowlds, Sir George". *Encyclopedia of New Zealand*.

———. "Socialist (N.Z.) Party". *Encyclopedia of New Zealand*, updated 22 April 2009.

Royle, Edward. "Bradlaugh, Charles (1833-1891)". ODNB.

———. "Foote, George William (1850-1915)". ODNB.

Ruston, Alan. "Henry Solly". DUUB. http://uudb.org/articles/henrysolly.html

———. "John Relly Beard". DUUB. http://uudb.org/articles/johnrellybeard.html

———. "Solly, Henry (1813-1903)". ODNB.

Schulman, Frank. "James Martineau". DUUB. http://uudb.org/articles/james-martineau.html

Sharfe, Jean. "Manning, George". DNZB, updated 1 September 2010.

Sinclair, Keith. "Reeves, William Pember 1857-1932". DNZB.

———. "Richmond, Christopher William". DNZB, updated 1 September 2010.

Slater, Michael. "Dickens, Charles John Huffam (1812-1870)". ODNB.

Sprigge, Timothy. "Mrs Humphry Ward". DUUB. http://uudb.org/articles/maryaugustaward.html

Sutherland, John. "Ward, Mary Augusta [Mrs Humphry Ward] (1851-1920)". ODNB.

Bibliography

Tennant, Margaret. "Neill, Elizabeth Grace 1846-1926". DNZB.
Tomes, Jason. "Joad, Cyril Edwin Mitchinson (1891-1953)". ODNB.
Vance, Norman. "Kingsley, Charles (1819-1875)". ODNB.
Vincent, Andrew, "Green, Thomas Hill (1836-1882)". ODNB.
Waller, Ralph, "Martineau, James (1805-1900)". ODNB.
Webb, R. K. "Martineau, Harriet (1802-1876)". ODNB.
———. "Trevor, John (1855-1930)". ODNB.
Whitby, Michael, "Bury, John Bagnell (1861-1927)". ODNB.
Wilson, Trevor. "Scott, Charles Prestwich (1846-1932)". ODNB.

Index

ABBREVIATIONS

The following abbreviations are used throughout the Index.

WJ	William Jellie
EJ	Ella Jellie
PW	Philip Wicksteed
FM	Forward Movement

Act of Toleration 1689, 199n.1
adult education. *See* Mechanics Institutes; Quaker Adult Schools; University Extension movement; Workers Educational Association (WEA); Working Men's Colleges
Airey, Willis (Bill), 108, 109
Anglicans
    Broad Church Anglicanism and Unitarianism, 29, 174
    See also Christian socialism
Archer, J. K., 227n.7
Armstrong, Richard Acland, 208n.65
Atkinson-Richmond family. *See* Richmond-Atkinson family
Atkinson, Arthur Richmond, 77-78, 86, 214n.20; FM lecture, 158
Atkinson, Arthur Samuel, 212n.12
Atkinson, Harry Albert, 37-38, 79, 195n.47, 195n.49, 215n.29, 241n.12
Atkinson, Hugh Ronald, 241n.12
Atkinson, Lily May Kirk (Mrs Arthur), 78, 81, 86, 214n.20

Atkinson, Rose Bell (Mrs Harry), 38, 195n.47, 241n.12
Auckland Unitarian Church, 51, 54-59, 61, 72-73, 127-129, 130-131, 132-133, 135
    activities, clubs, etc., 69-70, 72
    building, 57-59, 204n.32
    library, 65, 72
    ministers: *see* Constable, William and Wilna; Hall, Richard James; Jellie, William > ministry; Mitchell, Cyprus Richard; Morris, Ellis Henry; Thomas, Kenneth; Thornhill, Albert; Williams, William Edward
    office holders, 171-173
    organ, 64-65, 206nn.50-53
Ballance, John, 52-53, 201n.8
Barnett, Samuel, 30, 194n.30
Beaglehole, (David) Ernest, 78, 214n.20; FM lecture, 156
Beaglehole, John and Elsie, 123
Beard, James R., 39
Beard, John Relly, 28
Bell, Norman Murray, 231n.31
Bellamy, Edward (author of *Looking Backward 2000-1887*)*, 120-121, 165, 189n.44; in PW lectures, 23, 150
Belshaw, Horace, 108
Benbow, C. W., FM lectures, 156, 158
Bennie, James, 80, 216n.36
Bentham, Jeremy (author of *Introduction to the Principles of Morals and Legislation*), in PW lectures, 18, 187n.16
Besant, Annie, 188n.25

---

* This format is used when the reference is to a person's writings rather than to the person as an individual.

Index

Besant, Digby, 9
Bible in schools. *See* secular education
Binns, William, 28
Blackfriars Domestic Mission (London), 42-44, 46, 197n.1, 197n.10, 198n.13
Blackfriars Settlement. *See under* settlement movement > Women's University Settlement
Blackwell, Elizabeth (author of *The Human Element in Sex*), 187n.18; in PW lectures, 18, 143
Blanco White, Amber, 117
blasphemy, prosecution for, 20-21, 188nn.29-30
Blatchford, Robert, 37, 214n.24
Booth, Charles (author of *Life and Labour of the People of London*), 31, 193nn.25-26
Bowie, W. Copeland, 31, 42, 71-72, 89-90, 220n.62
Bradbury, Charles, 74-79, 211n.4, 212nn.10-11, 213n.16, 215n.27, 215n.29
Bradlaugh, Charles, 20, 187nn.24, 188n.25, 211n.6
Bradley, Franklin, 4
British & Foreign Unitarian Association. *See under* Unitarian organizations
Broad Church. *See under* Anglicans
Brooke, Stopford, 20, 32, 39, 47-48, 183n.25, 194n.30, 196n.51, 199n.31
Brown, James Shaw, 226n.4
Browning, Robert (author of *The Ring and the Book*), at Auckland Unitarian church, 72; at Wellington Unitarian church, 82; in WJ lectures and courses, 160, 161, 162, 163; in FM lectures, 157, 213n.15
Browning Hall. *See under* settlement movement
Burns, Robert (author of "A Man's a Man for A' That"), at Auckland Unitarian church, 72; in WJ lectures and courses, 115, 162
Bury, John Bagnell (author of *History of Freedom of Thought*), 119, 235n.21
Caird, Edward, 11
Cairnes, John Elliott, in PW lectures, 147
Carlisle, Earl and Countess of, 45, 194n.30, 198nn.19-20

Carpenter, J. Estlin, 6, 8, 11, 14-15, 53, 180n.4, 184n.1, 194n.33, 195n.44
Carpenter, Philip Herbert, 153, 190n.46
Carr, Clyde, 110, 121, 230n.29, 231n.31
Carrickfergus, Co. Antrim, Northern Ireland, 3-5, 45, 97
Catholic church, Catholicism, 86, 97-98, 130, 131, 228n.8, 235n.26; Catholic Emancipation Act 1829, 98
Chapple, James H. G., 73, 86, 105, 218nn.48-49, 219n.55, 230n.29, 231n.31, 242n.16; at Timaru Unitarian church, 83, 104, 107, 228n.10; at Christchurch Unitarian church, 110, 218n.48, 231n.31; at Auckland Unitarian church, 127, 128, 130-131, 238n.51; Rationalist Association lectures, 167-169, 242n.17; writings, xxiii-xxiv, 181n.11
Chartism, 13, 28, 29, 115, 163, 194n.35
Christchurch Socialist Church, 79, 195n.47, 215n.29
Christchurch Unitarian Church, 110, 218n.48, 230n.29, 231n.31
Christian Ethical Society, 75
Christian socialism, 28-30. *See also* Forward Movement
Churchill, Winston, 98, 193n.26, 221n.9
Clarion Club, 79, 214n.24
Cobbe, Frances Power, 194n.30
Colclough, Mary Ann ("Polly Plum"), 211n.3
Coleridge, John Duke, Lord Chief Justice, 9-10, 20, 188n.29
Collett, Clara, 31, 193n.26
Collins, William Whitehouse, 76, 203n.20, 211n.6
Communism, WJ lectures on, 107, 119, 165; James Chapple as Communist, 130-131
Comte, Auguste (author of *A General View of Positivism*), in PW lectures, 17-18, 139-140, 176
Condliffe, John Bell, 108-110
Congregationalists, 135, 185n.4; settlement/antipoverty work, 31-32, 37, 76-77, 193n.20. *See also* Forward Movement; Bradbury, Charles; Evans, W.A.; Fowlds, George
Constable, William and Wilna, 124-125, 127, 238n.48, 238n.51

Index

co-operative movement, 13, 29, 121, 175, 189n.41, 193n.19, 237n.36. *See also* Neale, E. V.; Owen, Robert
Coyne, Joseph Denis, 124, 128-129, 240n.5
Croft, George (organ maker), 64-65
Cross, Robert Nicol, 90
Csifo, Salomon, 24
Dante Alighieri (author of *Divina Commedia* and *De Monarchia*), 115-117
  PW as Dante scholar, 10; in PW lectures, 140, 145, 150, 151, 152
  WJ as Dante scholar and book collector, 89, 117, 235n.17, 243n.27; in WJ lectures and courses, 108, 115, 120, 122, 124, 159, 162, 164, 165, 166
Darwin, Charles (author of *On the Origin of Species*), 83, 189n.38, 208n.68; in PW lectures, 18, 142; in WJ sermons and courses, 67-68, 126, 164
de la Mare, Fred, 78, 123, 130
Dickens, Charles (author of *Little Dorrit*), 43, 198n.11; at Auckland church, 72; in WJ course, 161
Dissenters' Chapels Act 1844, 5, 98, 199n.1
Dr Williams' Library, 11, 32, 38, 183n.26
Drummond, James, 6, 12, 32
Drummond, William Hamilton, 218n.51
Duncan, Alfred W., FM lecture, 158
Dunedin Freethought Association, 66, 207n.60
Dunedin Unitarian Church, 83-84
Edger, Herbert Frank, 78
Edger, Kate Milligan. *See* Evans, Kate Edger
Edger, Samuel, 74, 211n.3
Edwards, Passmore. *See* settlement movement > Passmore Edwards Settlement
Ellis, John Gillies Whait, 107, 229n.13
Emerson, Ralph Waldo (author of *Essays*), at Wellington Unitarian church, 82; in WJ lectures and courses, 159, 161
Essex Hall. *See* Unitarian organizations > British & Foreign Unitarian Association
Evans, E. D. Priestley, 24
Evans, Kate Edger (Mrs W. A. Evans), 74-75, 78-79, 81, 211n.4, 214n.18; FM lecture, 156
Evans, William Albert, 74-80, 211n.4, 214n.26, 215n.28, 220n.56; FM lectures, 156-157

evolution, 186n.14, 190n.46, 208n.68; WJ view on, 67-69, 129; in PW lectures, 152-153; in Rationalist Association lecture, 167. *See also* Darwin, Charles
Fabian Society, 10, 37, 40, 52, 54, 75, 79, 117, 193n.19, 196n.51, 196n.62, 200n.7, 202n.17, 203n.19, 235n.25, 241n.6
Fell, Margaret Richmond, 77, 80, 81, 215n.35
Ferner, Ellen Elizabeth (Nellie), 114, 234n.14
Ferriar, John, 26-27, 191n.4
Findlay, John, 78; FM lectures, 157-158
Fleming, Mrs J. S., FM lectures, 156-158
Foote, George William, 20-21, 115, 144, 187n.24, 188nn.29-30, 191n.1
Forward Movement (Wellington, New Zealand), 74-80, 122-123, 214nn.19-20; Literary Society lectures, 77, 156-158. *See also* Bradbury, Charles; Evans, William Albert
Foster, Gregory, 9
Fowlds, Sir George, 61, 65-67, 81, 86, 113-114, 123, 207n.57, 207n.59, 207n.61, 208n.66, 238n.51
Fox, Arthur William, 24
Franklin, Miles, 239n.4
Fraser, Peter, 130, 241n.13, 242n.18
Free Religious Movement. *See* Christchurch Unitarian Church
freethought, 129, 174. *See also* Ballance, John; Collins, William; Dunedin Freethought Association; Foote, George; Rationalist Association; Stout, Sir Robert
Gain, D., FM lectures, 156-157
Gammell, John, 66, 82, 85-86, 208n.64, 217n.43, 218n.46, 218n.49
Gaskell, Elizabeth (author of *Mary Barton*), 27, 191n.6
Gaskell, William, 27, 28
Geddis, James McRoberts, 217n.43
General Assembly of Unitarian and Free Christian Churches. *See under* Unitarian organizations
George, Henry (author of *Progress and Poverty*), 63, 207n.57; in PW lectures, 14, 18, 23, 139, 149
Glasson, J. Reed, FM lectures, 157-158

Index

Green, Thomas Hill (author of *Prolegomena to Ethics*), 32, 187n.20, 189n.41; in PW lectures, 19, 143
Gribble family, 243n.26
Gribble, Lincoln Ashton, 133-135, 243n.26, 244n.28
Gribble, William, 64
Guy family, 233n.6
Guy, Charlotte Mary (Lottie), 69-70, 209nn.77-78, 233n.6
Guy, John, 123, 233n.6
Hall, Richard James, 83-84, 219n.55
Hannah, Sam, 93-94, 221n.14
Hargrove, Charles, 39, 72, 80, 90, 190n.46, 196n.52
Harris, Robert, 91, 224n.31
Harris Manchester College, 182n.12
See also Manchester College; Manchester New College
Haselden, W. R., FM lecture, 158
Hayes, Will ("Brother John"), 243n.26
Heath, Frank, 9
Heathcote, Wyndham, 104-105, 226n.4, 234n.15
Hemus, Charles and Gertrude, 79-80
Herford, Brooke, 40, 46, 196n.57
Herford, Charles, 15
Heywood, Jessie, 65
Hickson, James Moore, 106-107, 228n.12
Hill, G. F., 9
Hill, Octavia, 31, 193n.24
Hillier, William. *See* Onslow, Earl of
Hirst, Joseph Crowther, 90
Hislop, (Maria) Annie, 77, 78, 81, 214n.17
Hislop, Thomas, 78
Hoare, James O'Bryen, 75, 76, 211n.6
Hobbes, Thomas (author of *Leviathan*), in PW lectures, 140
Hogben, George, 78
Holding, H. Bond, 40
Holland, Thomas, 91
Holliwell, J. H., FM lecture, 157
Hopps, John Page, 211n.6
Howard, George and Rosalind. *See* Carlisle, Earl and Countess of
Hughes, Hugh Price, 19, 191n.1
Hughes, Thomas, 29
Independent Labour Party, 37-38, 193n.19, 214n.24

Ipswich Unitarian Chapel (Ipswich, Suffolk, England), 46-48
Ireland
controversy over Home Rule, 97-99, 106, 224n.28, 224nn.32-33, 228n.8
WJ birth and childhood, 3-5; identification as Irish, 223n.23; visit in 1918, 97
Isaac, Edmund Charles, 217n.43
Jacks, Lawrence Pearsall, 73
James, William (author of *Varieties of Religious Experience*), 195n.42
Jellie family
WJ family of origin, 3-5
WJ and EJ family life: engagement and marriage, 61-63; in England, 96-97; return to Auckland, 103-104; home in Auckland, 114
See also Jellie, Ella Macky; Macky family
Jellie, Ella Macky (wife of WJ), xxiii, 60, 61-63, 69-70, 72, 81, 89, 90, 91, 94-95, 96, 103-104, 114, 127, 181n.10
Jellie, Hilary Theodore (son of WJ and EJ), 70, 81, 91, 97, 103, 106, 209n.79, 223n.22
Jellie, John (uncle of WJ), 3-5, 97, 223n.22
Jellie, John Hugh (son of WJ and EJ), 99, 103, 114, 132, 225n.34
Jellie, Letitia Turkington (mother of WJ), 3-4
Jellie, Margaret Campbell (daughter of WJ and EJ), 81, 91, 96-97, 103, 106, 114, 216n.40
Jellie, Mary Isabella (daughter of WJ and EJ), 103, 114, 225n.1
Jellie, Robert (father of WJ), 3, 181n.4
Jellie, William
birth, family, and childhood, 3-5
education: Royal Belfast Academical Institution, 3-4; Manchester New College, London, 5-9; Manchester College, Oxford, 9-12; *see also* Wicksteed, Philip
ministry at Stamford Street Chapel and Blackfriars Domestic Mission, 42-46
ministry at Ipswich Unitarian Chapel, 46-48
ministry at Auckland Unitarian Church, 51, 54-59, 61, 64-65, 67-70, 72-73

Index

ministry at Wellington Unitarian Free Church, 80-83, 87, 88
ministry at Southport Unitarian Church, 90-91; church activities during WWI, 92; controversy over Irish Home Rule, 97-99, 224n.31
health crisis, 98-99, 103-104, 106
ministry at Timaru Unitarian Church, 104-107, 111
sermons: on Unitarianism, xxi-xxii, 46, 55-56, 116, 132; on science and religion, 67-69, 73; on politics and political theory, 106-107, 236n.27; on deity of Christ, 203n.27; list of extant sermons, 209n.74
adult education, 47, 107-110, 112-126; course descriptions, 159-166; *see also* Workers Educational Association
return to Auckland ministry, 127-128, 130-131, 132-133
old age and death, 134-135
See also Jellie family
Jevons, William Stanley (author of *Theory of Political Economy*), in PW lectures, 21, 144, 145, 146, 150
Joad, Cyril Edward Mitchinson, 118, 119-120, 235n.25
Jones, William Tudor, 70-72, 80
Joosten, Henry, 86
Jowett, Benjamin, 11
Kay, James Phillips, 26-27, 191n.4
Kennedy, William Fleming, 83-84, 86, 205n.40, 218n.51, 219n.55
Kenny, Courtney Stanhope, 20, 188n.31
Kingsley, Charles, 29
Kok, Mary. *See* Jellie, Mary Isabella
Koller, George Thurston, 107
Labour Church, 10, 25, 34-41, 44-45, 53, 55, 190n.53, 194n.37, 214n.24, 215n.29
Labour Party (New Zealand), 104-105, 106, 120-121, 227n.7, 230n.29, 231n.31, 242n.16
Lady Hewley's Charities case, 199n.1
Lambelle, W. H., 39
land ownership, in PW lectures, 18, 19, 22-23, 148-149. *See also* George, Henry; Walker, Francis Amasa; Wicksteed, Charles
Lankester, E. Ray (author of *Extinct Animals*), 68

Lee, Rosalind, 105, 106
literature: in FM lectures, 77, 156-158; in WJ lectures and courses, 113, 115, 122, 126, 159-166; in Unitarian sermons, 180n.7, 181n.11; in WJ radio talks, 238n.48
Lloyd George, David, 44, 193n.26
London Domestic Mission Society. *See under* Unitarian domestic missions
Ludlow, John M. F., 29
Lusitania, sinking of, 93-96, 221nn.14-15
Lyell, Charles (author of *Principles of Geology*), 83
Machiavelli (author of *The Prince*), in PW lectures, 144
Mackenzie, Hugh, 82, 86, 217n.41, 217n.43, 218n.49
Macky family, 59-60, 205n.37
Macky, Archibald Cameron (brother of EJ, d. in infancy), 60, 204n.36
Macky, Ella (wife of WJ). *See* Jellie, Ella Macky
Macky, Frank (brother of EJ), 60, 97, 223n.21
Macky, Isabella Campbell Kennedy (mother of EJ), 59-60, 204n.36
Macky, John (Jack) (brother of EJ), 60, 93-95, 96, 206n.53, 221n.9, 221nn.14-15
Macky, Joseph Cochrane (father of EJ), 59-62, 93-96, 204n.34, 205n.42, 205n.46, 221n.14; at Auckland Unitarian church, 61, 69, 208n.65, 209n.76, 210n.84; church organ, 64-65, 206n.50, 206n.53
Macky, Mary Birrell (stepmother of EJ), 60, 61, 63-64, 93-96, 205n.37, 205n.47, 221nn.14-15
Macky, Neil Lloyd (Polly), 96, 222n.20
Macky, Thomas Hugh (Tom) (brother of EJ), 60, 89, 94, 204n.35, 220n.1
Macky, Thomas Lindsay, 60
Macky, Thomas Roy Bayntun, 96, 222n.19
Malthus, Thomas Robert (author of *An Essay on the Principle of Population*), in PW lectures, 22, 147, 189n.38
Manchester College, Oxford, 9-12, 125, 182n.12, 183nn.34-35. *See also* Manchester New College
Manchester Domestic Mission. *See under* Unitarian domestic missions

275

Index

Manchester New College (London), 5-9
moves to Oxford; changes name to Manchester College, Oxford, 9, 182n.12
University Hall, 2, 5-9, 11
WJ as undergraduate, 5-8; as theological student, 8-12
See also Manchester College, Oxford; Unitarian domestic missions > service by students for Unitarian ministry; Wicksteed, Philip
Mander, Linden Alfred, 113, 233n.11
Manning, George, 109-110, 230n.27
Mansbridge, Albert, 108, 113, 229n.20
Mansfield Settlement. *See under* settlement movement
Marchmont Hall. *See under* settlement movement
Martineau, Harriet, 189n.38
Martineau, James, 5-7, 9, 19, 33, 40
Marx, Karl (author of *Capital*), 23; in WJ lectures and courses, 120, 126, 164, 165; in PW lectures, 150
Marxism, 33, 122, 124
Mason, R. A. K. (Ron), 124, 128, 238n.49, 241n.6
Mason, Rex, 131, 242n.18
Massey, Gerald, 115
Maurice, F. D., 29-30, 193n.24, 196n.51, 212n.12
McCabe, Joseph, 83, 85, 218n.49
McCready, Hugh Clyde, 59, 66, 204n.33
McDonnell, E., 105, 227n.6
Mechanics Institutes, 27, 112, 113, 232n.2
Middle Ages, in WJ lectures, 108, 159
Mill, John Stuart (author of *Principles of Political Economy*), in PW lectures, 16, 140, 145, 146, 148
Miller, Harold Gladstone, 109-110
Milton, John (author of *Paradise Lost*), in WJ lectures and courses, 115, 160, 161, 162, 163, 164
Mitchell, Cyprus Richard, 127, 239n.4
Morley College for Working Men and Women, 117
Morley, Henry, 6, 8-9
Morris, Ellis Henry, 127, 243n.26
Morris, William (author of *News from Nowhere*), in WJ lectures and courses, 115, 120, 165

Mulgan, John, 200n.6
Muller, Max, 11
Murray, Gilbert, 11
Neale, Edward Vansittart, 29, 35
Neill, Elizabeth Grace, 201n.12
Neill, Lillie (Mrs Samuel), 205n.40
Neill, Samuel James, 60-61, 205n.40, 205n.42
New Zealand
labour, labour movement, labour relations legislation, 52-53, 201n.12; Sweating Commission, 52, 66, 201n..10
poverty, depression, unemployment, 52, 74, 127, 201n.9, 239nn.1-2
progressive social reform, socialism, social mobility, 51-54, 120-121, 200n.3, 200n.6, 202n.16; old age pension, 54, 201n.12, 203n.20; universal health care, 128
religion: freedom of religion, 51, 130, 199n.1; decline of religion, 111, 232n.33; *see also* secular education
New Zealand Educational Institute. *See* secular education
New Zealand National Schools Defence League. *See* secular education
New Zealand Rationalist Association. *See* Rationalist Association
New Zealand Unitarian Association. *See under* Unitarian organizations
Newland, Charles and Annie, 56, 203n.29
newspapers and magazines
Citizen, 76-77
Clarion, 37; *see also* Clarion Club
Freethinker, 20, 188n.29
Freethought Review, 201n.8, 201n.12
Inquirer, 36, 73, 106
Labour Prophet, 36
Motive, 134, 243n.26
Standard, 120, 235n.26
Triad, 73, 210n.87
Nicholson, (Richard) Thomas, 24
Noble, John Ashcroft, 91
Non-subscribing Presbyterian Church, 3-4
Odgers, Blake, 194n.30
Oliver, Richard, 196n.62
Onslow, Earl of, 53, 202n.16
Our Father's Church, 211n.6

Index

Owen, Robert, 121; Owenism, 175, 236n.34, 237n.36
Oxford House. *See under* settlement movement
Oxford University. *See* Manchester College, Oxford
Parker, Theodore, in PW lectures, 150
Parnell, Frank, 24
Passmore Edwards Settlement. *See under* settlement movement
Paterson, Alexander McLean, 104-105, 106
peace and pacifism, in WJ sermons and lectures, 106, 119, 132-133, 235n.24
peace and pacifist organizations (National Peace and Anti-Militarism League, National Peace Council, etc.), 218n.51, 219n.55, 235n.25
Pegler, George and Mary, 69
Pemberton, Robert (author of *The Happy Colony*), in WJ lectures and courses, 120-121, 165, 236nn.33-34
Percival, Thomas, 26-27, 191n.2, 191n.4
Perris, H. W., 39
Phillips, William Priestly, 110
Pinkerton, David, 208n.63
Poel, William, 45
Plato (author of *The Republic*), in WJ sermons, lectures and courses, 106, 120, 164, 165
poetry, in WJ lectures and courses, 160, 161
Potter, Beatrice. *See* Webb, Beatrice
poverty, Unitarian response to, 26-34, 39-41. *See also* settlement movement; Unitarian domestic missions; Wicksteed, Philip
Presbyterians, 60-61, 64, 66, 73, 83, 96, 135, 199n.1, 219n.54, 232n.32
Quaker Adult Schools, 112, 233nn.5-6
Ranstead, William, 214n.24
Rationalist Association, 123, 130, 131, 211n.6, 230n.21, 238n.49; lectures by James Chapple, 167-169, 242n.17
Rees, Daniel, 24
Reeves, Magdalene Stuart (Maud), 54, 202n.17
Reeves, William Pember, 52-54, 75-76, 120, 200n.7
Ricardo, David, in PW lectures, 22, 150

Richmond-Atkinson family, 76, 77-78, 122, 212n.12, 214n.19, 241n.12
Richmond, Christopher William (Judge), 76, 212n.12, 213n.15; FM lecture, 157
Richmond, Dorothy Kate (Dolla), 78, 214n.18
Richmond, Mary Elizabeth, 77, 81-82
Richmond, Maurice Wilson, 78, 122, 214n.20
Richmond, Norman Macdonald, 122, 124, 237n.41
Rothenstein, William, 8-9, 118, 183n.25
Rowe, T. W., FM lectures, 157-158
Royal Belfast Academical Institution, 3-5
Royal Holloway College, University of London, 31, 62
Ruskin, John (author of *Unto This Last*), 115, 123, 163, 237n.43; in PW lecture, 140; in FM lectures, 157
Salvation Army, 44
Samuel, Sir Herbert, 117
Savage, Michael, 121
Sayce, Archibald Henry (author of *Introduction to the Science of Language*), in PW lectures, 18, 140
secular education, 67, 85-87, 107, 130, 131-132, 218n.49, 241nn.11-12, 242n.14
Seddon, Richard, 53, 201n.12, 203n.20
Senior, Nassau W. (author of *Outline of the Science of Political Economy*), in PW lectures, 21, 145
settlement movement, 30-34, 41, 194n.28
  Browning Hall, 31, 194n.27
  Mansfield Settlement, 31, 76-77
  Marchmont Hall, 34
  Oxford House, 31
  Passmore Edwards Settlement, 34, 194n.35
  Toynbee Hall, 30-32
  University Hall (London), 32-34. *See also* Ward, Mrs Humphry
  University Settlement (Manchester), 193n.21
  Women's University Settlement / Blackfriars Settlement, 31, 44, 193n.22
Sewell, Arthur, 124, 238n.49
sexuality, in PW lectures, 18, 142-143
Seyb, J., 107-108

Index

Shakespeare, William, WJ interest in, 45, 54, 109; at Auckland church, 72, 210n.85; in WJ lectures and courses, 115, 122, 160, 161, 162, 164, 165, 166
Sharman, William, 20
Shaw, George Bernard, 10, 43, 52, 54, 117. *See also* Fabian Society
Shawcross, Annie and Edward, 70-72, 204n.33
Shelley, James, 108-109, 230n.21, 237n.41
Sidgwick, Henry (author of *The Principles of Political Economy*), in PW lectures, 140
Sinclaire, Frederick, xxiii, xxiv, 181n.10
Smith, Adam (author of *Wealth of Nations*), in PW lectures, 147
socialism
  in PW lectures, 23, 142, 144, 150-151
  in WJ lectures and courses, 115, 119, 163, 165
  See also Bellamy, Edward; Christchurch Socialist Church; Christian socialism; Clarion Club; co-operative movement; Fabian Society; Forward Movement; Independent Labour Party; Labour Church; New Zealand > progressive social reform, socialism, social mobility; settlement movement; utopianism
Socialist Church. *See* Christchurch Socialist Church
Socialist Party, 73, 79
Socialist Sunday School / Socialist Guild of Youth, 231n.31
Society for the Protection of Women and Children, 81
Solly, Henry, 13, 29-30, 112
Southport Unitarian Chapel (Southport, Lancashire, England), 90-92, 98-99, 224n.31
Spanish Civil War, 235n.26
Spears, Robert, 42
Spencer, Herbert (author of *Principles of Sociology*), 186n.14, 207n.58; in PW lectures, 18, 139, 140-141, 143-144, 148, 153
St Clair, G., 40
Stafford, Edward, 212n.12
Stamford Street Chapel (London), 42-46, 197n.2, 197n.10, 205n.47
Stout, Anna Logan, 81, 207n.58

Stout, Sir Robert, 65-67, 78, 82, 88, 98, 112, 129, 180n.6, 202n.16, 207nn.58-60, 207n.62, 208nn.64-66, 217n.43, 218n.49, 227n.7, 241n.10; FM lectures, 156-157
Strong, Charles, 63-64, 205n.47, 239n.4
Sweating Commission: Report of the Royal Commission. *See* New Zealand > labour > Sweating Commission
Sydney Unitarian Church. *See under* Unitarian churches and chapels
Tarrant, William George, 73
Tawney, R. H., 108, 232n.4
temperance movement, 44, 45, 77, 180n.6, 207n.58, 211nn.5-6
Tennyson, Alfred (author of *In Memoriam*), at Wellington Unitarian church, 82; in WJ lectures and courses, 115, 160, 163
theatre (Little Theatre Society; People's Theatre; WEA Dramatic Club), 124, 240n.5, 241n.6
Thomas, Kenneth, 127, 128, 131, 198n.20, 200n.4
Thomson, (John) Arthur (author of *The Bible of Nature*), 67, 208n.69
Thornhill, Albert, 104, 226n.3, 228n.9, 231n.30, 234n.15
Thornhill, Daisy (Mrs Albert), 104, 226n.3
Tillett, Benjamin, 34, 194n.37
Timaru Unitarian Church, 83, 104-107, 111, 210n.84, 227n.6, 228nn.9-11, 231n.30, 236n.27. *See also* Unitarian Hall, Timaru
Tosh, James Westwood, 197n.10
Toynbee Hall. *See under* settlement movement
Toynbee, Arnold (author of *A Study of History*), 189n.41; in PW lectures, 23, 149, in FM lecture, 157
Tregear, Edward Robert, 53, 81, 201n.12
Trevor, Hugh Mostyn, 211n.6
Trevor, John, 10, 25, 34-39, 79, 190n.53, 195n.39, 195n.42
Tudor Jones, William. *See* Jones, William Tudor
Tullyhubbert, Co. Down, Northern Ireland (birthplace of WJ), 3
Unitarian beliefs (reason, tolerance, free inquiry, freedom of thought, etc.), 15, 55-56, 90-91, 119, 129, 185n.6

278

Index

Unitarian churches and chapels
   Australia
      Adelaide Unitarian Church, 226n.4
      Melbourne Unitarian Church, 125, 224n.33, 226nn.3-4, 239n.4
      Sydney Unitarian Church, 61, 105, 114, 226nn.3- 4, 234n.15
   Canada
      Ottawa Unitarian Church, 226n.4
      Vancouver Unitarian Church, 238n.51
   England
      Barnard Castle Free Christian Church, 218n.51
      Birmingham: Church of the Messiah, 24
      Liverpool: Hope Street Unitarian Church, 208n.65
      London: Little Portland Street, 10, 25, 197n.1
      Loughborough Unitarian Chapel, 24
      Manchester: Brookfield Church, 226n.3; Longsight Unitarian Chapel, 24; Strangeways Unitarian Chapel, 24; Upper Brook Street, 25, 35, 190n.53, 191n.4
      Rochdale: Clover Street Unitarian Chapel, 237n.36
      Warwick Unitarian Chapel, 238n.51
      See also: Ipswich Unitarian Chapel; Southport Unitarian Chapel; Stamford Street Chapel
   Ireland
      Belfast: Rosemary Street Presbyterian Church, 45
      Dublin: Strand Street Meeting House, 218n.51
      See also Non-subscribing Presbyterian Church
   New Zealand
      See Auckland Unitarian Church; Christchurch Unitarian Church; Dunedin Unitarian Church; Timaru Unitarian Church; Unitarian Hall, Timaru; Wellington Unitarian Free Church
   South Africa
      Free Protestant Church, Cape Town, 204n.32, 238n.51
   United States
      Orlando, Florida, 238n.51
      Pullman, Washington, 239n.4

Unitarian College, Manchester. *See* Unitarian domestic missions > Unitarian Home Missionary Board
Unitarian domestic missions, 27-29, 41
   London Domestic Mission Society, 32-34
   Manchester Domestic Mission, 27
   service by students for Unitarian ministry, 12, 32-34
   Unitarian Home Missionary Board, 27-28, 41, 192n.11
   See also Blackfriars Domestic Mission; Christian socialism; settlement movement
Unitarian Hall, Timaru, 83, 106, 219n.52, 228n.10
Unitarian Home Missionary Board. *See under* Unitarian domestic missions
Unitarian organizations
   British & Foreign Unitarian Association (B&FUA), 31, 39, 42, 44-45, 46, 47, 51, 71-72, 82, 89, 105, 110, 184n.3, 188n.30, 194n.34, 220n.62, 228n.9
   Eastern Union of Unitarian and Free Christian Churches, 46-47
   General Assembly of Unitarian and Free Christian Churches, 184n.3
   National Conference of Unitarian, Liberal Christian, Free Christian, Presbyterian and other Non-Subscribing or Kindred Congregations, 34-35, 39, 184n.3
   New Zealand Unitarian Association, 83, 107, 133, 226n.3, 227n.6, 229n.13, 231n.31, 242n.20
   Unitarian Lay Preachers Association, 42
Universities Tests Act 1871, 9-10, 176
University Extension movement, 11, 31, 47, 112, 187n.20, 226n.3, 229n.20, 232n.4
University Hall. *See under* Manchester New College
University Hall settlement. *See under* settlement movement
University Settlement (Manchester). *See under* settlement movement
University of London, 2, 5-9, 31, 185n.5, 235n.25
   See also Manchester New College; Royal Holloway College

Index

university settlement movement. *See* settlement movement
Upton, Charles Barnes, 6, 7
utopianism, in PW lectures, 23; in WJ sermons, lectures and courses, 106, 119-121, 165, 236n.27
Waddell, Rutherford, 74, 201n.10, 208n.63
Waiheke Island, New Zealand, 69-70, 103-104, 106, 234n.14
Walker, Francis Amasa (author of *The Wages Question*), in PW lecture, 21, 145, 147, 149, 150
Walker, Robert, 96
Wallace, Alfred Russel (author of *Man's Place in the Universe*), 83
Walters, Frank, 129
Walters, George, 61, 224n.33, 226n.4, 234n.15
Ward, Mrs Humphry (Mary Augusta Arnold), 32-34, 194n.30, 194nn.33-34
Webb, Beatrice and Sidney (co-authors of *The History of Trade Unionism*), 31, 40-41, 54, 117, 180n.4, 193n.25, 196n.60, 200n.5
Wellington Unitarian Free Church, 70-72, 80-83, 87, 104, 123, 207n.58, 216n.37, 217nn.43-44, 226n.4, 229n.13
Wells, H. G. (author of *A Modern Utopia*), 54, 106, 120
White, Thomas Henry, 57, 69, 204n.32
Wicksteed, Charles (author of *The Land for the People*), in PW lecture, 23, 149
Wicksteed, Philip
 influence on WJ, 6, 10-11, 52, 55, 113, 116, 183n.32
 lectures on *Social Problems in the Light of Economic Theory*, 13-24, 180n.4, 185n.4, 186n.7, 186n.14, 190n.46; WJ synopsis, 139-153; bibliography, 153-155
 and Labour Church, 25, 34, 36-40, 190n.53, 200n.5
 and settlement movement, 31, 33-34, 194n.30, 194n.33
Williams, William Edward, 96, 222n.16
Williams, William James (author of "The Bitter Cry of Christchurch"), 74
Wilsie, Maurice James, 243n.26
Wilson, C., FM lecture, 158

women
 higher education, 62; FM lecture, 157
 in PW lectures, 18-19, 142-143
 in Unitarian ministry, 73, 125
 voting rights, 42, 45, 54, 75, 201n.8, 202n.17
Women's University Settlement. *See under* settlement movement
Wooding, William and Emily, 82-83, 210n.84
Workers Educational Association (WEA), 107-110, 112-117, 119-126, 130, 229n.20, 233n.8
 drama classes and Dramatic Club, 123-124
 summer school, 121-123
 students: breakdown by gender, occupation, etc., 125-126
 WJ lectures and courses, 159-165
Workers Union, 78, 214n.22
Working Men's Clubs, 29, 64
Working Men's Colleges, 29-30, 112, 216n.36
World War I, 91-98
World War II, 127, 130-131, 132-133
YMCA, 108, 239n.4

www.ingramcontent.com/pod-product-compliance
Lightning Source LLC
Chambersburg PA
CBHW050625300426
44112CB00012B/1659